NAMED A BEST B

FINANCIAL TIMES
FORTUNE
NEW YORK POST
YAHOO! FINANCE

LONGLISTED FOR THE 2018
FT & McKINSEY BUSINESS BOOK OF THE YEAR AWARD

"Take one chubby Malaysian business school graduate.
Mix with Middle Eastern sheikhs and greedy Southeast Asian
politicians. Add Wall Street investment banks, law firms,
and Swiss wealth managers. Then mix in superyachts, five-star
hotels, luxury apartments, nightclubs, models, A-list movie
stars. . . . [A] richly reported page-turner."

—*Reuters*

"If you like global intrigue, financial crime, wealth porn,
and absurdity, *Billion Dollar Whale* is for you."

—*New Yorker*

"Like all good business stories, *Billion Dollar Whale* is bigger than
the immediate one it tells. It is a story of emerging markets crippled
by corruption and . . . mostly punishment-free banking."

—*Financial Times*

"A scintillating and prodigiously reported tale of a
globe-spanning modern Gatsby and his audacious fraud."

—JESSE EISINGER, Pulitzer Prize–winning reporter for
ProPublica and author of *The Chickenshit Club*

More Praise for

BILLION DOLLAR WHALE

"The book unpacks—in detail—the 1MDB scandal and Goldman Sachs's involvement in it. The book features Hollywood movie stars, including Leonardo DiCaprio and Jamie Foxx, Saudi Princes, fancy yachts and piles and piles of money being laundered in shell companies around the world. What's not to love?"
                                                            —Yahoo Finance

"What a blast to read! A true-life thriller that reads like a Hollywood movie, *Billion Dollar Whale* traces the exploits of the most mercurial, mysterious big player in history. Jho Low is Gatsby with twice the bank account and ten times the ambition, and the stories surrounding his exploits leap right off the page!"
                            —Ben Mezrich, *New York Times* bestselling
                                    author of *The Accidental Billionaires*

"Even the most skilled fiction writer would have trouble conjuring the corrupt and colorful protagonist of *Billion Dollar Whale*. Bradley Hope and Tom Wright's gripping portrait of Jho Low and his enablers throughout the global financial system will both fascinate and enrage you."
                    —Sheelah Kolhatkar, staff writer for *The New Yorker*
                                and bestselling author of *Black Edge*

"I highly recommend this rip-roaring story of brazen fraud…, political corruption…, and investment-banker callousness."
                                            —Adam Lashinsky, *Fortune*

"Well-researched and well-documented...reveals how Low used a bag of tricks, including financial fraud, to make himself seem more powerful, more influential, and more successful than he actually was....This is a must-read."   —*Booklist*

"An incredible story...If you need some billionaires to despise— look no further than these charlatans."
                    —Alexis Ohanian, co-founder of Reddit

"An amazing tale of greed...juicy and entertaining."
                    —*Library Journal* (starred review)

"Wright and Hope transform their investigation of a mind-boggling financial fraud into a nonfiction thriller....This is an epic tale of white-collar crime on a global scale."
                    —*Publishers Weekly* (starred review)

"*Billion Dollar Whale* does more than dissect a financial fraud of epic proportions; it takes the reader on a fascinating journey inside the heart of a con that was years in the making."
                    —Gregory A. Coleman, retired FBI special agent and case agent in *The Wolf of Wall Street* investigation

"Compelling."   —*Minneapolis Star Tribune*

"An incredible story."   —Knowledge@Wharton

BILLION DOLLAR WHALE

BILLION DOLLAR WHALE

THE MAN WHO FOOLED WALL STREET, HOLLYWOOD, *and the* WORLD

TOM WRIGHT & BRADLEY HOPE

hachette
BOOKS

NEW YORK

Hachette Books
Hachette Book Group
1290 Avenue of the Americas, New York, NY 10104
hachettebooks.com
twitter.com/hachettebooks

First trade paperback edition: October 2019
Originally published in hardcover, international trade paperback, and ebook by Hachette Books.

Hachette Books is an imprint of Perseus Books, LLC, a subsidiary of Hachette Book Group, Inc. The Hachette Books name and logo are trademarks of Hachette Book Group, Inc.

The publisher is not responsible for websites (or their content) that are not owned by the publisher.

The Hachette Speakers Bureau provides a wide range of authors for speaking events. To find out more, go to www.hachettespeakersbureau.com or call (866) 376-6591.

LCCN: 2018011725

ISBNs: 978-0-316-43647-2 (trade paperback); 978-0-316-43648-9 (ebook)

Printed in the United States of America

LSC-C

10 9 8 7 6

To Mum, Nina, Julia, and Laurence—TW

To Farah, Joumana, and Sufiyan—BH

Contents

PART III
EMPIRE

PART IV
BONFIRE OF SECRETS

PART V
THE CAPTAIN'S RESOLVE

Authors' Note

In 2015, we began reporting on a Malaysian sovereign wealth fund after rumors started swirling about its towering debts and shadowy dealings. It was an intriguing story. Goldman Sachs had made unfathomably large profits helping the fund raise money, and the ensuing scandal over the fate of the cash threatened to topple Malaysia's prime minister. But this was no run-of-the-mill corruption case in yet another developing country. Media reports—and sources we began speaking to—suggested that Jho Low, a little-known, twenty-seven-year-old associate of the prime minister, had himself taken the money, possibly hundreds of millions, if not billions, of dollars, and used it to build a Hollywood production company, commission one of the world's grandest yachts, and throw wildly decadent parties around the globe. If true, the Low affair would represent one of the greatest financial heists in history.

Who was Jho Low? And how did he emerge from obscurity to become the alleged mastermind of a multi-billion-dollar scam—one seemingly pulled off under the noses of the financial world? We set out to uncover Low's true identity, and what we found was astonishing. Behind the plain outward appearance and mild manners of Low was a serial fabulist who figured out how the world really works. He was everyone's friend, but few truly knew him beyond his reputation as one of the greatest spenders of money the jet-setting class had seen in a generation. It was not just a wild story involving Wall Street bankers, celebrities, and a silver-tongued con man. Low's very success, at its core, was rooted in the failures of the twenty-first-century global economy. His ability to take so much, fooling Wall Street banks, auditors, and regulators; his success in using untold wealth to buy his way into friendships with the world's most famous actors and models; and the ease with which he made everyone believe he belonged. In all of this, Low was the product of a society preoccupied with wealth and glamor.

We realized the amazing life of Jho Low was too incredible to fit neatly into the pages of the *Wall Street Journal*. By writing a book, we hoped to show in detail how Low did it, but also what drove him, and how he got away with it for so long. That larger portrait, about capitalism and inequality, told through the life of Low, would be of enduring value, we agreed.

The material in these pages is the result of four years of research. We interviewed more than one hundred individuals in more than a dozen countries, from the tiny city of Willemstad on the island of Curaçao to Shanghai in China. The majority of people named in the book agreed to talk to us either directly or through legal representation, although a small number declined.

Many of our sources insisted on anonymity for fear of physical or legal harm. Every anecdote is based on the recollection of multiple sources and, in some cases, backed up by photographs, videos, and other documentation. We have reviewed tens of thousands of documents, including public court records and confidential investigative documents and financial records as well as hundreds of thousands of emails provided to authorities during the course of investigating the case. We also relied on the official allegations contained in the U.S. Justice Department's civil asset-forfeiture cases and criminal indictments against Goldman Sachs bankers and a former Justice Department official, as well as court proceedings in Singapore and official reports by Swiss authorities.

As of this writing in April 2019 (as we prepared updates for the paperback edition), public charges of criminal wrongdoing have been filed against Jho Low in Malaysia and the United States. Former Malaysian Prime Minister Najib Razak's trial for money laundering and other offenses began in April 2019. Tim Leissner of Goldman has pleaded guilty in the United States to money laundering and bribing foreign officials. While only a handful of bankers in Singapore have served jail time, the Justice Department is in the throes of a massive criminal investigation into Jho Low and others at the center of the case. Authorities in Malaysia, Switzerland, Singapore, and other nations continue to investigate.

Most of the principal characters in this book, including Jho Low and Najib Razak, have denied committing crimes and maintained the transactions were legal, but they have yet to provide any thorough explanation for their dealings. Other figures readers will get to know, including Patrick Mahony and Tarek Obaid of a Swiss oil company called PetroSaudi International have maintained, via lawyers, that they did nothing wrong. Any errors are our own.

Cast of Characters

The Low Family

Low Taek Jho, "Jho Low"
Low Taek Szen, "Szen Low," his older brother
Low May-Lin, his older sister
Goh Gaik Ewe, his mother
Low Hock Peng, "Larry Low," his father
Jesselynn Chuan Teik Ying, Jho Low's girlfriend

Low's Associates

Jasmine Loo Ai Swan, legal counsel at 1Malaysia Development, or
    1MDB, a Malaysian state investment fund
Casey Tang Keng Chee, 1MDB's executive director
Seet Li Lin, Wharton friend and vice president of Jynwel Capital,
    Low's Hong Kong firm
Eric Tan, "Fat Eric," party boy and Low associate
Nik Faisal Ariff Kamil, 1MDB's investment director
Hamad Al Wazzan, Kuwaiti friend

Malaysia

Najib Razak, Malaysia's prime minister
Rosmah Mansor, Najib's wife
Riza Aziz, Rosmah's son by an earlier marriage; cofounder of Red
    Granite Pictures
Mahathir Mohamad, former prime minister and Najib nemesis
Anwar Ibrahim, opposition leader

Goldman Sachs

Timothy Leissner, chairman, Southeast Asia

Andrea Vella, head of Goldman's structured finance business in Asia; later cohead of investment banking, Asia

Lloyd Blankfein, chief executive

Gary Cohn, president

PetroSaudi International

Prince Turki Bin Abdullah Al Saud, cofounder

Tarek Obaid, cofounder and chief executive officer

Nawaf Obaid, Tarek's brother

Patrick Mahony, chief investment officer

Xavier Justo, head of London office

Abu Dhabi

Khadem Al Qubaisi, managing director, IPIC

Yousef Al Otaiba, UAE ambassador to the United States

Mohamed Badawy Al Husseiny, chief executive, Aabar Investments

Sheikh Mohammed Bin Zayed Al Nahyan, crown prince of Abu Dhabi

Sheikh Mansour Bin Zayed Al Nahyan, brother of Sheikh Mohammed and chairman of IPIC

Khaldoon Khalifa Al Mubarak, chief executive of Mubadala Development

BSI

Hanspeter Brunner, chief executive, Asia

Yak Yew Chee, chief relationship banker for Jho Low and 1MDB

Yeo Jiawei, a wealth management banker who leaves to work for Jho Low

Kevin Swampillai, head of wealth management

AmBank

Cheah Tek Kuang, chief executive

Joanna Yu, banker handling Prime Minister Najib Razak's accounts

Falcon Bank

Eduardo Leemann, chief executive

Hollywood/Entertainment

Joey McFarland, friend of Low's; cofounder of Red Granite Pictures

Paris Hilton, socialite

Leonardo DiCaprio, actor

Jamie Foxx, actor, musician

Kasseem Dean, "Swizz Beatz," husband of Alicia Keys; music producer

Busta Rhymes, musician

Noah Tepperberg and Jason Strauss, owners of the Strategic Hospitality Group nightclub empire

Miranda Kerr, model

Prakazrel Samuel Michél, "Pras," musician

Kate Upton, model

Martin Scorsese, director

Elva Hsiao, Taiwanese musician and sometime Low girlfriend

Nicole Scherzinger, musician

Journalists

Clare Rewcastle-Brown, founder of Sarawak Report

Tong Kooi Ong, owner of the Edge

Ho Kay Tat, publisher of the Edge

Federal Bureau of Investigation

William "Bill" McMurry, head of international corruption squad, New York

Robert Heuchling, lead FBI agent on the 1MDB case

Justin McNair, FBI agent and forensic accountant on the case

Steal a little and they throw you in jail
Steal a lot and they make you king.

—*Bob Dylan, "Sweetheart Like You"*

You get so deep into things sometimes that the
abnormal seems normal and normal seems like a
distant memory.

—*Jordan Belfort*

BILLION
DOLLAR
WHALE

Prologue

Around 6 p.m. on a warm, cloudless November night, Pras Michél, a former member of the nineties hip-hop trio the Fugees, approached one of the Chairman Suites on the fifth floor of the Palazzo hotel. Pras knocked and the door opened, revealing a rotund man, dressed in a black tuxedo, who flashed a warm smile. The man, glowing slightly with perspiration, was known to his friends as Jho Low, and he spoke in the soft-voiced lilt common to Malaysians. "Here's my boy," Low said, embracing the rapper.

The Chairman Suites, at $25,000 per night, were the most opulent the Palazzo had to offer, with a pool terrace overlooking the Strip, and a modern white interior, including a karaoke room with wraparound sofas and padded walls. But the host didn't plan to spend much time in the room tonight; Low had a much grander celebration in store for his thirty-first birthday. This was just the preparty for his inner circle, who had jetted in from across the globe. Guzzling champagne, the guests, an eclectic mix of celebrities and hangers-on, buzzed around Low, as more people arrived. Swizz Beatz, the hip-hop producer and husband of Alicia Keys, conversed animatedly with Low. At one point, Leonardo DiCaprio arrived alongside Benicio Del Toro to talk to Low about some film ideas.

What did the guests make of their host? To many at the gathering, Low cut a mysterious figure. Hailing from Malaysia, a small Southeast Asian country that many Westerners would struggle to pinpoint on a map, Low's round face was still boyish, with glasses, red cheeks, and barely a hint of facial hair. His unremarkable appearance was matched by an awkwardness and lack of ease in conversation, which the beautiful women around Low took to be shyness. Polite and courteous, he never seemed fully in the moment, often cutting short a conversation to take a call on one of his half a dozen cell phones.

But despite Low's unassuming appearance, word was that he was loaded—maybe a billionaire. Guests murmured to each other that just months earlier, Low's company had acquired a stake in EMI Music Publishing, and there was speculation that he was the money behind DiCaprio's latest movie, *The Wolf of Wall Street*, which was still filming. Low's bashful manners belied a hard core of ambition the like of which the world rarely sees. Look more closely, and Low was not so much timid as quietly calculating, as if computing every human interaction, sizing up what he could provide for someone and what they, in turn, could do for him. Despite his age, Low had a weird gravitas, allowing him to hold his own in a room of grizzled Wall Street bankers or pampered Hollywood types. For years, he'd methodically cultivated the wealthiest and most powerful people on the planet. The bold strategy had placed him in their orbit and landed him a seat here in the Palazzo. Now, he was the one doling out favors.

The night at the Palazzo marked the apex of Low's ascendancy. The guest list for his birthday included Hollywood stars, top bankers from Goldman Sachs, and powerful figures from the Middle East. In the aftermath of the U.S. financial crisis, they all wanted a piece of Low. Pras Michél had lost his place in the limelight since the Fugees disbanded, but was hoping to reinvent himself as a private-equity investor, and Low held out the promise of funding. Some celebrities had received hundreds of thousands of dollars in appearance fees from Low just to turn up at his events, and they were keen to keep him happy.

Swizz Beatz called for quiet in the hotel suite, before presenting expensive DJ equipment, emblazoned with images of a panda, to Low as a gift. The group burst into laughter. That was what Low's closest friends called him—"Panda"—a nod to his plump frame and cuddly demeanor. He'd loved *Kung Fu Panda*, and when gambling with his close friends from back home they'd each pretend to be a character from the film. But even those stars like Pras and Swizz Beatz, who had received multiple millions of dollars in appearance fees and other business deals from Low, could not really claim to know his story. If you entered "Jho Low" into Google, very little came up. Some people said he was an Asian arms dealer. Others claimed he was close to the prime minister of Malaysia. Or maybe he inherited billions from his Chinese grandfather. Casino operators and nightclubs refer to their highest rollers as "whales," and one thing was certain about Low: He was the most extravagant whale that Vegas, New York, and St. Tropez had seen in a long time—maybe ever.

A few hours later, just after 9 p.m., Low's guests began the journey to the evening's main event. To avoid the paparazzi, they strode through staff-only areas, including a kitchen, before emerging into a concrete tunnel leading to the hotel's parking garage. A fleet of black limousines stood ready, engines purring. This was a special arrangement the Palazzo permitted for only its most lucrative guests.

Every move felt seamlessly scripted, doors opening at the right moment and young, smiling women gesturing the way. As the limousines drove up the Strip, it was clear they weren't heading to the desert, as some guests thought, instead pulling up at what looked like a giant aircraft hangar, specially constructed on a vacant parcel of land. Even the VIPs were in the dark. The cars sailed through security checkpoints before stopping at a red carpet entrance, manned by burly security personnel in black suits and the first of scores of young models wearing red dresses, some of whom handed out drinks and food, while others—in the crude language of nightclubs—acted as "ambient" decorations.

This was how the super-VIPs arrived, but most of the three hundred or so guests, some clutching bright red invitations with "Everyday Birthday" stylishly rendered in gold lettering, checked in earlier at LAVO nightclub in the Palazzo or at a security post. There, they signed nondisclosure agreements, binding them to secrecy, and handed in their phones, before getting into mini-buses for the short distance to the venue. Among them was Robin Leach, who for decades, as host of the TV show *Lifestyles of the Rich and Famous*, had chronicled the spending of rappers, Hollywood stars, and old-money dynasties. But that was the 1980s and 1990s, and nothing had prepared him for the intemperance of the night. A gossip columnist for the *Las Vegas Sun*, Leach was among the few guests who had gleaned some details of what was coming. "Wicked whispers EXCLUSIVE: Britney Spears flying into Vegas tomorrow for secret concert, biggest big bucks private party ever thrown," he tweeted.

One puzzling requirement of Leach's invitation was that he could write about the party, but not name the host. He'd made his career from the desire of rich people to brag about their affluence; what made this guy want to spend so much cash in secret? he wondered. A nightlife veteran, Leach was stunned by the audacity of the construction on the site. As he surveyed the arch of the party venue, which was ample enough to house a Ferris wheel, carousel, circus trampoline, cigar lounge, and plush white couches scattered throughout, he did some calculations. One side was circus themed, with the other half transformed into an ultrachic nightclub. With the lighting, and devices that sent explosions of fire into the air periodically, it felt like a major concert, not a private event.

It must have cost *millions*, Leach estimated. Here were new lovers Kanye West and Kim Kardashian canoodling under a canopy; Paris Hilton and heartthrob River Viiperi whispering by a bar; actors Bradley Cooper and Zach Galifianakis, on a break from filming *The Hangover Part III*, laughed as they took in the scene. It was rare to get so many top actors and musicians together at a single event outside of a big awards show. "We're used to extravagant parties in Las Vegas, but this was the *ultimate* party," Leach said. "I've never been to one like it."

As the guests chatted, Cirque du Soleil–type entertainers walked among them on stilts, while acrobats in lingerie swung on hoops overhead. There were several monster trucks parked on the fringes and a troupe of about twenty little people dressed as Oompa-Loompas beating a path through the revelers. In a cordoned-off VIP area, Low held court with DiCaprio and Martin Scorsese, who was directing *The Wolf of Wall Street*. As the night wore on, other guests came by, including Robert De Niro, Tobey Maguire, and Olympic gold medalist Michael Phelps.

Not every guest that night was a celebrity. Low was careful not to overlook his less well-known friends and key business contacts. Among them were Tim Leissner, a German-born banker who was a star dealmaker for Goldman Sachs in Asia, and Mohamed Al Husseiny, the CEO of one of Abu Dhabi's richest investment funds. There were whispers among Wall Street bankers about the huge profits Goldman had been making in Malaysia, hundreds of millions of dollars arranging bonds for a state investment fund, but they hadn't reached insular Hollywood. Low's usual entourage was on hand as well, including "Fat Eric," whom the Malaysian had gotten to know from the nightclub world in Malaysia, his cousin Howie, and older brother Szen.

Waitresses handed out mini-bottles of champagne with

straws. Bartenders, standing behind the twenty-four-foot ice bar, doled out top-shelf liquor and flutes of Cristal. The crowd was already lively when Jamie Foxx started off the show with a video projected on huge screens. It appeared as if friends from around the world had volunteered to help make a surprise birthday video for their good friend Low, each dancing a bit of the hit song "Gangnam Style." Investment bankers from Low's Hong Kong–based investment company performed in a conference room. Al Husseiny danced on a jet ski off Abu Dhabi. In truth, the video was partly Low's idea, and like every aspect of the evening, from the color of the flowers to the drinks at the bar, it had been carefully orchestrated at his direction. Although the clips came as little surprise to him, Low was beaming.

As the video ended, Psy, the South Korean singer who had shot to stardom that year for "Gangnam Style," played the song live as the crowd erupted. Over the following hour and a half, there were performances from Redfoo and the Party Rock Crew, Busta Rhymes, Q-Tip, Pharrell, and Swizz Beatz, with Ludacris and Chris Brown, who debuted the song "Everyday Birthday." During Q-Tip's session, a drunk DiCaprio got on stage and rapped alongside him. Then, a giant faux wedding cake was wheeled on stage. After a few moments, Britney Spears, wearing a skimpy, gold-colored outfit, burst out and, joined by dancers, serenaded Low with "Happy Birthday," as a troupe of women began doling out slices of real chocolate cake. Each of the performers earned a fat check, with Spears reportedly taking a six-figure sum for her brief cameo.

Then the gifts. The nightlife impresarios who helped set up the party, Noah Tepperberg and Jason Strauss, stopped the music and took a microphone. Low had spent tens of millions of dollars in their clubs Marquee, TAO, and LAVO over the past few years, just as the financial crisis hit and Wall Street high rollers were feeling the pinch. He was their number one client, and they did everything to ensure other nightclub owners didn't steal him away. As Tepperberg and Strauss motioned to staff, a bright red Lamborghini was driven out into the middle of the marquee. Someone gave not one but three high-end Ducati motorcycles. Finally, a ribbon-wrapped $2.5 million Bugatti Veyron was presented by Szen Low to his brother.

Even the low-end presents were elaborate. A former talent booker whom Low had helped transform into a big movie producer, Joey McFarland, presented Low with a custom wine box with an image of Kung Fu Panda from the animated film, and the words "Vintage 1981" and "Product of Malaysia" engraved in wood. It came with a $1,000 bottle of 1981 Petrus wine, made the year of Low's birth. Just after 12:20 a.m., the sky lit up with fireworks. Partying went into the early hours, with performances by Usher, DJ Chuckie, and Kanye West. Surrounded by celebrities and friends, Low piled into a limousine and brought the party back to the Palazzo, where he gambled well into the bright light of Sunday afternoon.

This was the world built by Jho Low.

"While you were sleeping, one Chinese billionaire was having the party of the year," began an article on the website of local radio station KROQ two days later, mistaking Low's nationality. It referred to him as "Jay Low." It wasn't the first time Low's name seeped into the tabloids or was associated with extravagance—and it wasn't the last—but the Vegas birthday party was a peak moment in his strange and eventful life.

Many of those who came across Low wrote him off as a big-talking scion of a rich Asian family, a spoiled princeling from the booming region and economy of *Crazy Rich Asians*. Few people asked questions about him, and those who bothered to do so discovered only fragments of the real person. But Low wasn't the child of wealth, at least not the kind that would finance a celebrity-studded party. His money came from a series of events that are so unlikely, they appear made up. Even today, the scale of what he achieved—the global heists he pulled off, allowing him to pay for that night's party and much, much more—is hard to fathom.

Low might have hailed from Malaysia, but his was a twenty-first-century global scheme. His conspirators came from the world's wealthiest 0.1 percent, the richest of the rich, or people who aspired to enter its ranks: young Americans, Europeans, and Asians who studied for MBAs together, took jobs in finance, and partied in New York, Las Vegas, London, Cannes, and Hong Kong. The backdrop was the global financial crisis, which had sent the U.S. economy plummeting into recession, adding to the allure of a spendthrift Asian billionaire like Low.

Armed with more liquid cash than possibly any individual in history, Low infiltrated the very heart of U.S. power. He was enabled by his obscure origins and the fact that people had only a vague notion of Malaysia. If he claimed to be a Malaysian prince, then it was true. The heir to a billion-dollar fortune? Sure, it might be right, but nobody seemed to care. Not Leonardo DiCaprio and Martin Scorsese, who were promised tens of millions of dollars to make films. Not Paris Hilton, Jamie Foxx, and other stars who were paid handsomely to appear at events. Not Jason Strauss and Noah Tepperberg, whose nightclub empire was thriving. Not the supermodels on whom Low lavished multi-million-dollar jewelry. Not the Wall Street bankers who made tens of millions of dollars in bonuses. And certainly not Low's protector, Malaysian Prime Minister Najib Razak.

Low's scheme involved the purchase of storied companies, friendships with the world's most celebrated people, trysts with extraordinarily beautiful women, and even a visit to the White House—most of all, it involved an extraordinary and complex manipulation of global finance. As of this writing, the FBI is still attempting to unravel exactly what occurred. Billions of dollars in Malaysian government money, raised with the help of Goldman Sachs, has disappeared into a byzantine labyrinth of bank accounts, offshore companies, and other complex financial structures. As the scheme began to crash down around them, Malaysia's prime minister turned his back on democracy in an attempt to cling to power. Wanted for questioning by the FBI, Low disappeared into thin air.

Jho Low's story epitomizes the shocking power of those who learn how to master the levers of international finance in the twenty-first century. How he thrived, and what it says about the failure of global capitalism, is the subject of this book.

The story begins on the palm-fringed island of Penang.

PART I

THE INVENTION OF JHO LOW

Chapter 1

Fake Photos

Penang, Malaysia, Summer 1999

As he moved around the *Lady Catalina*, a 160-foot yacht docked at a government marina on Penang island, Jho Low periodically checked he wasn't being observed. Stashed in his pocket were a handful of photographs of his family: his father, Larry Low, a businessman who had made millions of dollars through his stake in a local garment manufacturer; his mother, Goh Gaik Ewe, a proud housewife who doted on her children; and his two elder siblings. Locating photos of the boat's owner, a Penang-based billionaire, he eased the snapshots one by one from their frames, replacing them with those of his own family. Later, he did the same at a British colonial-era holiday home on Penang Hill, which he also had borrowed from the billionaire, a friend of Low's family.

From Penang Hill, covered in rainforest, Low could see down to George Town, the British colonial capital named for George III, a warren of whitewashed mansions and crumbling Chinese shophouses. Beyond, the narrow straits that separated Penang island from continental Asia came into view. Situated at the mouth of the Strait of Malacca, an important sea lane linking Europe and the Middle East to China, Penang had attracted its share of adventurers, from British colonial officers to Chinese traders and other assorted carpetbaggers. The streets bustled with Penangites, mainly Chinese-Malaysians, who loved eating out at the many street-side stalls or walking along the seaside promenade.

Low's grandfather washed up in Penang in the 1960s from China, by way of Thailand, and the family had built a small fortune. They were a wealthy clan by any standard, but Low recently had begun attending Harrow, the elite boarding school in England, where some of his classmates counted their families' wealth in billions, not mere millions.

Larry's shares in the garment company, which he recently had sold, were worth around $15 million—a huge sum in the Southeast Asian nation, where many people lived on $1,000 per month. But Low had begun to mix with members of the royal families of Brunei and Kuwait at Harrow, where he had arrived in 1998 for the last two years of high school. The Low home, a palm-tree-fringed modernist mansion on the north coast of Penang, was impressive and had its own central cooling system, but it was no royal palace.

In a few days, some of Low's new school pals would be arriving. He had convinced them to spend part of their summer vacation in Malaysia, and he was eager to impress. Just as his father had raised the family's station in Penang, earning enough to send his son to one of the world's most expensive boarding schools, so Low harbored ambitions. He was somewhat embarrassed by the backwater of Penang, and he used the boat and holiday home to compensate. His Harrow friends were none the wiser. With his pudgy frame and glasses, Low never found it easy to attract women, so he clamored to be respected in other ways. He told his Harrow friends he was a "prince of Malaysia," an attempt to keep up with the blue bloods around him.

In reality, the ethnic Chinese of the nation, like the Lows, were not the aristocrats, but traders who came later to the country in big waves during the nineteenth and twentieth centuries.

The majority of Malaysia's 30 million people were Muslim Malays, who typically treated the Chinese as newcomers, even if their families had lived in Malaysia for generations. Some of the older Chinese of Penang began to wonder about this strange kid. After Low's Harrow friends had come and gone, the story of the photos began to circulate around the island, as did Low's claims to an aristocratic lineage. People laughed over the sheer chutzpah. *Who did this kid think he was?*

In the 1960s, Penang island was a ramshackle place. The British granted independence in 1957 to its colony of Malaya—a tropical Southeast Asian territory rich in tin and palm oil—after fighting an inconclusive and sapping war against a Communist insurgency. From their jungle redoubts near the Thai border, Communist rebels bided their time, and soon would start a years-long guerilla war against the untested forces of the newly established nation of Malaysia. This lawless frontier region was an area that Meng Tak, Low's grandfather, knew well. He'd left his native Guangdong province in China in the 1940s—a time of great upheaval due to the Second World War, Japanese occupation, and a civil war that led millions to flee the country—and settled in southern Thailand, near Malaya. He made some money as a minor investor in an iron ore mine, and married a local woman of Chinese ancestry, before moving on again to Penang in the 1960s.

The Low family lived in a modest bungalow in George Town, the capital of Penang, just a few blocks back from the peeling British-era colonnaded villas and warehouses on the shoreline. Many Chinese had emigrated here during colonial times to trade in commodities like tin and opium, a narcotic whose sale the British had monopolized but which now was illegal. There were dark rumors in George Town's close-knit community about the origin of Meng Tak's money. Some old-timers remembered him running a cookware shop in the city. But perhaps the story about iron-ore mining in Thailand was only part of the truth. Others whispered that he'd made money smuggling opium over the border.

For each version of the Low family's history, there was an alternate recounting. Decades later, Low started telling his own story about Meng Tak, one he fabricated to explain how he was in possession of enormous wealth. The money, he told anyone who would listen, came from his grandfather's investments in mining, liquor trading, and property. There was only one problem. Few in Malaysia—neither top bankers nor business leaders— had ever heard of this fabulously rich family. With Low's father, Larry, the family story comes into sharper focus.

Born in Thailand in 1952, Larry Low moved as a young child to Penang and went on to study at the London School of Economics and the University of California, Los Angeles, for an MBA. On returning to Malaysia, he took over Meng Tak's business. Despite his elite school, Larry made a disastrous investment in the 1980s in cocoa plantations that almost wiped out the family wealth. After commodity prices dropped, he used what was left to buy a minority stake in a company that produced clothes for export to the United States and Europe. This time Larry hit the jackpot.

The 1990s were anything-goes years for Malaysia's nascent stock market. "Asian Tiger" economies like South Korea and Taiwan had taken off from the 1960s, and now it was the turn of other Asian nations. Malaysia's economy was growing at over 5 percent annually, powered by the export of commodities like palm oil, as well as garments, computer chips, and electronic devices. Attracted by the hot growth, foreign investors poured money into Malaysian stocks and bonds. But there was no oversight. Insiders regularly broke securities laws, as if taking their cues from the excesses of 1980s figures such as Michael Milken, the U.S. junk bond king, and insider trader Ivan Boesky. Malaysians who knew how to play the system became incredibly rich, while minority shareholders lost out.

People who worked with Larry considered him charming and a wheeler-dealer, albeit with a lazy streak, preferring drinking late in nightclubs to work, but he benefited nevertheless from a run-up in the garment company's stock. In the early 1990s, he was involved in an acquisition by MWE, the garment company in which he owned a minority stake, of a Canadian technology firm. The deal overvalued the target firm, and Larry arranged for some of the excess cash to go into an offshore bank account he controlled.

Using such accounts, often owned by anonymous shell companies set up in places like the British Virgin Islands, was common for Malaysian companies at the time. The younger Lows learned from their father about this world of secret finance, and May-Lin, Low's sister, became a lawyer with an expertise in offshore vehicles.

When he uncovered that Larry had funneled off the money, the owner of MWE was furious and, not long after, Larry sold his stake in the company. But there was a silver lining: The increase in MWE's stock price in the 1990s had made the Low family millionaires many times over.

Flush with cash, Larry, now in his forties, indulged his desire to party. For one celebration on a yacht, he arranged for Swedish models to fly into Penang, the kind of arrangement for which his son later would be known. The family was a big fish in a small pond—and acting the part. Larry drove around town in a Lexus, and was a member of the Penang Club, an exclusive sports club founded by the British in 1868 and whose members included well-known business families and politicians from the island. The younger Low was a keen swimmer, often doing laps on Sundays in the pool by the ocean before eating a Chinese dinner with his family.

But Larry saw all this as parochial, and he had ambitions to raise his family's social standing. So, in 1994, when Low was thirteen, his father moved him out of the local education system to Uplands, an international school that rich Penangites chose to prepare their children for boarding school in Britain. Many elite Malaysians had gotten their education in the former colonial power, and it was still the country of choice for overseas schooling.

Larry Low opted to put down roots in England. Around this time, developers of a new gated community in London's posh South Kensington neighborhood began to advertise in Malaysia. Some of the most powerful Malaysian politicians owned homes in the Kensington Green development, and Larry sensed it could only be beneficial for an ambitious family like the Lows to develop friendships with these people. He bought an apartment in the complex, and the family began to vacation there, which gave Low the opportunity to meet the children of Malaysia's elite.

Larry's alertness to status seemed to rub off on his sons, who began to forge a friendship with Riza Aziz, a college student whose family also had a place in Kensington Green. Riza's stepfather was Defense Minister Najib Razak, who was tipped as a future prime minister. A few years older, Riza would be the key to Low's entry into the upper echelons of Malaysia's power structure.

Back home, in Penang, Larry ordered a beautiful cream-colored mansion built on a hill outside George Town, which with its sleek steel-and-glass look could have been plucked from the streets of Miami. The modern edifice was a step up from the somewhat modest family house that Meng Tak had constructed.

As Larry acquired the trappings of an upper-class life, the teenage Jho Low was busying himself exploring the nascent online world. Low took to spending hours at his computer, hiding behind the anonymity of the web. He began to fib in an offhand way, offering himself on an online chat site for modeling "in any part of the world." On the forum, Low described himself as "muscular, well proportioned" but received no modeling offers. A class photo from 1994 shows Low as a slight middle-school student dressed in a white short-sleeved shirt and blue shorts, with a neat but unstylish haircut. His online activities suggested a longing to be cool. He asked people on chat rooms what hard-core techno music they suggested or which haircuts were popular in different countries.

Although he vacationed in England, Low appeared more pulled toward American culture, as was typical among younger Malaysians. One of his favorite shows was *The X-Files*, and he traded photos of Mulder and Scully with other fans online. Since selling out of MWE, Larry had begun to dabble in property investment and stock trading, and Low showed an interest in this world. He devoured Hollywood films like *Wall Street*, with its tale of insider trading and corporate raiding, and at Uplands he pooled resources with fellow students to invest in the stock market, even though he was only fifteen years old. Many adults remember Low as smooth and deferential, but adept at using this charm to get what he wanted. On occasion, he would borrow small sums of money from Larry's friends, many of them wealthy businessmen, and then not pay them back.

Larry was plotting the next phase of the family's rise. He had the apartment in London and the swish mansion in Penang. Low's elder brother, Szen, had studied at Sevenoaks, a prestigious school in England. Now, he was about to send his youngest son to one of the world's premier boarding schools. It was a decision that would catapult Low into the exclusive club of the world's richest people.

For decades, Harrow, situated on a bucolic hill to the northwest of London, had churned out British prime ministers such as Sir

Winston Churchill, but by the late 1990s it was attracting new money from Asia and the Middle East. For wealthy Malaysians, Harrow in the late 1990s had a reputation as easier to get into than Eton, another of Britain's top boarding schools, but still an effective way to grease entry into Oxford or Cambridge and to make contacts. To reduce costs, Malaysians often would attend only the final two years of high school—to prepare for A-level exams—and that was exactly what Larry chose for his son.

In 1998, sixteen-year-old Jho Low arrived at Harrow, some of whose buildings date to the 1600s. In Penang, the Uplands uniforms consisted of short-sleeved shirts and slacks. At Harrow, pupils were required to don navy blazers and ties, topped with a cream-colored boater hat. The fees were high, more than $20,000 each year, but for the Lows it was an investment worth making.

At Harrow, Low thrived as a member of Newlands, one of the school's twelve houses of seventy or so pupils. Newlands pupils, which had included members of the Rothschild family, the Anglo-French banking dynasty, lived in a four-story redbrick detached building from the 1800s, much like the town house of a well-to-do Victorian-era businessman. Although Low was relatively wealthy himself, he quickly fell in with a new group of friends from Middle Eastern and Asian royal families, and was struck by the cash at their disposal. These were people, including the son of the sultan of Brunei, a small oil-rich country abutting Malaysia, who were picked up by drivers in Rolls-Royce cars at the end of term.

Surrounded by his elite new friends, Low began to display a more risk-taking side to his personality. He sneaked into Harrow's library with a group of students who had a mini roulette wheel and played for small amounts of money. On another occasion, he procured the letterhead of the Brunei Embassy from his friend and forged a letter to Chinawhite, the famous nightclub near Piccadilly Circus that in the 1990s was one of the city's hottest spots. In the letter, supposedly from staff at the embassy, Low asked for tables to be reserved at Chinawhite for members of Brunei's royal family. The gambit worked, and Low and his underage friends went partying alongside Premier League soccer players and models.

It was a lesson that power and prestige—or at least the appearance of it—opened all kinds of doors. Low positioned himself in the group as someone who could get things done. He'd make the bookings and collect money when it came time for the bill, making it appear like he was the one paying. He became the fixer, trading off his proximity to the truly powerful, and it had the effect of making him a focus of attention.

On vacations, Low headed to the Kensington Green apartment, where he spent more time with Riza Aziz. He knew that Malaysian politicians like Riza's stepfather, paid only moderate official government salaries, could never afford to live in multi-million-pound homes in London's toniest district. Everyone was aware that Malaysia's ruling party, the United Malays National Organization, demanded kickbacks from businesses for granting everything from gambling licenses to infrastructure contracts. Many of those businesses were controlled by Chinese Malaysians, like the Lows. The situation stirred in him a moral relativism. If everyone was taking a cut, then what was the problem?

After Harrow, Low opted to attend college in the United States. He had business ambitions, and America was his choice over stuffy Oxford and Cambridge. There, on the campus of an Ivy League school, he would enter the next stage of his metamorphosis.

Chapter 2

Asian Great Gatsby

Philadelphia, November 2001

Low stood in the nightclub he'd rented for his twentieth birthday—Shampoo, one of Philadelphia's most popular—and surveyed his domain. He'd agreed to pay around $40,000 for a full bar and canapés, and to keep out regular guests, giving the club an air of exclusivity. Only in his sophomore year, Low had spent weeks flicking through the student directory at the University of Pennsylvania. He had cold-called the social chairs of sororities to ensure the club was crammed with sought-after women. This wasn't a normal student night of beer-pong, and everyone turned up, from the jocks to the artsy crowd and the foreign students. The bar was stocked with champagne in sufficient supply to keep everyone's glass brimming all night.

Tipsy and swaying self-consciously to the pounding music under a gigantic disco ball, Low made awkward small talk with the women, asking them if they were enjoying the party. He seemed extremely anxious to please. At one point during the evening, a coterie of models wearing only bikinis made of lettuce leaves walked across the dance floor and reclined on a bar top. The waiting staff covered their near-naked bodies in sushi for the guests to eat with chopsticks. A Marilyn Monroe look-alike strutted out to sing happy birthday in a sultry voice.

Low looked on at the spectacle, smiling as the crowd roared with laughter.

Among themselves, some partygoers that night referred to Low as the "Asian Great Gatsby," a reflection of how their host seemed to observe his own parties, rather than partake in them. Like Jay Gatsby's, Low's origins were shrouded in mystery. The guests felt the need to talk to their benefactor, but conversations were stilted and trailed off. He was friendly enough but really didn't have anything interesting to say, instead preferring to repeatedly ensure his guests were sated. *Do you like the champagne? How's the sushi?* He wasn't hitting on women in the way other male students did when they hosted parties. In fact, he wasn't even flirting.

Low chose the university's business-focused Wharton School, whose alumni included Warren Buffett and Donald Trump, for its reputation as a production line for top financiers. For $25,000 a year, students in the economics department, where Low was studying, learned the mechanics of capitalism. Many of his classmates, wealthy students from across the globe, envisioned a career on Wall Street. Low majored in finance rather than dry macroeconomics, but he wasn't planning on a regular banking career. The Malaysian worked hard in his first year—he was a quick study with a prodigious memory—but he began to see Wharton foremost as a place to socialize and build his contacts.

That night in Shampoo—like the many others he would organize over the ensuing fifteen years in nightclubs and casinos across the world—was pure performance, orchestrated by Low to impress. For sure, he enjoyed partying, and he liked having pretty women around, but more than anything this was an investment, one that made him appear successful and indispensable. That was why, before the night in Shampoo, he had made an ostentatious request: The fliers for the party should have JHO LOW emblazoned in big letters next to those of the sororities. Low handed out two types of invites, standard and

VIP, promising a complimentary "premium open bar," and with details of shuttle buses from campus to the club. He intuitively understood that people desire to feel important, part of an exclusive club, and he played on it. "Fashionable attire is a must. No jeans or sneakers," the invites read.

Sure, Low was rich, with a family wealth in the millions. While at Wharton, he would receive regular wire transfers of tens of thousands of dollars from Larry Low to finance gambling trips to Atlantic City and to pay for partying. The money was a gift from a wealthy, doting father, ensuring Low made a name for himself with the children of influential families who attended Wharton. But even with his father's backing, Low was stretched to afford the cost of the night at Shampoo. Unknown to his guests, he had put down only a portion of the costs up front and later stalled on paying the balance to the club's owners, haggling for months before finally settling on a steep discount.

Low began to invite sorority members and his Asian and Middle Eastern friends to gamble, hiring stretch limos for the one-hour drive to Atlantic City. The group often gambled at the Trump Plaza Hotel and Casino, wagering a few hundred dollars a hand. Low even wrote Ivanka Trump, then a student at Wharton, inviting her to attend. Low told his friends she declined the offer on the grounds she would never set foot in one of her father's "skeevy" casinos. The group returned to Atlantic City several times, and Low at one point was up some $200,000, but he lost all of the gains during one heady night of gambling in 2002. Those around him were shocked at the cavalier attitude he exhibited while betting the equivalent of a year's tuition. This guy, they thought, must have money to burn.

The Malaysian worked in other ways to build his brand. He wrote articles on stocks for the *Wharton Journal*, the business school's student newspaper. One of Low's pieces, in the November 6, 2000, issue, argued Enron was no longer a conservative gas pipeline firm but a profitable financial company that had made new markets in commodities. It was only a year before Enron collapsed amid an accounting scandal, sending its top executives to jail. But it wasn't just that the analysis was faulty; many bankers had fallen for Enron's lies. Low had plagiarized entire sections of his piece, word for word, from a Salomon Smith Barney report. He wrote many more such pieces, copying most of them from analyst reports on Wall Street. Somehow this got past editors at the paper, and Low began to develop a reputa-tion as a stock picker, despite being only a freshman with zero experience analyzing companies.

He began to foster an aura of a rich prodigy. On campus, he drove around in a maroon-red SC-430 Lexus convertible, which he had leased but passed off as his own. He deliberately didn't correct rumors that he was a "prince of Malaysia," a claim that made the other Malaysian students laugh when they heard it. Low was playing a part—and it was not just to overcome any insecurity about his provincial background, but was aimed at getting him into the right social circle. He identified the wealthi-est students and pursued friendships with them. He got to know Hamad Al Wazzan, the son of a Kuwaiti construction and energy magnate, and he befriended students from the rich Gulf states of the Middle East.

Alongside this social striver, there was another Low, one whose friends were from humbler origins, and with whom he'd spend time in the dorm room eating buckets of KFC fried chicken and watching pirated DVD movies from Malaysia. This group included Seet Li Lin, a whip-smart Singaporean who was on a government scholarship at Wharton. With Seet and their group, Low would drop the act. They watched boxing on cable, Low lounging around in a baggy tracksuit, and would spend the odd evening at a Philly strip club called Delilah's or at one of the jock bars on campus. At one point, Low dated an exotic dancer from the club, whom he lavished with gifts. He fantasized about blonde stars like Paris Hilton and Britney Spears, and watched Hilton's debut film, *House of Wax*, half a dozen times, spurring eye rolls from roommates.

With his soft way of talking, almost inaudible at times, it was easy to forget you were doing what Low desired. In 2003, he persuaded his Arab friends to help him set up a tour around the Middle East, introducing him to the richest families and most influential firms. Taking a semester off, Low went to Kuwait, where Al Wazzan arranged meetings with businesspeople and minor royals.

Then, in Abu Dhabi, in one of these meetings—enabled by his years of cash-fueled networking—Low made a connection that would change the course of his life.

Chapter 3

Win Tons of Money

Abu Dhabi, United Arab Emirates, Fall 2003

In a seafood restaurant overlooking the sparkling Persian Gulf, a twenty-two-year-old Low sat down for lunch with Yousef Al Otaiba, a fresh-faced foreign policy adviser to the country's sheikhs. The Malaysian had begged a mutual friend to set up the meeting, and, as they ate, Low peppered Otaiba with questions. During the lunch, Otaiba noted that Low was no mere student on a world tour. Instead, the young Malaysian was eager for specific information about power structures in the United Arab Emirates: which sheikhs held the ear of the crown prince and who controlled the biggest pots of money. Low sensed that Otaiba, an inner-circle figure, could help guide him through the hallways of power in an up-and-coming nation.

Situated on an island in the Persian Gulf, just off the Arabian Peninsula, Abu Dhabi wasn't yet an impressive sight to behold, with its 1970s-era buildings and generic glass office towers. But the emirate was in the midst of big changes. Oil prices were on an upward trajectory that would fill the coffers of Middle East governments, and Abu Dhabi's royal family was overhauling the city, the capital of the UAE. Not far from the seafood restaurant, the Emirates Palace, a $3 billion edifice slated to become one of the world's ritziest hotels, was under construction.

With intelligent, piercing brown eyes and a closely shaved head that accentuated his angular features, Otaiba already had tasted more success by thirty than many men do in a lifetime. Yet his ambition, for power and money, was anything but sated. One of at least twelve children, from different wives, of Abu Dhabi's former oil minister, Otaiba had a privileged upbringing, attending the Cairo American College in Egypt—his mother's country—before studying at Georgetown (where he attended four years but did not graduate), and later, at Washington's National Defense University. Eloquent and charming, he positioned himself back home as an interpreter of the West for the emirate's royal family. At age twenty-six, he became an adviser to Abu Dhabi's crown prince, Mohammed Bin Zayed Al Nahyan, and he assumed the role of national security liaison with foreign governments.

Otaiba was always dressed impeccably in a Western business suit, and he had a perfect American accent, so officials in Washington often forgot he was a foreigner, and the young emirati became a trusted ally during the George W. Bush era. Over dinners, he expounded to journalists, diplomats, and White House officials about the need for the United States to take a hard line on Iran and Islamist militants, both of which he saw as an existential threat to Abu Dhabi's authoritarian government. By galvanizing support among Arab nations for the escalation of Bush's war in Iraq, Otaiba cemented his influence in Washington.

A regular on nightly cable news programs, he exhibited poise and charm, which masked a stony self-belief and a tendency to curtness with those who reported to him. In an email exchange with Mohamed El-Erian, then-CEO of PIMCO, the giant U.S. investment firm, and one of the world's most recognizable Arab businessmen, Otaiba warned him: "As you get to know me, you will find out that I'm brutally honest and blunt."

Otaiba was not as wealthy as many emiratis. His father, also a businessman with interests in finance and real estate, had accrued a fortune. But as one among so many children, Otaiba did not have the wealth to keep up with the royals, with their mansions, yachts, and other luxuries. The emirati led a second life that was costly to maintain, and he needed cash to compete with the princes of the Gulf. In conservative Abu Dhabi, Otaiba dressed in billowing robes and a *gutrah*, the traditional emirati headdress. But in the United States, like many senior Arab figures once they escape the strictures of life at home, he lived a decidedly more rakish lifestyle.

Not yet married, he supplied a Florida modeling agency with lists of his preferred women, mainly brunettes. Professionally successful, he still had an interest in self-enrichment. While well versed in Arab politics, Otaiba was a novice at business. To make money, he became involved with a construction company set up by a partner. The pair co-invested in projects in the Middle East, but Otaiba remained in the shadows: His main contribution to the business was to provide *wasta*, or "connections" in Arabic.

Here was just the kind of contact Low was seeking out: an influential figure, yet a striver, one who was still on the rise, knew nothing about business, and was amenable to a meeting with an unknown Malaysian. Over the lunch, Low held out the prospect of deals between the Middle East and Southeast Asia, especially Malaysia, which he talked up to Otaiba as a growing economy. It was mainly bluster—outside of throwing college parties, Low had no experience of brokering deals and, apart from his previous knack for borrowing money from family friends, no real special access in Malaysia. But Low did not let those facts stop him. As he listened to the persuasive Malaysian, Otaiba was intrigued by his talk of potential business relationships, and he began to open doors for Low in Abu Dhabi.

Soon after their first meeting, Otaiba introduced the young Malaysian to Khaldoon Khalifa Al Mubarak, another young, ambitious emirati who ran an investment fund called Mubadala Development. With prominent, arching eyebrows and sleek, frameless glasses, Al Mubarak was a charming figure who spoke calmly and easily broke into a smile. The son of an emirati ambassador murdered on the streets of Paris by a Palestinian terrorist group in 1984, Al Mubarak was—like Otaiba—a trusted aide to Abu Dhabi's most powerful sheikh, Crown Prince Mohammed Bin Zayed Al Nahyan.

At Wharton, Low could be indolent, scraping through with the bare minimum of effort. Yet here in Abu Dhabi he was getting a genuine education in how the world worked. Abu Dhabi had formed Mubadala a year earlier, in 2002, to diversify its oil-dependent economy. The idea was to raise capital from international markets, plowing the money into industries like real estate and semiconductors. Low could see how Al Mubarak, only in his late twenties and a smooth talker, was in a position of considerable power, with control over big chunks of Abu Dhabi's economy.

Mubadala was part of a trend in which rich states were playing a greater role in the global economy. Sovereign wealth funds had been around since the 1950s, when Saudi Arabia and Kuwait set up entities to find ways to invest their oil wealth with a long-term outlook. Other examples followed, from Norway's Government Pension Fund to the Abu Dhabi Investment Authority, the emirate's main wealth fund. By Low's visit, sovereign wealth funds controlled $3.5 trillion in assets, larger than the annual GDP of most Western nations.

But Mubadala was novel: Rather than simply invest oil profits, securing them for future generations, the fund was borrowing from global markets and actively trying to move the economy in new directions.

What Low saw in Abu Dhabi planted a seed in his mind. Malaysia had a sovereign wealth fund, Khazanah Nasional, but nothing like Mubadala. It would take six years for Low to establish himself as an Al Mubarak–like figure controlling his own fund in Malaysia. In the near term, he had a more achievable goal: to turn his newfound Arab contacts into business opportunities. Whatever Al Mubarak made of this cocksure young Malaysian, it would not be long before they found common ground on which to operate.

Back at Wharton for his final semester, Low set up his first company, the British Virgin Islands–based Wynton Group. The name stood for "win tons" of money, he told friends, who were unsure if it was a joke. Ivy League schools draw students from across the globe, whose families pay the huge fees in return for the networking opportunities and the brand name. In their senior years, the best students compete for jobs at Goldman Sachs or McKinsey & Company. Low's brother, Szen Low, who studied at Cambridge University in England, joined Goldman out of college.

But Low had no time for the well-trodden path, figuring he could make more money without the constrictions of an office job, and he set about pitching Wynton as a vehicle for Middle Eastern investors to get involved in projects in Malaysia. It started small, with some seed capital from the families of friends from Kuwait and other countries, and bought some stocks, but it wouldn't do any major deals until Low left Wharton for good.

As his senior year ended, in 2005, Low had a plan in mind: to return to Malaysia and look for ways to do business with his Wharton and Harrow contacts. A young financier with his own company, Low was ambitious. But he needed to find an influential backer at home.

Fortunately, from his father's real estate investment in London, he had one: the powerful family of Najib Razak.

Chapter 4

We're Going to Need a Bigger Van

Hong Kong, China, December 2007

In the lobby of Hong Kong's opulent Shangri-La Hotel, perched on a steep hill with views over the city's skyscrapers and the narrow harbor below, there was a commotion. The throng of handlers, security personnel, and assorted sycophants who clung around Malaysian Deputy Prime Minister Najib Razak and his wife, Rosmah Mansor, were trying to load the car taking them to the airport, but there was a problem. And Rosmah, her hair in a bouffant, the product of hours at the salon, and bedecked in expensive jewelry, was losing patience.

Najib had spent the past couple of days meeting fund managers with Credit Suisse, the investment bank, aimed at drumming up foreign investment. Malaysia's commodities-heavy economy was beginning to attract the attention of Wall Street banks. While Najib sat in conference rooms, Rosmah had indulged in Hong Kong's plethora of luxury boutiques. Now there was a problem. Rosmah's towering pile of boxes and shopping bags would not fit into the car taking them to the Malaysian government jet that was on standby in the VIP hangar at Chek Lap Kok airport. Scrambling, Rosmah's staff eventually found a van to haul the excess baggage. It took so long to make the arrangements and load the cargo hold, the jet did not take off for Malaysia until after midnight.

As the heir to a Malaysian political dynasty—his father and uncle had both been prime ministers—Najib and his wife were accustomed to a retinue of handlers who looked after their every need. In his midfifties with thick red lips and a salt-and-pepper mustache, his face often wearing a look of happy befuddlement, Najib was the epitome of an entitled politician. His father, Abdul Razak, tried to instill an old-fashioned morality into Najib and his four younger brothers. When the boys asked for a swimming pool at the prime minister's official residence, their father rejected the proposal, lecturing his children on how a public servant should not use state funds for personal pleasure. But Abdul Razak died young, when Najib was only twenty-two, and with him any restraining influence also vanished. From then on, the boys, and especially Najib, were enveloped in the privileged bubble of the ruling United Malays National Organization, or UMNO.

Educated at Malvern College, an illustrious British boarding school, and the University of Nottingham, Najib preferred English to Malay. Like an English gentleman, he had a penchant for expensive cigars and watched English TV shows like *Yes Minister*, a sitcom about a bumbling government minister. On the back of his revered father's name, he held a string of plum government positions. A deputy minister by his midtwenties, Najib didn't bother himself much with the mundane details of governance, preferring to attend events and make speeches. From the outset, he was surrounded by yes men.

UMNO had ruled Malaysia since its independence from Britain in 1957. Malaysia held regular elections, but the system was deeply flawed and corrupt. In the 1970s, Najib's father ushered in policies whose effect was to help Malays, the majority ethnic group. The government reserved university places for Malays, gave special financial handouts to Malays, and even favored Malay-owned companies for state contracts. By 2007, these policies had spawned a thick web of graft in which businesses, many controlled by Chinese and Indian Malaysians, had to pay kickbacks to the likes of Najib and Rosmah in order to operate.

Rosmah's origins were somewhat more humble. Her parents were middle-class school teachers, but she had partly grown up on the grounds of the palace of a Malaysian sultan, who had adopted the family as his own. The experience had exposed Rosmah to wealth from a young age but also instilled in her a sense of insecurity, of not truly belonging to the aristocratic world she inhabited, according to people who know her. Fascinated by royalty, Rosmah reportedly eyed members of Brunei's royal family for marriage before she met Najib in the 1980s. She was working for a property company and he was a chief minister. They married soon after, a second union for them both.

When Rosmah first boarded a government private jet, she was enthralled by her new surroundings. To compensate for her common origins, she began to dress in fine silks and precious jewels. She could be humorous, but she also exhibited a draconian streak, yelling at aides and cutting off contact with a daughter from her first marriage because she disliked her choice of husband. Relationships for her appeared to be transactional. Foreign businessmen seeking government support for a new venture would often meet her first, and she'd set up a follow-up encounter with Najib.

Grandees from the ruling UMNO party grew concerned about the deputy prime minister and his wife. Most politicians had made money through kickbacks for government contracts and property deals, and Najib was no exception. But by the mid-2000s Rosmah's spending had reached new extremes, even for

Malaysia. One story that made the rounds involved her breezing into a Hermès store and informing the clerks of the few items she did not want to buy, before ordering one of everything else.

To finance her penchant for luxury items, Rosmah was pilfering the state coffers. One Malaysian businessman detailed how it worked: He would buy properties from state-owned companies before selling them at a markup to other state firms, sharing the profit with Rosmah. She was already an unpopular figure in Malaysia, having developed a reputation as a social climber and modern-day Imelda Marcos, whose penchant for high-end accessories, like Birkin handbags by Hermès, which cost tens of thousands of dollars apiece, seemed beyond the reach of Najib's official salary.

She couldn't walk around in public with multi-million-dollar pieces of jewelry, so she'd spend hours pulling items out of a collection of safes around her home. "She'd just sit polishing them, trying them on, admiring them," said a family member. "It was almost like 'my precious' from *Lord of the Rings*."

In late 2006, a Mongolian model, a girlfriend of a Najib aide, was shot dead, and her corpse was then blown up with C4 explosives. At the time she was killed, the dead woman's boyfriend, an aide in Najib's Defense Ministry, was facing accusations of accepting bribes worth more than $100 million from a French submarine company. A Malaysian court later convicted two police officers for the murder. At the time, the officers were part of Najib's personal security detail. Najib denied any knowledge of the killing, but the sordid affair stuck to him like a rotting smell.

By 2007, with Najib harboring ambitions for the nation's top office, one once held by his father, the ambitious couple needed some good news. It arrived in the form of a friend of Rosmah's son, a young man called Jho Low whom they had met in London.

On his return to Malaysia, after graduating from Wharton in the spring of 2005, Low set up offices on the seventieth floor of the Petronas Towers in Kuala Lumpur for his company, Wynton. The pair of futuristic skyscrapers, the tallest buildings in the world in the late 1990s and early 2000s, were the premier address in Malaysia's capital—a symbol of the country's emergence from agrarian poverty within a generation. Encased in shiny chrome steel cladding, with a sky bridge linking the forty-first floors, the towers featured in the 1999 film *Entrapment* with Sean Connery and Catherine Zeta-Jones. In the lobby, iron bars inserted into the black marble floor traced a swirling Islamic-inspired geometric pattern.

Only the best-known Malaysian firms could afford an office in the towers. Chief among them was Petronas, the state oil company, whose profits had fueled Malaysia's economic transformation. Jho Low, his college graduation barely behind him, couldn't really afford such a prestigious address, but managed to arrange a loan from a local bank. Using the bank's money, he decorated the office, sparing no expense. The space featured an "island" boardroom in the center of the floor, with glass that frosted over at the touch of a button. A whiteboard inside printed out whatever was written on it. In the restrooms, the toilet seats adjusted automatically to the height of the occupant. There was even a wading pool for tired feet. For Malaysia at the time, this was more than cutting-edge technology: It was the most luxurious office space in the country.

Low splashed money on staff, even though he had few investment deals in the pipeline. One of his first hires was Seet Li Lin, the Singaporean whom he had befriended at Wharton. Seet had a sound understanding of finance, having gone to work for Singapore's central bank after college, before Low convinced him to join Wynton. Extremely young looking, with a cheerful smile, Seet acted as Low's details guy. Often, Low would begin a negotiation before asking Seet to take care of the details. Like his boss, Seet was impatient to get ahead. The key to his success at Wharton, he once boasted, was turning in essays that were big on buzzwords and short on substance.

Eric Tan—a Malaysian whom Low referred to as "Fat Eric"—also became a key member of Low's entourage. A Malaysian who spoke heavily accented English, Tan would become Low's de facto body man, a partner so trusting of Low that he would sign any document without question. Low had met Tan in the nightclub world in Malaysia, and they would travel everywhere together, for work and vacations.

Now all Low needed was business. While at Wharton, he'd made contacts in the Middle East. Now, he wanted to bring rich Arabs to invest in Malaysia, perhaps making a fee for brokering a deal. To build allegiances, Low sent chocolates and flowers to prospective partners, and offered personal favors, securing appointments with sought-after doctors. But as a Chinese Malaysian, Low knew he needed a Malay protector if he were to really succeed in business. He had one in mind: the family of Najib Razak, whose stepson, Riza Aziz, he had gotten to know in London. The deputy prime minister himself was still out of reach, but a mutual friend introduced him to Nizam Razak, one of the politician's four brothers, and Low offered him space for free in Wynton's office. Low enticed Nizam to co-invest in a high-end condominium project near the Petronas Towers that some contacts from Penang were developing.

The problem with the co-investment was that Low didn't have any money—in fact, he had sizable debts from his bank loans. When it came time for the down payment, a businessman fixer of the Najib family came in to arrange financing and bail Low and Nizam out of the situation. Low was at a low ebb. After failing to pay the rent on the Petronas Towers office for several months, he had to give it up. Rather than getting him close to Najib's family, his efforts appeared to be in vain.

"They had disdain for him," one close aide of Najib said of Low.

But Low was tenacious and resourceful, using every failure as an opportunity. He had gotten to know executives from the

Kuwait Finance House, an Islamic bank, which had come in on the condominium property deal. In 2007, he tried to broker a deal for the Kuwait Finance House to take over a Malaysian bank. He failed again, but had added to his contact book. Low was becoming adept at obtaining meetings with powerful figures, putting himself in the room even though he had no track record.

Later that year, he heard Khazanah, Malaysia's powerful sovereign wealth fund, was looking for partners to develop a gigantic construction project in the southern state of Johor, near the border with Singapore, to be known as the Iskandar Development Region. The project was an ambitious effort to create a financial and lifestyle center to rival wealthier Singapore, Southeast Asia's financial and commercial hub.

Here was Low's chance. In Abu Dhabi, Low had observed firsthand the huge amounts of money that sovereign wealth funds control, and he saw an opportunity to broker a deal. Since Low's Middle East tour, Khaldoon Al Mubarak, the chief executive of Mubadala, had grown in prestige. Buoyed by sky-high oil prices, Mubadala had taken sizable minority stakes in firms like Ferrari and Advanced Micro Devices, and Al Mubarak controlled a multi-billion-dollar empire.

Low's main contact in Abu Dhabi remained Yousef Al Otaiba, the political adviser to the emirate's crown prince. On June 17, 2007, Low wrote an email to Otaiba with details of the plans for the Iskandar development, and suggested Mubadala could invest. He then arranged for Khazanah executives to fly to Abu Dhabi, where he set up meetings with Otaiba and others.

"Otaiba's name card is the only one you need in Abu Dhabi," Low joked as he introduced the emirati to Khazanah executives.

Low was punctilious, stage-managing meetings and phone calls between Mubadala and Khazanah, and sending around emails ahead of time with subject lines like "sequence of events."

He also acted as if the deal would go off the table if both sides didn't pounce now. Situating himself at the nexus of the deal-making, Low's behavior served to deepen the impression that he could deliver powerful Middle Eastern contacts.

Low's ability to bring Mubadala to the table marked a revival after the mess of the failed condominium deal. He latched onto the opportunity it presented to build his political contacts in Malaysia. He already knew Deputy Prime Minister Najib's brother and his stepson, and he set about getting close to Najib and Rosmah themselves. In 2007, Low formed an offshore company for Rosmah and Najib to help pay for their daughter's expenses while studying at Georgetown.

The Iskandar land project, with a big investment from the Middle East, offered Low a chance to show his worth. The young Malaysian told the politician about the deal, and offered for Najib to take credit for it—all without having to do the legwork. The Iskandar project, right on Singapore's doorstep, would burnish Najib's credentials as a doer, a politician who could attract investment and finally propel Malaysia into the ranks of developed nations.

As Rosmah Mansor took the microphone, she beamed at the crowd. Clad in colorful traditional Malay silks, the wife of the deputy prime minister was enjoying playing host. The guests, soft drinks in hand, milled around the huge stateroom of Rosmah and Najib's official residence, an impersonal, cavernous building, with a pointed red-tiled roof and floor-to-ceiling windows that offered a sweeping view of gardens bordered by a man-made lake. Outside a tropical downpour threatened to break out. At the back of the room, scurrying around, making sure everyone was having a good time and meeting the right people, was Jho Low.

That night, in late August 2007, marked a new turn for Najib and Rosmah—and they had the young Malaysian to thank for it. The guests had assembled at Najib's residence in the new city of Putrajaya, just outside Kuala Lumpur. Malaysia had moved the government there in the 1990s, hoping to develop a global technology hub. An impressive sight of modern skyscrapers and Islamic-inspired domed edifices set around a huge lake, Putrajaya had never attracted sufficient capital or companies and felt somewhat forlorn, its multilane highways largely empty.

Inside the residence, however, the mood was celebratory. The party was to mark the deal for Mubadala and the Kuwait Finance House to take a stake in the Iskandar land project. "I'd like to thank Jho Low for bringing Middle Eastern investment to Malaysia," Rosmah told the room. Then, accompanied by a live band, she began to sing a number of ballads, as the bemused delegation from Abu Dhabi looked on.

Afterward, guests waited in line as Najib introduced Mubadala's chief executive around the room. Wearing a head-dress, and with a confident yet polite demeanor, Al Mubarak had added another investment to his growing empire, all thanks to Low. The next morning, Mubadala signed a contract to invest half a billion dollars in the Johor project of five-star hotels, residences, and a "golf village."

For Low, the deal was a seminal moment. His ability to source Middle Eastern money put him in good stead with Najib and Rosmah, reinforcing his claims to hold sway in the Arab world. The couple was fascinated by the Gulf, where rulers enjoyed lives of exceptional luxury. In parallel, Low was making other efforts to ensure he became enmeshed with the family. A few weeks earlier he had flown to London for the high school graduation party of Nooryana Najib, Najib and Rosmah's daughter, who was leaving the exclusive Sevenoaks School to study at Georgetown in the United States.

But there was a problem. Low had expected to make serious

money for himself from the deal, and he was incensed when Khazanah turned down his request to be paid a broker fee. Run by professionals, the fund was too clean for Low's purposes. Going forward, he really needed to control his own pot of investment money. To do so, Low prepared to dive deeply into the world of offshore finance.

Chapter 5

A Nice Toy

Washington, DC, August 2008

In the fall of 2008, Otaiba's business partner, a Jordanian named Shaher Awartani, wrote him an email containing some very welcome news. The pair was about to make around $10 million through a deal that Low had set up in Malaysia. Perhaps worried about too many direct interactions with this Malaysian broker, Otaiba relied on Awartani to communicate with Low. Yet the Malaysian was starting to prove a very lucrative connection.

"Great news. It's nice to see our efforts finally paying off," Otaiba wrote back.

Soon after, Awartani suggested buying a Ferrari after what Otaiba described as a "transfer from Jho."

"I think we each deserve to buy a nice toy in celebration, what do you think? The 458 ITALIA maybe?" Awartani wrote in an email to Otaiba. The ambassador responded that such ostentatious consumption in Abu Dhabi "will just attract unnecessary attention."

Otaiba had reason to keep his dealings with Low under wraps. A few months earlier, he had become the UAE's ambassador to the United States, fast establishing himself as one of Washington's most prominent diplomats. His dinner parties, at the ambassador's palatial residence on the Virginia bank of the

Potomac River, catered by celebrity chefs such as Wolfgang Puck, attracted White House staffers, members of Congress, and top cable-news hosts. Sometimes, the ambassador invited guests down to his man cave—a basement area with a huge flat-screen television—to watch basketball. Accompanied by his glamorous wife, Abeer, an Egyptian-born civil engineer, Otaiba seemed to attend every social event in the capital. With his Western ways, and Abu Dhabi's support of the fight against militant Islam, the ambassador was a popular figure, whether at cocktail parties or propounding his views on *Morning Joe.*

But Otaiba, only in his midthirties, had a hidden side, a business life, one which he kept away from the limelight. The ambassador had been right to bet on Jho Low. His association with the Malaysian looked like it would make him exceptionally rich.

Denied a broker fee in the Iskandar land deal, Low had cast around for another way to profit. He had started out trying to be a classic deal maker, angling to earn a fee for bringing Mubadala into the investment. But he had been blocked. To get the payoff he believed he deserved, and to repay Ambassador Otaiba, Low would do whatever it took.

He came up with a convoluted yet brilliant scheme. Malaysia was abuzz over Mubadala's plans for the giant Iskandar project. With blueprints calling for new roads, homes, malls, and industrial developments, builders would be jockeying to win lucrative contracts. At this time, Low heard about two Malaysian construction companies that were for sale. Perhaps he could buy them cheaply, and win contracts on the Iskandar development? To finance the multi-million-dollar purchase price, Low needed more loans. But he was still a nobody in the eyes of banks, a low-level businessman with a poor track record. To burnish his image and get his hands on the banks' money, he once again turned to powerful friends.

As a vehicle to make the purchase, Low set up a British Virgin Islands entity called the Abu Dhabi-Kuwait-Malaysia Investment Company and gave free shares to Ambassador Otaiba and minor aristocrats from Kuwait and Malaysia. He was creating the impression that prominent individuals were behind the company. With such illustrious backing now in place, Low had no trouble persuading Malaysian banks to lend tens of millions of dollars. He used some of the debt to fund the investment group's acquisition of the construction companies. At the same time, a subsidiary of Wynton, Low's company, took out further loans to finance the purchase of a minority stake in the Iskandar land project alongside Mubadala. Instead of receiving a broker fee, Low became a co-investor.

He then set about creating a fiction that major Middle Eastern sovereign wealth funds also were involved in the purchase of the construction companies. If Low could make it appear as if his personal ventures were backed by powerful Middle Eastern funds, he could attract even more money. To create the illusion, he turned to the opaque world of offshore finance. Low knew about offshore financial centers from his father, Larry, who had a myriad of overseas accounts. It was normal for rich Asians, fearing instability at home, or just to evade taxes, to set up offshore accounts in secretive jurisdictions like the British Virgin Islands and the Cayman Islands.

The "offshore" designation typically refers to jurisdictions whose financial systems are much larger than their domestic economies; in other words, the banking system exists purely for nonresidents to stash cash, unlike international financial centers in London and New York that also service local citizens and companies. In recent years, offshore centers have come under pressure to share information on their clients. But many of these centers, reliant on annual fees from the thousands of companies seeking a cloak of secrecy, remain safe harbors for money launderers and other criminals to wash cash and avoid taxes. One recent estimate puts the money stashed in offshore financial centers since 1970 at $32 trillion—a figure equal to the combined economies of the United States and China—with hundreds of billions lost in tax revenues.

The now twenty-six-year-old Low was already mastering this hidden realm of the global economy. He would have known that the Cayman Islands, home to branches of U.S. banks and hedge funds, had improved its information sharing with Washington. The British Virgin Islands in the Caribbean, however, had a no-questions-asked approach to company incorporation, and was where he had set up Wynton. (In 2007, his sister Low May-Lin became a solicitor of the Supreme Court of the British Virgin Islands.) And tiny Seychelles, in the Indian Ocean, had the advantage of not seeming to care who owned its shell companies.

Most importantly, Low had experienced the ease of setting up an offshore account—almost anyone could do it. For only a few thousand dollars, a corporate-services firm like U.S.-headquartered Trident Trust or Mossack Fonseca of Panama would open an account or form a company, and deal with all the paperwork. (The Panama Papers, a leak in 2016 of hundreds of thousands of Mossack Fonseca client records going back to the 1970s, showed the extent of the use of offshore accounts by the global elite, from the family of Chinese president Xi Jinping to actress Emma Watson.)

Without this secrecy, the scam that was about to unfold would have been impossible. For the next step of his scheme, Low set up two shell companies in the Seychelles. The firms—ADIA Investment Corporation and KIA Investment Corporation—appeared, given their names, to be related to the Abu Dhabi Investment Authority, or ADIA, and Kuwait Investment Authority, or KIA, two of the most famous, multi-billion-dollar sovereign wealth funds in the world. But the look-alike companies were purely Low's creation, with no links to Abu Dhabi or Kuwait.

In setting up ADIA Investment Corporation, Low experimented with another financial trick that he would add to his repertoire. The company issued just one unregistered share, valued at $1, and it was controlled by whoever physically held the stock certificate. These "bearer shares" were banned in many jurisdictions, including Great Britain and the United States—Nevada and Wyoming in 2007 became the last states to abolish their use—because they allowed owners of companies to hide behind layers of secrecy and made it nearly impossible for regulators to determine the owner of an asset at a given point in time. Seeking to find tax cheats in the early 2000s, the United States started to pressure offshore centers to hand over details of the beneficial owners of companies and accounts. Even the British Virgin Islands had recently outlawed the practice of bearer shares. But in the Seychelles, Low learned, they were still permitted.

Next, Low had these look-alike offshore companies take minority stakes in the Malaysian construction firms. It now would appear to any prospective business partner doing due diligence that royals from Kuwait and Malaysia, as well as Ambassador Otaiba, and two major sovereign wealth funds, were Low's partners in plans to develop the Iskandar project.

With this elaborate structure in place, Low went fishing. He needed a mark, a rich but financially naive businessman who would buy the companies and land from his supposedly illustrious investment group for a high price. He found one in Taib Mahmud, the seventy-one-year-old chief minister of Sarawak, a remote, jungle-covered Malaysian state on Borneo Island, separated from the rest of the country by hundreds of miles of sea. Short and elfish, with silver-gray hair, Taib was one of Malaysia's richest individuals—the product of decades in businesses such as logging and palm-oil plantations that had led to the deforestation of his state. A wily and long-serving politician, Taib dressed in white suits, drove a white Rolls-Royce, and owned a white grand piano, which had once belonged to Liberace. He was not, however, a skilled financier.

The chief minister had come to hear of Low, who was touting Mubadala's ambitions to invest more widely in Malaysia after the Iskandar deal. Taib was keen for investment to build palm-oil refineries and other energy projects in Sarawak. Low held out the possibility of huge Middle Eastern outlays. But in the meantime, Low persuaded Taib to buy the construction companies and the Iskandar land.

A few months later, Wynton, Low's company, completed the sale of its stake in the Iskandar land to UBG, a holding company controlled by Chief Minister Taib, in return for cash and shares. The deal made Low the largest shareholder of UBG. He crowed to friends that the sale had netted a $110 million profit for Wynton by selling to Taib at a significant markup. The Malaysian had made his first killing, and he traded in his E-series Mercedes for a black-colored Ferrari, taking his new toy for nightime joy rides around Kuala Lumpur.

But there were problems on the horizon. Low's haul was staggering, and Taib, who still held a stake in UBG, would be furious when he found out the premium he had paid. Otaiba, too, started to hear talk of these huge profits that Low had reaped and worried that he was only being fed scraps. It was Otaiba, after all, who had lent his name to this deal, embellishing the fiction that Abu Dhabi officially was involved.

"Our friend Jho may be shafting us on the Iskandar Development region issue," Awartani wrote to Otaiba. "My opinion is we may be getting just a bone to keep us happy and [quiet]."

On U.S. nightly cable news, Otaiba had a charming demeanor as he explained Middle East affairs to American audiences, but, used to wielding power, he could be stony in private, and Low's perceived double-dealing infuriated him. He viewed Low as a useful contact, one who offered access to potentially lucrative deals in Malaysia, but it was the Malaysian who ultimately needed him—and his high-level contacts in Abu Dhabi—far more than he relied on Low.

"He needs to understand VERY clearly that he can't do much without us knowing," Otaiba replied to Awartani, urging him to confront Low. "Personally, I prefer the direct approach cuz it will scare him a bit."

Even his partners were starting to distrust Low. But at that moment, he had finally hit a gusher of cash, all without holding down a regular job. He was twenty-seven years old—only three years out of college. While most of his Wharton classmates were grappling with the turmoil engulfing Wall Street and the world financial system in late 2008, Low was already sitting on a fortune that most of his finance industry classmates from Wharton could only dream of. Without producing anything, Low had shown an unusual ability to navigate the chambers of power and persuade investors by holding out the promise of large returns. He had made money for Otaiba and his other influential sponsors, strengthening his web of contacts. Not all the cash was really his—he'd have to figure out a way to get some money back to Taib—but Low was starting to develop a deal-making reputation.

He was no longer a nobody, but an investor with a track record who was now a fixture at events—business meetings but also society gatherings—held by Kuala Lumpur's elite. It was this precocious renown that landed him on the radar screen of an ambitious banker at Wall Street's most powerful financial institution.

Chapter 6

Doctor Leissner, I Presume

The Great Wall of China, June 2006

Waiters bustled around Chinese banquet tables, which had been set up under a tent at the Great Wall near Beijing for a celebration with a very special guest of honor. Moments later, Lloyd Blankfein, the aggressive former trader who recently had been named chief executive of Goldman Sachs Group, arrived with an entourage of senior American and Chinese bankers. Blankfein was the new king of Wall Street, and Goldman was holding a symbolic global board meeting on the Great Wall, a sign of the importance of China—and Asia more broadly—for the powerful bank.

Hank Paulson, who had just left the chief executive role, had steered Goldman deep into China, where it made money advising the Communist government on how to privatize companies and became one of the first foreign banks to set up a local securities joint venture. Paulson had quit weeks earlier to become President George W. Bush's Treasury secretary, and Blankfein was keen to keep the focus turned on Asia. The region remained somewhat of a backwater. Wall Street banks still earned well over half of their profit in the United States, raising capital for clients, advising on mergers and acquisitions, and selling profitable derivative products, not to mention making hefty bets with their own money, including on the teetering housing market. Before the financial crisis, Asia accounted for only around a tenth of Wall Street's profits, of which China was a major driver.

By 2006, however, the winds were shifting. The board meeting on the Great Wall was largely a symbolic affair, but as the attendees looked out from their perch down over the plains toward Beijing, the talk was tinged with optimism about the future of Asia. There was growing interest in the region, as China's economy, churning out toys, clothes, machine parts, and other manufactured goods for the United States and Europe, grew at double-digit rates. Southeast Asian neighbors like Malaysia, which supplied China with raw materials, were registering their own solid economic expansions of more than 5 percent annually. Goldman's honchos began telling staff they had better chances of promotion if they moved to Asia, a sweetener to get employees to uproot their families from New York and London and relocate to Hong Kong or Singapore.

In early 2009, Tim Leissner, a rising star at Goldman in Asia, stepped out of a car at the Istana Negara in Kuala Lumpur. With mustard-colored domes, the imposing hillside official residence of Malaysia's king evoked an Indian maharaja's palace. It was an incongruous location for Leissner, a thirty-nine-year-old German, to be holding a meeting. Six foot three tall and dashing, Leissner, head of investment banking in Southeast Asia, had spent a decade generating new business for Goldman throughout the region.

Today's meeting was different. After flying in from his base in Hong Kong, Leissner went to purchase a *songkok*, a traditional Malay hat, a piece of headgear that was de rigueur when meeting Malaysia's king. He was there to talk with the sultan of Terengganu, Mizan Zainal Abidin, one of the country's nine hereditary princes, who at the time was also king of Malaysia under a system that rotates the crown among the sultans. Mizan often received guests in ceremonial Malay attire—a headdress made from folded embroidered silk, a short golden-threaded sarong over black pants, with a kris dagger tucked into a waistband—but for this meeting he was dressed in a Western business suit.

Typically Leissner would scout for deals in Malaysia by maintaining close ties with chief executives and politicians. The country's economy was a minnow compared to China, where Goldman was focusing most of its attention in Asia, but Leissner had spent almost a decade building connections in Malaysia, and Goldman had started to make respectable money advising on deals. Sometimes he would rely on middlemen, politically connected Malaysian brokers, who took a fee for making introductions, a normal practice in Asia. This meeting had been organized by Jho Low, who was only twenty-seven years old but seemed extremely well connected.

Leissner had met Low through Roger Ng, a well-connected local banker at Goldman, and the young Malaysian registered an unfavorable first impression. Low seemed like a striver, someone who tried to set up deals and take a cut without doing the legwork or risking any money of his own. Leissner told friends that he considered Low a "dodgy" character. Still, Low had investment ideas, and the Goldman banker was ambitious and hungry for the next big thing. Low had told Leissner about the sultan's plans to set up an investment fund to manage his state's oil and gas wealth. The sultan, Low had said, wanted to hire Goldman.

A good talker, Leissner knew how to charm Asian dignitaries, and he hit it off with the sultan. By the end of the meeting, Goldman had clinched a contract to advise on the formation of the new fund, which was to be known as the Terengganu Investment Authority. Goldman's fee for setting up the authority was a paltry $300,000—a sum barely worth getting out of bed for, by Wall Street's standards. But Leissner knew how to play the long game. The Terengganu deal was the beginning of a line of business that in short order would earn hundreds of millions of dollars for Goldman. Suddenly, the one-time backwater of Malaysia would become one of Goldman's biggest profit centers anywhere in the world.

Growing up in the northern German town of Wolfsburg, close to Hanover, Leissner led a privileged childhood as the middle of three brothers. His father was a senior executive with Volkswagen, which is based in the town, and he attended a local high school, playing tennis most afternoons at a private club from the age of ten. In the summers, the family would send him to exclusive training camps in Europe and the United States, where he hit with star players such as Steffi Graf.

When he was seventeen, Leissner spent a year as an exchange student at the private Millbrook School in upstate New York. His host family considered him reserved, a trait they took to be typically German, but he quickly dove into his new American life. He played basketball and wide receiver for the football team. The local newspaper described his "slew of life's gifts" that included "confidence, intelligence, looks, affluence and athletic talent." The sports coach praised him as the most coachable student he had ever taught and a "great role player." He attracted women easily, almost without trying, and had a tennis-playing American girlfriend.

The trip gave Leissner a taste for life abroad. After college in Germany he headed to the States—to the University of Hartford in Connecticut for an MBA. The class was filled with international students, and he met a French woman of Iranian descent. They moved to London and married, and Leissner joined J.P. Morgan as an associate, the lowest level of banker. He was hungry for success, and despite his gifts there were signs of a willingness to cut corners.

In 1993, while employed at J.P. Morgan, Leissner acquired a doctorate in business administration from the University of Somerset. The college, which closed down a few years later, was known for selling degrees for a few thousand dollars, especially to Americans looking to burnish their credentials with a certificate from a serious-sounding British institution. Leissner began using the title "Dr." at speaking engagements and soon after he secured a promotion to vice president at J.P. Morgan.

While in London, he was involved in a deal to finance a power plant in Indonesia, and the work got him interested in Asia. His marriage was falling apart, and by 1997 he moved to Hong Kong, where he had secured a job with Lehman Brothers.

In the 1990s Hong Kong was a city in flux. The territory of 7 million, situated on mountainous islands and part of the Chinese mainland, had become a playground for expatriate financiers. Asian economies like Thailand and South Korea had been through a decade of heady growth, and bankers worked long hours, partied in the bars and fleshpots of Wanchai, the city's entertainment district, and took jaunts to Hong Kong's outer islands in private yachts on the weekends.

By 1997, however, the party atmosphere was souring. After 156 years of colonial rule, Britain was handing Hong Kong back to China. The Asian financial crisis was in full swing, the result of years of reckless borrowing to finance investments in property and other risky sectors. It was a typical financial bubble, and when speculators like George Soros attacked the region's overvalued currencies, angering Malaysia's then prime minister, Mahathir Mohamad, foreign banks were forced to book losses on loans that went bad.

For a financier like Leissner, there was an upside to all that volatility. Among foreign bankers, Asia had developed a reputation as a place to turbocharge a Wall Street career. Competition out in Hong Kong and Singapore was less fierce, and bankers were given more latitude to make big financial trades. In 1995 a rogue trader at Britain's Barings Bank named Nick Leeson made unauthorized bets on Japanese stocks that led to the bank's collapse. But as Leissner was arriving, activity in capital markets—the raising of money through selling stocks and bonds—was drying up thanks to the crisis. Lehman wasn't too exposed, though, and it began to advise the region's cash-strapped governments on a wave of privatizations to raise money.

Hong Kong–based bankers often kept a blistering pace, traveling nonstop around the region, and Leissner was no exception. On one deal, he worked alongside Goldman bankers to help a state-owned Thai petroleum company sell a chunk of shares. The bankers worked eighteen-hour days, finishing at 2 a.m. and partying in Bangkok's notorious bars for a couple more hours before starting over. The crisis forged close links between the Wall Street bankers who had chosen the less crowded field of Asia to further their careers. Leissner's work ethic impressed Goldman, considered top of the pile of global banks, and he was offered a job. He accepted.

Shortly after Leissner joined, Goldman moved its Asian headquarters into gleaming new offices in Hong Kong's Cheung Kong Center, a seventy-floor skyscraper with breathtaking views of the Peak, a mountain that towers over the central financial district, and Victoria Harbor, a busy sea channel separating Hong Kong island from the mainland. One floor had meeting rooms adorned with multi-million-dollar Chinese art, including ancient calligraphy and ink drawings of mist-shrouded mountains. An antique terra-cotta horse donated by Li Ka-shing, the Hong Kong billionaire who owned the building, stood inside the reception area.

At Goldman, Leissner met and fell in love with Judy Chan,

a junior analyst at the bank, and they married after the German banker's divorce from his first wife. Chan was from an Indonesian-Chinese family that had made a fortune in coal mining—and the first of many connected women that Leissner would court. The wedding ceremony at a luxury Hong Kong hotel featured suckling pigs with flashing lights in their eye sockets. The couple had two daughters together, but he was rarely at home. As an executive director in the mergers and acquisitions division, Leissner practically lived on planes, incessantly looking for deals on which Goldman could advise or offer financing.

After a few lean years, as Asia picked itself up from the crisis, Leissner began to strike gold. In 2002, Goldman sold shares for a Malaysian cell phone company owned by Ananda Krishnan, a billionaire whom Leissner had gotten to know. The $800 million IPO was the largest offering in Asia that year, and Leissner was promoted to managing director. The following year, he helped bring in another Krishnan-related deal, this time selling IPO shares for a satellite-television company called Astro. Then, in May 2006, Leissner beat out other banks to snag a role advising on Malaysia's largest-ever corporate takeover, a $2 billion deal for a local power company. Goldman's fee on the deal, $9 million, was respectable, even by U.S. norms, and much fatter than run-of-the-mill Malaysian payouts.

Goldman colleagues noticed how Leissner had an uncanny ability to make clients feel like they had a deep, personal connection with him. He was a relationship banker, skilled at reeling in important executives through a kind of personal magnetism, rather than a "structuring guy," one of the mathematical whizzes who priced and sold complex derivative products.

Since coming to Asia, Leissner had deepened his connections, especially in Malaysia. He was funny and animated, speaking in German-accented English, and a consummate networker who told people what they wanted to hear. He would sit next to clients in the boardroom rather than across the table. At one society wedding in Kuala Lumpur, he spent the entire dinner out of his seat, making the rounds of the hotel ballroom.

"He loved clients and he loved deals," said Joe Stevens, a senior banker who worked with him at Goldman.

As Goldman Sachs ramped up its Asia business under Hank Paulson and now Lloyd Blankfein, Tim Leissner was a benefi- ciary. In October 2006, he made partner, one of 115 staff that year to be invited into Goldman's inner sanctum. The bank kept the partner pool to only a few hundred people, or no more than 2 percent of its thirty thousand full-time employees, and those anointed were personally called by Blankfein. The honor came with a pay bump, to a base salary of almost $1 million, and access to larger bonuses and proprietary investments—deals that Goldman's top bankers reserved for themselves. Leissner had begun to make real money for Goldman in Malaysia, and he was reaping the benefits of the bank's Asia focus. Of those who made partner in 2006, more than a fifth were from the region, out of whack with the fees generated there. It was a signal from Blankfein that Goldman saw a bright future.

But there were whispers about Leissner. Some Goldman bankers greeted him with, "Dr. Leissner, I presume," an ironic allusion to his questionable academic credentials. And there was his string of affairs, which struck some colleagues as unprofes- sional. He didn't so much engage in one-night stands as fall in love easily, floating from one serious relationship to another. He had begun a romantic liaison with the chief financial officer of Astro during negotiations for the IPO. The relationship, which was not hidden, led rival bankers to complain to Astro's chief executive that it gave Goldman an unfair advantage. After an internal complaint, Goldman launched an investigation. But

Leissner denied any involvement with the woman, and Goldman dropped the matter.

He also was prone to go off the reservation. As a junior banker, he would overstep his authority. "He never operated within boundaries. He would offer clients, and get permission later. It was tolerated because he brought in deals," said one Goldman banker who worked with him. In one deal that caused concern, Leissner gave a written assurance to the chief executive of Maybank, a large Malaysian commercial bank, that Goldman would underwrite a $1 billion rights issue, meaning it would pledge its own capital to buy up the shares and later sell them into the market. But he didn't inform his bosses in Hong Kong, despite the huge risks involved. Another time, Goldman cut Leissner's pay for passing information outside the company without authorization. It was a warning sign, but Leissner was making money for Goldman and the bank took no further action.

Leissner took little notice of the admonishments—this was Asia, the Wild West of capitalism, after all—and, seemingly as long as the profits kept rolling in, Goldman bosses in the region allowed him a very long leash. In 2009 that led Leissner to an upstart Malaysian businessman named Jho Low.

In early 2009, after the triumph of his Iskandar land deal, Low was looking for the next big thing. He'd built a quick reputation in Malaysia as a deal maker, but, as always, Low was keenly aware of how his success stacked up on a global stage. Low had observed the power and status of Khaldoon Al Mubarak of Mubadala, who ran the emirati sovereign wealth fund. A fund like that had billions of dollars in investments, not mere millions. Why, Jho Low wondered, couldn't he put together a sovereign wealth fund of his own—one based in Malaysia? But where could he find the initial funds?

Traditional sovereign wealth funds invest oil profits, and so Low honed in on the Malaysian state of Terengganu, which was rich in offshore oil and gas fields.

Malaysia's nine hereditary Malay royal families, each ruling a different state, coexisted with the nation's elected officials. These sultans had wide-ranging political powers, in some cases including control of local state revenues, creating ample opportunity for corruption. How Low settled upon Mizan Zainal Abidin, the sultan of Terengganu, was typical of his ability to spot opportunities, moving from one deal to the next.

The sultan, who had been educated in the United Kingdom, was from a conservative Islamic family. While some royals in Malaysia are entitled and lazy, he was considered to be smart. Low had met Mizan's sister, who sat on the board of the construction companies, and had used that connection to offer the sultan free shares in the Abu Dhabi–Kuwait–Malaysia Investment Company. This was the entity which had generated massive profits by flipping the construction firms.

After this initial success, Low now suggested a more ambitious investment plan to Mizan. Why didn't the sultan set up a sovereign wealth fund, based on Abu Dhabi's Mubadala, which borrowed money against the state's oil wealth? Low said he knew bankers at Goldman who could advise and tap global investors, creating a huge war chest for the state to fund development.

To buy legitimacy, Low also needed the involvement of Goldman, and Leissner, despite his initial concerns about the young Malaysian, was eager for the business. Low soon arranged for Leissner and Roger Ng, the local Goldman banker, to meet Mizan and accompanied them to the palace in Kuala Lumpur.

Within months of the meeting with the sultan, after which Goldman became an adviser, Low was sending bankers emails that referred to them informally as "Bro" and discussing ways to portray the fund in Malaysia's media. Low's official role at the fund, which began operations in February 2009, was as adviser, but in reality he controlled the show, and he hired a handful of people he knew as staff. Emails between Low and Leissner referred to the endeavor as Project Tiara. But Leissner and Ng knew the presence of Low, a "dodgy"—and young—broker, could cause trouble with Goldman's compliance department, and so they disclosed his role to only a select few at the bank. Indeed, Low himself asked them to conceal his activities to the Goldman bosses, and they were happy to oblige.

Low talked Mizan into allowing the fund to issue $1.4 billion in Islamic bonds—structured to avoid violating Islamic rules against charging interest—backed by the state's future oil receipts. But as the fund was preparing to raise the money, in May 2009, the sultan got cold feet. Low was rushing to get the deal through, but without a clear investment plan. Mizan saw no reason for such alacrity, especially as the fund didn't even have a full management team in place. His representative on the board ordered a delay in the fund-raising, but Low took no notice, and pushed for the bonds to go through.

But now Mizan, fearful of gambling away the state's oil wealth, threatened to shut down the whole thing. Mizan's reticence was further fueled by rumors in banking circles that Low had siphoned away some of the bond money, and the sultan scotched Low's plans before they even got off the ground.

Low was on the cusp of transforming into a powerful figure, the kind of young fund manager he had watched up close in the Middle East, deploying billions of dollars in investments. But now he was seemingly back to square one, with Mizan ordering the fund be shuttered. He quickly had to figure out what to do. At that moment, he got the luckiest break of his career so far.

For years, Najib Razak had been groomed for the nation's highest office. With his recognizable family name, and years of government service, many Malaysians assumed one day he would become prime minister. The ruling UMNO party was in crisis. In the 2008 elections, its coalition had barely held onto power. Ethnic Indian and Chinese Malaysians, sick of living as second-class citizens, voted in droves for the opposition. To revive its flagging fortunes, the party turned to the heir of the Razak political dynasty. In April 2009, Najib became Malaysia's sixth prime minister, as if laying claim to a birthright.

Suddenly, Low's cultivation of Najib and his wife was paying dividends. Overnight, the ambitious Malaysian had the ear of the most powerful man in the country. And Najib needed a pot of money to help restore his party's popularity. Low moved fast to cash in and save his stillborn investment fund.

Chapter 7

Saudi "Royalty" (The First Heist)

Aboard the Alfa Nero, *French Riviera, August 2009*

As he took in the opulence of the *Alfa Nero*, cruising off the coast of Monaco in the French Riviera, Prime Minister Najib Razak was under the impression the yacht belonged to a son of Saudi Arabia's king, Abdullah Abdulaziz Al Saud. With a movie theater and a huge swimming pool that transformed into a helipad, the 269-foot boat, estimated to be worth $190 million, was an impressive sight.

In the stateroom, with comfy sofas and a view out to the Mediterranean, Najib was greeted by the purported owner, His Royal Highness, Prince Turki Bin Abdullah. Wearing a white baseball cap and matching blue linen pants and shirt, Prince Turki, a broadly built thirty-seven-year-old with a mustache and stubble, gave off a relaxed air. A former Saudi Air Force pilot, who had begun to dabble in business, he jovially clasped Najib by the hand.

Casually dressed in a short-sleeved white shirt, the prime minister laughed as he handed Prince Turki a gift in a green box. Najib's wife, Rosmah, in a black-and-white leopard-print shirt, who had joined the trip accompanied by their two children, smiled and joked with their host. Rosmah looked thrilled to be in the presence of Saudi royalty, especially in such an intimate setting. Respecting Islamic tradition, the guests drank fresh juices. A photographer snapped pictures of the meeting. Najib and Prince Turki then sat, each perched on the end of a sofa, to discuss ways in which Malaysia and Saudi Arabia could foster deeper economic ties.

On the periphery of the group, also dressed casually in a green polo shirt, stood Jho Low. Only he knew what this meeting was really about.

In the few months since Najib became prime minister, he and Low had spoken frequently. Low had convinced Malaysia's new leader to focus on the Middle East. He'd already delivered Abu Dhabi financing for the Iskandar land project, and now Low held out the prospect of access to Saudi's inordinate wealth. Aged only twenty-seven, the young Malaysian had managed to persuade Najib and, just as important, Rosmah, that he held the key to future Middle East investment.

In the first few weeks of the new administration, Low acted as an unofficial aide to Najib, helping the prime minister organize a visit to the Middle East. Najib had grand ambitions to turn Malaysia into a developed nation within a few years, and for that he would need a major source of capital. Low persuaded him it would come from Arab nations. Najib and Rosmah, accompanied by Low, toured the Middle East, meeting King Abdullah in Saudi Arabia and Crown Prince Sheikh Mohammed Bin Zayed Al Nahyan of Abu Dhabi. To many onlookers, Low seemed to be an official emissary for Najib, such was his proximity to the prime minister, and some businesspeople who met Low on the trip mistook him for a minister of investment.

In Abu Dhabi, after a dinner with the crown prince at the sumptuous Emirates Palace hotel, Najib announced the formation of a new Malaysian sovereign wealth fund to be called 1Malaysia Development Berhad, or 1MDB. The 1MDB fund was simply the Terengganu Investment Authority, which had recently raised $1.4 billion in Islamic bonds, transformed into a federal entity. The 1MDB fund would be responsible for repaying the bonds.

Once Najib came to power, Low convinced him to take over the fund, broaden its remit, and look for Middle East backing. From here on, the sultan washed his hands of the whole affair.

Low had pulled on his connections with Ambassador Otaiba to help fast-track Najib's meeting with the crown prince and to obtain a pledge from Abu Dhabi, however vague, to invest in Malaysian projects alongside the fund.

The 1MDB fund was supposed to invest in green energy and tourism to create high-quality jobs for all Malaysians, whether of Malay, Indian, or Chinese heritage, hence the slogan "1Malaysia." The fund, Low promised the prime minister, would suck in money from the Middle East and borrow more from global markets. But he had another selling point, one which Najib, who was ambitious, found extremely attractive: *Why not also use the fund as a political-financing vehicle?* Profits from 1MDB would fill a war chest that Najib could use to pay off political supporters and voters, restoring UMNO's popularity, Low promised.

On the surface, such spending by 1MDB would be packaged as "corporate social responsibility," to borrow a phrase from the corporate world. The fund's charitable arm would award scholarships and build affordable housing in areas where UMNO needed votes. On top of that, Low told Najib that Middle Eastern nations, through their investments in the fund, would come to see Malaysia as a coveted ally in Asia, and also back Najib's administration with a flow of political donations.

Was this young businessman, barely out of school and with a pretty short track record, really able to deliver Arab investment? He seemed well connected, but would these powerful Middle Eastern kingdoms pour billions of dollars into the 1MDB fund just because Low wanted it to be so? Why did they need him as a broker? Low was doing his all to give the impression that he was indispensable, and the meeting with Prince Turki on the *Alfa Nero* in August was meant to deepen that feeling.

Unbeknownst to Najib and Rosmah, it was a setup, a facade of officialdom, aimed at making the prime minister and his wife feel they were getting close to Saudi Arabia's royal family. Luckily for Low, Najib wasn't one to scratch the surface too deeply. After a lifetime of enjoying the perks afforded to a leading Malaysian politician—the VIP limousines, hotel suites, and yachts—he didn't ask many questions at all.

In truth, Prince Turki was a new contact of Low's rather than an official emissary of Saudi Arabia. Many people think of Saudi princes as having almost unlimited funds, but Prince Turki faced a precarious future. His father, King Abdullah, was around ninety and had twenty children, and it was uncertain Prince Turki would remain close to power once his father died. After his military career, he'd tried his hand at business but had achieved little success. In the early 2000s, Prince Turki set up PetroSaudi International, an oil exploration firm, in an attempt to leverage his royal connections. The idea was that PetroSaudi, nominally based in Al Khobar, a Saudi city, would win oil-exploration rights in foreign countries that were keen to get close to Saudi Arabia.

Like many minor aristocrats, Prince Turki was trading off his name, and PetroSaudi was little more than a shell, with negligible business to speak of. The company's success was constrained by the laid-back approach of Turki and his partner, Tarek Obaid, a thirty-three-year-old Saudi financier. The son of a Saudi banker who moved his family to Geneva, Obaid had a round face, bushy eyebrows, and a stubbly beard. His father had made and lost a fortune wheeling and dealing alongside prominent Saudi families, including the ruling Al Sauds.

Obaid attended international school in Geneva before

Georgetown in Washington, and spoke fluent French and English, as well as Arabic. After studying, he had worked in finance, including for a small Swiss private bank, where he was considered lazy by some coworkers. As chief executive of Petro-Saudi, whose operations were run out of a nondescript Geneva office building, Obaid played at being a Saudi royal, allowing his bankers in Geneva to refer to him as "Sheikh"—a designation for royals or religious clerics—though he was of common stock. The young Saudi liked to drink heavily and party in Geneva's nightclubs, and it had aged him prematurely. He also was a hypochondriac, perpetually complaining of phantom illnesses.

Prince Turki was just the kind of figure Jho Low was seeking out: a bona fide Saudi royal to dazzle the newly installed Prime Minister Najib, but one whose need for cash made him malleable. Low recently had befriended the prince and Obaid through a thirty-nine-year-old Eritrean-American called Sahle Ghebreyesus. In a former life, Ghebreyesus owned Lamu, a high-end African restaurant in Manhattan that attracted minor celebrities and bankers. The business had shuttered and, to build himself back up, he began doing favors for some of his former customers—arranging private jets, getting reservations at sought-after restaurants, and fulfilling other whims of the superrich.

Before long, he found a new calling: concierge for millionaire Middle Easterners who traveled to the West to enjoy the company of models, alcohol, and other vices not easily available at home. He would arrange boats and hotels, and make reservations.

This line of work brought Ghebreyesus into contact with Prince Turki. He also came to know Low, whose parties had grown in size since Wharton, fueled by the money he made on the Iskandar deal.

Low wanted to shore up his budding relationship with Najib,

and he relied on Ghebreyesus to see to the details. In August 2009, he asked Ghebreyesus to arrange a sumptuous vacation for Najib and Rosmah and their children off the coast of France aboard the RM *Elegant*, a superyacht which came with fifteen staterooms and an Art Deco–style dining room.

At the same time, Prince Turki and his entourage chartered the *Alfa Nero* at more than $500,000 a week. Low's plan was to bring Najib and his family together with the prince, again making it appear like he could order up Saudi royalty on a whim. As planned, Najib and his family boarded the *Alfa Nero* and met Turki.

On the boat, Prince Turki and Najib began discussing the possibility of PetroSaudi partnering with the new 1MDB fund. After the meeting, Low and Tarek Obaid seized on the interest Najib had shown, quickly hammering out a rough outline of how a partnership might work. Only a matter of days after the meeting on the *Alfa Nero*, Prince Turki wrote Najib on official Saudi government letterhead, proposing "a potential business combination." With his missive, dated August 28, he included a proposal from Chief Executive Obaid outlining a business venture. The plan, according to Obaid, was for PetroSaudi to put its oil assets—supposedly rights to develop fields in Turkmenistan and Argentina worth $2.5 billion—into a joint venture.

1MDB, meanwhile, would contribute $1 billion in *cash*—tapping some of the money it had sitting in its bank account in Malaysia.

Chapter 8

Hitting a Gold Mine

New York, September 2009

From the thirty-fifth-floor lobby of the Mandarin Oriental on Columbus Circle, Patrick Mahony took in panoramic views across the green canopy of Central Park. Located in one of the two towers of the Time Warner Center, the hotel's sleek lounge, with floor-to-ceiling windows and a cream-and-marble-themed interior, was the kind of place Mahony was used to inhabiting. The Mandarin was a favorite of Jho Low, who liked to be close to a good Asian meal, and he'd arranged to meet Mahony in the lounge.

The British banker worked for Ashmore, a British investment fund, but he also had taken on a role at PetroSaudi as director of investments. After his meeting with Prince Turki on the yacht, Prime Minister Najib had agreed to the outline of the deal presented by Obaid, Turki's business partner at PetroSaudi, and Mahony and Low were at the Mandarin to get the ball rolling.

Handsome, with hair swept back to just above his shirt collar, Mahony had a reputation for being smart but cold, often taking a peremptory tone in business dealings, first as a banker at Goldman Sachs and later at Ashmore. Older bankers who came across Mahony, dressed in tailor-cut suits and full of bluster, found the thirty-two-year-old talented and ambitious, if a bit pretentious. He liked to email banker friends about expensive watches. When his niece cheated at cards, Mahony joked that she shared his genes. A product of the rootless global elite, he communicated with Obaid in a mixture of English and French. In English, he spoke with a transatlantic accent common among deracinated Anglophones.

Born in 1977, Mahony met Tarek Obaid at the international school they attended in Geneva. In 2009, Obaid persuaded his ambitious friend to join PetroSaudi, and Mahony jumped at the chance of a position of power in a smaller firm. Mahony's role at PetroSaudi was to work on a plan to ramp up PetroSaudi's business. Quickly he became the driving force behind the company, enticing Richard Haythornthwaite, a well-known former BP executive who was chairman of MasterCard International, to come on board to run the oil-and-gas business. In 2008, Petro-Saudi had bought the rights to fields in Argentina and reached an agreement with a Canadian company to develop a potentially huge offshore field in Turkmenistan. Now, this Malaysian businessman called Jho Low was promising to bring $1 billion in sovereign money into a deal.

Mahony knew little about Low before their meeting at the Mandarin, occurring less than two weeks after Obaid had written to Najib suggesting the joint venture, but—with the prospect of a giant deal in the making—he made it a priority. In the hotel lounge the pair sketched the contours of a plan. PetroSaudi would put in its oil assets, with the 1MDB fund contributing $1 billion in funds. On the surface, the idea was to use the money to explore for oil. But Low sensed there was an opportunity to make a financial killing, and he left the meeting in the Mandarin Oriental ecstatic. Soon after, he emailed his father, mother, brother, and sister, with whom he often shared details of his deal making.

"Just closed the deal with petrosaudi—looks like we have hit a goldmin[e]," Low wrote.

With a billion-dollar deal in the works, it was time for 1MDB to staff up. Prime Minister Najib himself held the highest position as chairman of the board of advisers, with power to appoint board members and veto decisions. The fund appointed Shahrol Halmi, a former consultant at Accenture in Malaysia, as chief executive. Other hires included Casey Tang, a finance director at a Malaysian retailer, who became an executive director, and Jasmine Loo, a smart Malaysian lawyer, as legal counsel.

One name was missing from the list of positions, however: Jho Low. Low decided to take no official role, but in truth, he was behind every decision. Najib had given Low a free hand to run the fund, and Low had stuffed it with his associates. Tang and Loo were among the Malaysians Low had gotten to know while doing deals after returning from Wharton. Plucked from relative obscurity, Shahrol would soon show he could be relied on to blindly follow orders. With staff in place, things began to move quickly.

Just days after the Mandarin Oriental meeting between Mahony and Low, a larger group assembled in Geneva. Obaid, Low, Mahony, and Seet Li Lin, Low's Wharton school friend who worked for Wynton, met for breakfast in Geneva near the lake at the center of the city. The small city for years had been accepting fugitives, at one time Protestants escaping persecution from the Catholic Inquisition—and, more recently, financiers from the world over, looking to stash their wealth in property and private bank accounts.

Before the Geneva meeting Low had sent an email to his inner circle, ordering them to "move fast" to get the joint venture off the ground. After breakfast, Low took out his BlackBerry and connected Obaid with Shahrol Halmi by email. Although the two heads of the organizations had never met, Low informed them both the joint venture was on track, making it clear who was boss, while insisting he remain in the background.

"I trust all of you can now officially communicate and don't need to cc me for proper governance purposes," wrote Low, who also began to ask his inner circle to destroy emails after reading them. Without a formal position at 1MDB, Low didn't want compliance issues with banks or lawyers.

Shahrol replied to Low's email asking for more information about PetroSaudi, and Mahony appeared to try and cover for the paucity of business.

"PSI is very press shy and usually never announces our investments (one of the main reasons governments like to work with us)," he wrote.

He attached a presentation, which he said "should give you a sense of what we are about," but it included no detailed information about the size of the firm's assets.

After the group left the breakfast in Geneva, the participants wasted no time in setting up the joint venture. Mahony emailed PetroSaudi's bank, BSI, a small Swiss private bank, to start the process of arranging a business account for the new entity. Low went to meet BSI staff in Geneva, and Mahony explained to the bankers how the new venture would soon be receiving $1 billion from a Malaysian fund, and Low would be taking a cut as a fee for helping put the deal together—just as he had attempted to do, but without success, during the Mubadala investment in Malaysia.

Yet again, however, Low was thwarted. BSI balked at such a strange arrangement, and turned down the account request. "I don't like the transaction at all! In particular the role and involvement of Mr. Low Taek Jho 'looks and feels' very [suspicious] to me," one BSI banker wrote in an email to colleagues.

Even at this early stage, any competent bank official could sense something was off. Bankers are supposed to catch wrong-doing and report it to authorities. But this self-policing system doesn't work. Turned down by one institution, financiers can simply shop around until they find someone willing to assist them. After facing problems with BSI, Mahony turned to his private bank, J.P. Morgan (Suisse). J.P. Morgan agreed to open an account, seemingly asking few questions about why a sovereign wealth fund needed a relationship with a Swiss private bank.

If the Swiss bankers had asked Low and Mahony more about their intentions—and the pair had told the truth—what would they have said? Perhaps in the beginning Low and the Petro-Saudi principals meant only to take broker fees for setting up 1MDB with PetroSaudi—a questionable practice which nevertheless is common in emerging markets. Or maybe they planned to invest what they saw as government money—not anyone's personal piggy bank—making returns and putting the cash back. What's for sure is that Low was improvising, searching out ways to make money at each twist and turn, and the scope of his endeavors would soon broaden considerably.

As Low's group forged ahead, they worked hard to ensure the pillars of capitalism—lawyers, investment bankers, auditors, and valuation experts—were involved at every turn. The effect was to give the deal between PetroSaudi and 1MDB a patina of respectability. For a fee, most were happy to oblige. Just over a week after the Geneva meeting, Mahony reached out to Edward Morse, a former senior U.S. State Department official and energy analyst at Lehman Brothers, to conduct an independent valuation of PetroSaudi's assets, which 1MDB's board had requested before the fund sent its $1 billion investment. One of the world's foremost experts on global oil, Morse had worked with Obaid's elder brother, Nawaf Obaid, who had written a book-length study on Saudi energy markets. Mahony told Morse he was seeking a valuation of $2.5 billion.

"Ok. Got it!" Morse replied.

Only two days later, Morse was done with his report, a technical analysis of reserves and prices based on numbers that PetroSaudi had provided.

"I think you won't be displeased with our conclusions either on Turkmenistan or Argentina," Morse wrote Mahony.

His valuation range went up to $3.6 billion, more than Mahony had requested, and a high number given the Turkmenistan fields were in waters of the Caspian Sea that were disputed with Azerbaijan. In the report, Morse made it clear his analysis was purely an economic valuation of the oil contained in the fields. He was paid $100,000 for the work.

Others involved were happy to facilitate the deal, even when aspects of it made no sense at all. Timothy Buckland, a New Zealand national who worked for the London office of U.S. law firm White & Case, counsel for PetroSaudi, was eager to please his client. On September 22, Mahony, in an email to Buckland, copying other White & Case lawyers, asked the law firm to prepare a document to send $2 million to an unnamed "broker" for helping put the joint venture deal together. Buckland simply replied, "Will do." It's unclear whether the broker fee was ever paid. (Buckland later left the firm to take a new position as in-house counsel at PetroSaudi UK.)

White & Case also helped PetroSaudi prepare a presentation of the proposed deal. The slides, replete with professional-looking diagrams of money flows, showed how PetroSaudi would inject its assets and 1MDB would put in $1 billion for a minority stake in the joint venture, based in the British Virgin Islands—all as agreed. But the presentation also indicated a strange payment of $700 million that the joint venture would make back to PetroSaudi. The payment supposedly was to repay a loan that

PetroSaudi had extended to the joint venture. In fact, the loan could not have existed; the joint venture hadn't even been set up and didn't have a bank account.

On September 26, 1MDB's newly constituted board met in Kuala Lumpur to approve the initial $1 billion transfer from the fund to the Swiss account set up for the joint venture with Petro-Saudi. Before the meeting, Low telephoned Najib to apprise him of what was about to transpire. Then Low attended the meeting, one of the few times he was physically present at a 1MDB official gathering. At the meeting, Low explained the plan. He did not mention the $700 million payment. The board agreed to fund the joint venture.

In the space of a month, since Prince Turki had written Najib with his proposal in late August, a multi-billion-dollar joint-venture agreement had been completed. Such a time frame—to complete due diligence, asset valuations, and other legal checks—was virtually without parallel. Such deals normally take months, if not a year, to wrap up. A 1MDB employee later compared the process to attempting to read the entire works of Shakespeare in an hour.

Chapter 9

"I Feel the Earth Move"

Kuala Lumpur, September 2009

Shortly after lunch on September 30, Jacqueline Ho, an employee with Deutsche Bank in Malaysia, was in a quandary. She was the relationship manager for a new client, 1MDB, and Casey Tang, the fund's executive director, was on the phone pressuring her to push ahead with a series of substantial payments out of the country.

Earlier that day Deutsche had received a letter from Tang, oddly delivered by hand, which asked for the bank to complete the transfers. But Deutsche's compliance department had some queries. *Why wasn't $1 billion flowing to the joint venture with PetroSaudi, as agreed by the 1MDB board? And how come Tang was asking for $700 million to be put into an unnamed account with RBS Coutts in Zurich?*

Tang replied that the account, identified in the wire request only by a number, was owned by PetroSaudi, and the transfer was to repay a loan.

"If they're going to overkill on the compliance thing, uh, they have to be responsible you know," Tang told Ho, according to a transcript. He seemed agitated, warning the banker that the joint venture might fail if Deutsche Bank didn't hurry up and transfer the funds.

"Yes that's, that's fine. But just one question as to why this is going to [PetroSaudi] itself? Is there any particular reason," Ho asked.

"For us, we don't care. Because $700 million I mean it's an advance [that's] owed to them," he replied. "This is where they want to send. They want to send to Timbuktu also, we don't care."

"Yeah that's fine. Alright. We just wanted to understand the background."

Ho's supervisor called Bank Negara Malaysia, the central bank, to check if it was okay to proceed with the enormous transaction. The bank gave the green light, as long as the money was going to the joint venture. Despite the confusion, Deutsche sent two wires around 3 p.m., one of $300 million to the joint venture's new account at J.P. Morgan (Suisse) and another of $700 million to the mysterious account at Coutts in Zurich. As it was a dollar transaction, the money needed to pass through a U.S. bank. Under American anti-money-laundering laws, these correspondent banks are obliged to check the source and use of funds. But with trillions of dollars flowing daily through the global foreign-exchange markets, such checks are little more than perfunctory, and in this case, J.P. Morgan let the money through.

Two days later, an employee from Coutts's regulatory risk department in Zurich sent an urgent email to 1MDB. The employee was confused by Deutsche Bank's omission of the full name of the beneficiary of the $700 million transfer, which is required on bank-transfer requests. When pushed, Shahrol Halmi, the fund's chief executive, acknowledged the account was owned by a Seychelles company called Good Star Ltd.

"Good Star is owned 100% by PetroSaudi International Ltd," he wrote.

Shahrol was parroting what Low told him. In truth, Good

Star was another bearer-share company, the kind made illegal in many jurisdictions, and its single share was held by Jho Low, who also was signatory to its accounts. Only months before, he had set up the shell company, using the services of a trust company. It was a simulacrum of a bona fide business, a front the perpetrators hoped would shield them from detection.

Still, Coutts bankers were not satisfied, and Low and Casey Tang flew to the bank's headquarters in Zurich to smooth things over. Here they told a different story from the one Tang had spun to Deutsche Bank about the PetroSaudi loan: Good Star was an investment management company, and 1MDB had decided to put in $700 million of its money. Why would a Malaysian state fund put so much cash into an unknown Seychelles fund management company? Whatever the Coutts bankers' concerns, however, the bank pushed the transfer through.

The 1MDB money began to move across the world. Low had carried off a move so brazen, it was hard to fathom how no one had stopped him. Several years before, in Abu Dhabi, he'd learned how sovereign wealth funds like Mubadala were pots of gold, and he yearned to control one. Drawing on the Abu Dhabi model, Low had convinced Prime Minister Najib that Malaysia needed its own powerful fund to tap global markets, and that he, a twenty-eight-year-old, should be permitted to run its affairs.

Low had tried to earn a commission for putting 1MDB and PetroSaudi together, but he'd been stymied by BSI. At some point, Low's scheme had evolved. Maybe PetroSaudi had been planning to invest the money in oil-field development with the hopes of earning a fat share of profits using Malaysian government money.

But Najib was giving Low so much room to maneuver, he dared to think on a grander scale. His people were running 1MDB, with cover from the prime minister. The involvement of

Prince Turki, the co-owner of PetroSaudi, and a Malaysian state fund offered a sheen of officialdom. (Indeed, PetroSaudi would later argue that it was an arms-length transaction between sophisticated and well-represented sovereign parties.) An idea had taken shape in Low's mind. Perhaps, he wondered, it was possible to take hundreds of millions of dollars in broad daylight, fooling Western banks and regulators.

For Saudi royalty, the boundaries between state and personal wealth were blurred, and so it was becoming for Low. What if someone caught on? Did Low have a deeply thought-out plan about what to do when someone noticed the financial hole? The events of the past month had happened at a rapid pace, and he was ad-libbing. It was an opportunistic move, and Low had pulled it off. Like he had always done, Low would rely on his ability to think on the fly.

In this age of social sharing, the conspirators could not even hide their glee. Seet Li Lin, Low's Wharton friend, took to Facebook on the day Deutsche Bank sent the $700 million to Good Star.

"i feel the earth move...," he wrote in a public message on his wall.

From Good Star's account at Coutts, Low distributed money among the group. In early October, he transferred $85 million to Tarek Obaid's J.P. Morgan account in Switzerland, under the pretense the amount was a private-equity investment. Coutts permitted the transfers, and three months later the bank similarly let through another payment of $68 million from Good Star to Obaid.

Weeks after, Obaid paid $33 million to Patrick Mahony, and over 2009 and 2010, sent $77 million from his account to Prince Turki.

Low had pulled off his first major heist, and even after paying off his partners, enjoyed virtually sole control over hundreds of millions of dollars. Armed with inordinate wealth, he set off to see what was for sale in the United States. The answer was almost anything he wanted.

PART II

OVERNIGHT BILLIONAIRE

Chapter 10

An Evening with the Playmates

Las Vegas, October 2009

The Playmates were nervous as they made their way across the casino floor of the Palazzo. The young women, about twenty of them, a mix of blonde and dark-haired models, had worked in Las Vegas on multiple occasions. But the instructions for this job were especially secretive: Check into your room, put on a black cocktail dress, and pack a bikini. The women had no idea who had hired them.

It was October 22, 2009, only three weeks since Low took $700 million from 1MDB. Hours earlier, the Playmates had flown in—first class—from across the United States. One of the newest hotels on the Strip, the Palazzo was an impressive sight, with stately stone staircases that brought visitors up to a lobby with an indoor waterfall. Beyond that was the casino floor, one of the largest in the country.

Clouds that afternoon had dispersed, and it was a beautifully clear late-fall evening. At around 8 p.m., the Playmates arrived at the door of a VIP room and entered. Inside, around a long card table, were a handful of Asian men playing poker, accompanied by Leonardo DiCaprio. Some of the models had met the actor before, but his presence in this gathering struck some of them as peculiar. The party, the women quickly learned, was an early celebration for the birthday of a portly Asian man who introduced himself as Jho Low. What, some of them wondered, was the actor doing in the company of these anonymous and rather dull men?

After about twenty minutes of watching the group play, Low began to pass $1,000 chips down the table, one for each woman, and made a signal for the party to move to a suite in the hotel. With a huge security entourage, the group made its way across the gaming floor, as tourists looked on. No one appeared to recognize DiCaprio, who was wearing his trademark battered baseball cap, pulled down tightly to assure anonymity.

At the doors of the Chairman Suites on the fifth floor, the most opulent at the Palazzo, security guards waited. The burly men in dark suits and earpieces required the Playmates to hand over their bags, phones, and driver's licenses, and then sign a nondisclosure agreement before finally entering the suite. The women were used to attending openings and nightclub events, but this high-security atmosphere was strange. Nonetheless, the $3,000 fee they had been promised to hang out for just a few hours overcame any qualms they might have had.

In the suite's living room, with a wood fire, plush couches, and doors that opened out to a pool terrace overlooking the Strip, the atmosphere was somber. The lights were off, and hotel staff had constructed a makeshift dance floor of white tiles, with a disco ball hanging overhead. The Palazzo also had set up a card table in the suite, and Low, DiCaprio, and the few other Asian men went off to play baccarat, which they taught to some of the Playmates who didn't know the game. With the ice broken, the gambling took off. Baccarat was Low's favorite. It involves little skill, revolving around whether the player or the "bank" gets the highest hand in a complicated scoring system, but rewards—or punishes—those willing to wager big.

Stephanie Larimore, a dark-haired model, wearing a black

dress with silver material around the bust, tried to make conversation with Low. He was polite, but shy and almost unable to think of what to say. Boxes of German chocolates were stacked round the room, and Low offered her one, saying the gold-wrapped squares were his favorite. *He's intimidated by women. Why have they hired us to be here?* Larimore thought.

The men, smoking cigars, began to gamble large amounts of money, putting down chips of $5,000, and after an early winning streak against the house, some of the Asian men began to throw chips around the room. Some of the Playmates, who were mingling on the sofas and around the table, chased after them, down on their hands and knees. After a couple of hours, a birthday cake came out, and the women crowded around Low.

Later, DiCaprio and Low sat on a sofa in the dark, smoking cigars and talking, as they watched three or four women dancing in the living room under disco lighting. Low then asked for some of the girls to change into bikinis and swim in a small pool on a balcony outside.

"I think he was selecting people," said Starz Ramirez, a makeup artist who was present that evening, referring to Low. "It was weird we were there. He didn't socialize with us."

Around the pool were trays filled with barbecued food and ice cream, but no one ate much. Everything had been selected in advance by Low, who quietly orchestrated the night's activities with a few words to staff standing by to cater to his every whim.

Someone took off DiCaprio's baseball cap and wore it. But there wasn't really a party atmosphere. The actor was in the process of filming *Inception*, a science fiction film, and, to some of the models, he still seemed to be in character, focused and distant. DiCaprio drank some bourbon, but there wasn't much alcohol flowing.

"They weren't crazy party guys," Larimore said.

Then Low asked Larimore whether she'd like to spend a few days longer with him in Vegas. He would pay $10,000 and take her shopping on the Strip. Some of the women stayed the night in the suite, but Larimore declined the offer and left to her own room around midnight.

"It was like he was bribing you to stay."

At that moment, in late 2009, Low had access to more liquid cash than almost anyone on earth—and he wasn't shy about spending it. Even before his big haul, Low had made a splash in New York and Las Vegas, dropping exorbitant sums of cash, profits from the Iskandar deal. But in the fall of 2009, armed with almost endless amounts of money, Low embarked on a period of incessant partying—and networking. Even after the payments to Obaid and others, hundreds of millions of dollars were just sitting in the Good Star account he controlled in Switzerland, for Low to deploy in any way he saw fit. There were no shareholders, no co-investors.

His wasn't a Ponzi scheme like Bernie Madoff's, which used new money to pay "profits" to earlier investors. Madoff's fraud led to losses of at least $18 billion, but his take was a fraction of that, as the "profits" were shared among other investors. By the time the scheme imploded in late 2008, Madoff had amassed a paper fortune of $800 million, but most of this was the value of his market-making business; the amount he personally stole was a fraction of the amount lost. Low's mark—the little-known 1MDB, a Malaysian government fund—wasn't asking for any money back and it wouldn't so long as he controlled it through his proxies.

Low also wasn't like junk-bond king Michael Milken, who had amassed a personal fortune in the 1980s before going to prison for violating securities laws. The Malaysian had simply taken hundreds of millions of dollars. The excesses of Madoff or the 1980s would seem prosaic compared to the multiyear spending spree on which Low was about to embark.

His was a scheme for the twenty-first century, a truly global endeavor that produced nothing—a shift of cash from a poorly controlled state fund in the developing world, diverting it into the opaque corners of an underpoliced financial system that's all but broken.

Did he really think he could get away with it? Perhaps Low believed he could make investments that would more than cover for what he had taken. With the protection of a prime minister, who would stop him? To pull it off, Low relied on skills he'd honed for years. He knew that transactions between governments attracted less scrutiny from auditors and banks, and so he had set about building high-level connections in Malaysia, the UAE, and Saudi Arabia. He understood that once money was sent into an anonymous offshore account, it was difficult to trace, and he'd learned how to layer transactions—sending cash around in a whirl between shell companies. And to keep everything flowing, he constantly misrepresented money as investments or loans, giving his scheme a veneer of formality.

But it was one thing to take money from a Malaysian fund and funnel it to Swiss bank accounts under the guise of a sovereign investment, using friends in official positions to address any concerns of compliance executives at banks. Now, Low wanted to get the money into the United States so he could spend it on luxuries and begin building his empire. That was risky, because the United States had started clamping down on corrupt foreign officials buying assets in Western nations. To do so, Low turned to Shearman & Sterling. Founded in 1873, with its headquarters at 599 Lexington Avenue in Midtown Manhattan, Shearman was as white-shoe a law firm as they came, an organization more suited to handling major mergers and acquisitions than dealing with the likes of Low.

Low claimed to have a relationship with a large Malaysian sovereign fund, and he appeared to also be close to Mubadala, the Abu Dhabi fund, so Shearman's partners apparently felt comforted about his reputation. The fact that Low held money with Coutts, banker to the Queen, was another level of assurance, as if the funds had accrued their own integrity simply by passing through storied institutions.

Low informed his new legal team that he would be making a sequence of major investments, but he was very concerned about privacy. He opted to use the firm's Interest On Lawyer Trust Accounts, or IOLTAs, to help distribute the money. These trust accounts are typically formed by U.S. law firms to pool clients' money, say, when they are holding short-term funds for business deals or property purchases. This arcane corner of the financial world came into existence three decades ago as a way for law firms to earn short-term interest on client money to finance legal aid for the poor, but over time the accounts developed a reputation for shielding the identity of clients in transactions and helping to hide the origin of funds. Some states mandate that law firms set them up. IOLTAs are at once good for society and a powerful tool for crime.

Lawyers, unlike bankers, don't have to conduct due diligence on a client. Details of transfers through IOLTAs, meanwhile, are protected by lawyer-client privilege. While it is illegal for lawyers to abet money laundering, they are not required to report suspicious activity to regulators. The Financial Action Task Force, a Paris-based intergovernmental group that sets standards for stopping fraudulent use of the global finance system, has highlighted the United States's poor oversight of lawyers as a weak spot in its defenses against money launderers.

In just a few years since graduating from Wharton, Low was

becoming skilled in working out ways to use relatively unobserved parts of the financial system to avoid detection, darkened
corners where regulators don't have full visibility and others had
no reason or duty to be suspicious. These lawyer accounts fit
the bill perfectly, especially because wire transfers leaving an
IOLTA account generally denote only the name of a law firm,
not that of the client, making it hard for correspondent banks to
detect suspicious activity.

On October 21, 2009, Low wired $148 million from the
Good Star account in Switzerland to an IOLTA account at
Shearman in New York, part of a staggering total of $369 mil-
lion that would enter such accounts at the law firm over the next
twelve months. The reasons Low gave for the transfers, noted on
wire documents, ranged from property purchases to deals to buy
companies. But at first, he simply used this money to fund endless rounds of partying.

Between October 2009 and June 2010—a period of only
eight months—Low and his entourage spent $85 million on alco-
hol, gambling in Vegas, private jets, renting superyachts, and to
pay Playmates and Hollywood celebrities to hang out with them.
Low set himself up at the Park Imperial on 230 West Fifty-Sixth
Street in New York, a granite apartment building with geometric
angles that resemble bookends and sweeping views of Central
Park and the Hudson River. The move put Low in the company
of boldfaced names of entertainment. James Bond actor Daniel
Craig was staying in a $38,000-a-month apartment there while
starring in a Broadway play, and Sean "Diddy" Combs had a
place in the building.

Low rented a suite of rooms that cost $100,000 per month.
The flashy new resident showed up at the building in a convoy of
black Cadillac Escalades with a retinue of security, and he paid
for a number of other apartments in the building for his entourage, which included Hamad Al Wazzan, his wealthy Kuwaiti

friend from Wharton. Long-term residents complained about the bodyguards and the ostentation, but that was exactly Low's aim: to show he had arrived.

He began to spend eye-popping amounts, running up a $160,000 bar bill at Avenue, a new club in New York's Chelsea district, on a single night during fall Fashion Week in 2009. On another occasion, Low sent twenty-three bottles of Cristal to actress Lindsay Lohan's table when he spotted her during a night out in Manhattan. These enormous outlays landed Low in the *New York Post*, which called the "big-spending Malaysian . . . the mystery man of [the] city club scene."

Low wasn't a total newcomer to the party world. Since at least the mid-2000s, his behavior had raised eyebrows. He would appear at clubs and outspend even the biggest Wall Street bon vivants—ordering $900 bottles of Cristal for no seeming purpose on a midweek night. Tracy Hanna, a cocktail waitress who served him in the Hamptons, remembers Low around 2005 spending some $30,000, a sum nearly equivalent to the median U.S. annual income, in only one evening. In this era of inequality, however, Low's behavior wasn't so notable.

"We just thought he was some kind of royalty," Hanna recalled. "There were a lot of princes at the time, especially from Saudi. We thought they can't drink or party where they're from, so they go crazy in America."

On another occasion he flew waitresses from New York to Malaysia for a party.

When Nawaf Obaid, the brother of Tarek Obaid, the PetroSaudi cofounder, came across coverage of Low in the *New York Post*, he was livid. A security expert, Nawaf Obaid had spent decades at Washington think-tanks and advising Saudi ambassadors to the United States.

"Wow this is very dangerous, he needs to be curtailed cause

at any moment he can lose his mind and blow the whole thing!"
he wrote in an email to his brother.

Patrick Mahony and Tarek Obaid would have surely been happy
to remain anonymous and enjoy their riches. For Low, such
behavior would have rendered the scheme pointless. He desired
to exist—and be seen—at the center of a powerful world. The
very point, it seemed, was for him to get close to the rich and
famous, and to publicize it, just as he had wanted his name on
the sorority posters back at Wharton. In the days after his heist,
Low was driven by the need to live among celebrities, as if this
would validate his worth. In the future, he would see Hollywood
as an investment opportunity. But right now, flush from the success of his scheme, Low just wanted to enjoy the thrill of buying his way into celebrity friendships. To do so, he had to figure
out a way to cozy up to truly A-list Hollywood names. The key
would be a pair of nightclub entrepreneurs named Noah Tepperberg and Jason Strauss.

The men were co-owners of Strategic Hospitality Group, a
nightclub empire that included Avenue, as well as New York's
popular Marquee club and a part share in Las Vegas–based
LAVO and TAO. Tepperberg and Strauss were among the country's top nightlife entrepreneurs—*Harvard Business Review* had
even conducted a case study of their operations. Now in their
midthirties, the pair were native New Yorkers who had known
each other since working as club promoters while still in high
school. Strauss, who is tall and lean with a permanent tan, and
Tepperburg, who is heavyset with a shaved head, made an odd
couple, but they were nearly inseparable. After college, they
began opening clubs in the Hamptons and New York. They realized clubs lived or died on who attended, and built databases of
celebrities and big spenders.

The pair opened Marquee in 2003, and it quickly became the hottest place in town. On a Friday or Saturday night, to secure a spot at Marquee, with its huge video screens, modern lighting, and disco ball enclosed in a spherical frame, guests had to sign contracts to order a minimum of two bottles of champagne or liquor, costing hundreds or even thousands of dollars each. Hollywood celebrities like Leonardo DiCaprio and Tobey Maguire were regulars, and counted Tepperberg and Strauss as friends. But the financial crisis of 2007 and 2008 had dented business, as Wall Street bankers shied away from dropping huge amounts in New York clubs. Low's advent on the scene couldn't have been better timed.

Tepperberg and Strauss had seen high rollers spend thousands, even tens of thousands of dollars at a time, but Low was on another level. He was willing to part with *millions* of dollars in a night. The duo, who also owned a successful events and marketing business, made themselves available to cater to Low's every whim. Word of the big-spending Asian also began to spread around the Hollywood types who knew Tepperberg and Strauss.

It's a little-discussed secret that even the biggest movie stars take payment to attend events, and Low began to seek out the managers of top actors, or pull on the Strategic Group's network of club promoters, to get celebrities to his parties. The rumor that Low was a billionaire with unlimited funds made him an attractive person to know. Even for DiCaprio, one of the world's top-paid actors, with a sizable fortune of his own, the scope of Low's purported wealth was alluring. The night at the Palazzo in October 2009 was just the start of many parties the actor would enjoy with Low.

Low met DiCaprio through Danny Abeckaser, a club promoter for Strategic Group who was trying to carve out his own career as an actor. Top promoters like Abeckaser were powerful

figures in the nightlife world, bringing in big-spending customers in return for a fee. While still at Wharton, Low had gained
Abeckaser's attention by laying out $3,000 in a night. Those
sums had ramped up to $20,000, then $50,000. Now, Low
thought nothing of putting down $1 million. No one had ever
encountered such profligacy. The spending fed rumors among
this nightclub set that Low was a new Asian billionaire looking
to invest in Hollywood.

By early November 2009, fueled by the 1MDB money, Low
was ready to take his socializing to the next level. It was his
twenty-eighth birthday, and he wanted to mark his arrival on
the Hollywood scene with a splash. The festivities ran over several days, including a party at the pool area of Caesars Palace in
Vegas that featured caged tigers and lions, as well as bikini-clad
models frolicking in the pool. Guests played carnival games set
up at booths around the property. This was Low's magic—to
throw the craziest party, stunning even models and actors who
were used to the most sumptuous events. Some of Low's earliest
Hollywood friends were there, including DiCaprio, the musician
Usher, and Jamie Foxx, the actor and comedian.

On nights when he went clubbing, Low acted as much as a
master of ceremonies as a reveler. Often, he would hold a microphone and order waiting staff to deliver Cristal champagne or
Patrón tequila to the whole establishment, while only sipping on
a Corona himself. A poor small-talker, he nonetheless developed
a sense of showmanship, often shouting "Malaysia in the house"
into his microphone. He had the Strategic Group staff draw up
elaborate plans for events, including the smallest features of the
decor, the flowers on display, and the alcohol behind the bar. He
ensured the best-looking models were on hand to mingle with
the guests.

Was there a justification for all this conspicuous consumption? To Low, it was part of a larger design. If the parties were

successful, Low figured, he would grow in stature, enticing more powerful figures into his world. Even an up-and-coming rap star like O.T. Genasis, himself not short of cash and women, was in awe after witnessing Low one night buy multiple bottles of champagne costing $50,000 each.

"I'm like, 'What?' Never! This is not for real," he said.

Surrounded by women who looked like they came straight from a Victoria's Secret shoot, Genasis, who had accompanied Busta Rhymes to the party, was overwhelmed.

"I've never been in nothing like that."

Low was partly a calculating showman, but he struggled to be present in the moment. He was afflicted by a deep-seated compulsion that drove him to spend more, acquire more, and move incessantly. Once, he went to a mall to get juice and returned home with eight identical pairs of black shoes. He bought Hermès Birkin bags, which start at $12,000 and go up to six figures, for friends, friends of friends, and even people he had just met.

"He was the biggest spender I've ever met in my life," said one jet-setter along for the ride. "You could be having lunch in a restaurant in London and he'll say who wants to have dinner in New York. Then he'd charter a jet and before you know it, you're having dinner with the best wine of your life in Manhattan. Nothing was out of reach."

In addition to his binge spending, people noticed another trait of Low's: a seemingly photographic memory. Some friends noticed he had an ability to remember very specific details of what money was moving where, down to a decimal point. "He was always a bit extreme," said one person who knew him.

In the autumn of 2009, the Malaysian was achieving something remarkable. In just a few short months, he had infiltrated the world's most elite circles and was becoming friends with celebrities. Some of it came down to money—he was paying for stars to attend his parties. Partly, he knew how to throw an amazing event, and with the help of Strategic Group was building a reputation as a socialite. But he was also figuring out what motivated stars like DiCaprio, and how his money could assist them to do more than just party.

There was one star for whom partying and business were one and the same, a model and actor over whom he'd fantasized since his college days. It took Low no time to befriend her.

Chapter 11

Raining Cristal

Whistler, British Columbia, Canada, November 2009

Paris Hilton was getting increasingly agitated. Low had sent a leased private jet to LA to whisk her to Vancouver, the nearest international airport to Whistler, the Canadian ski resort, but it had sat for six hours on the tarmac while Canadian immigration decided whether to let her into the country. The holdup was due to Hilton's legal history—a DUI conviction in the United States, which had garnered worldwide press attention. Eventually she was waved through, and Low's staff ferried her to the Four Seasons. It was early ski season, and Low was treating Hilton.

Low had contacted Hilton's manager a few months earlier and arranged for her to come along to his parties, for which she told friends that Low paid around $100,000 per event. But there was more to Low than simply cash, and Hilton, herself from money and with a blossoming television career, would grow close to him over the months ahead. Many people who got to know Low described him as kind and good-hearted, and his desire to please, to ensure everyone was having a good time, compared favorably with the arrogance that often accompanies extreme wealth.

Hilton brought along a friend called Joey McFarland, a native of Louisville, Kentucky, who had moved to LA a few years before and began helping his friends out in a business that hired stars for parties and events. Tall with short-cropped blond hair and an approachable, open manner that reflected his Southern upbringing, McFarland got to know Hilton through the talent-booking business. Only a few years earlier, he had been a small-time investor in a building in Cincinnati that housed a gyros restaurant, and his change in station made him eager to please, obsequious even. McFarland became close to Hilton, allowing her at one point to tweet from his account that she was a "celebrity princess." He would run around taking photos of her at events. She gifted McFarland a Louis Vuitton toiletries bag.

At the hotel, Low was surrounded mainly by his family and Middle Eastern friends, including Al Wazzan, the Kuwaiti Wharton classmate, who bragged over drinks about a recent arms deal he claimed to have done, unsettling some of Hilton's entourage. This was the first of what would become annual end-of-year ski vacations, paid for by Low to treat his closest friends and celebrities. Most of the group was just learning to ski—Low was taking snowboarding lessons—so Hilton, a practiced skier, spent most of the days on the slopes with other friends.

Riza Aziz, the stepson of Prime Minister Najib, also was present. He was short, balding, and rarely said much, but his calmness was alluring to women. He was a talented tennis player and posted pictures on Facebook of himself with stars like Rafael Nadal. Relatively smart, he had entered banking after the London School of Economics, and had recently quit his job in the mergers-and-acquisitions department of London-based HSBC.

Rosmah's child from an earlier marriage, Riza was a few years older than Low, and even though the pair had known each other for years, their relationship was polite and formal. Since coming into Najib's orbit, Low was always careful to remain subservient to the prime minister, calling him "my PM," and this extended to Rosmah and her son.

Now, Riza was living in Los Angeles, ready to help Low invest some of the money at his disposal, and that evening in Whistler led to an idea. A film buff, Joey McFarland had helped produce some low-budget movies since relocating to Los Angeles and for months had been telling friends about his desire to start a full-fledged production company. McFarland and Riza shared an interest in cinema, and immediately hit it off on the ski trip, bonding over movies. Riza was a fan of Italian postwar neorealistic cinema, while McFarland preferred contemporary films with Hollwood A-listers like Brad Pitt and Leonardo DiCaprio. Nonetheless, a connection had been made, and over the coming weeks Low, Riza, and McFarland got talking about an idea. *Why not leverage Low's money to get into the film business?*

The rise of McFarland and Riza in the filmmaking world would be unexpected and meteoric. As he reinvented himself, McFarland soon would be disavowing his talent-booking past, even to those closest to him. And like others, amid the excitement of money and recognition, he would ask very few questions about the origin of Low's funds.

On February 20, 2010, a Saturday night, a few months after the Whistler getaway, Paris Hilton laughed while putting down bets on the baccarat table at a private room on the floor of the Palazzo in Vegas. In a matching white dress and heels, with Chanel earrings and her hair parted tightly to one side, she was celebrating her twenty-ninth birthday, carrying herself with the assurance of wealth. But even such a monied heritage—her family had founded the Hilton hotel chain—had not prepared her to sit in front of a quarter-million dollars in gambling chips.

Earlier in the evening, Hilton had partied at TAO nightclub in the complex, cutting a tiered birthday cake that advertised her new line in shoes. It was a typical public-private performance for the heiress, part family celebration and part promotion in front of the cameras. The after-party downstairs was more intimate, the portion that wasn't curated for the paparazzi. There, in a private gambling room, Low surprised her with a very generous birthday present: a Cartier watch. As if that was insufficient, he then handed her the $250,000 in gambling chips and asked her to join him at the baccarat table.

Jho Low's party crew had begun to assemble. Apart from the celebrities, there were models. Some of these women had fallen in with the group at Las Vegas or New York clubs; some knew the nightclub owners Tepperberg and Strauss, while others were recruited through their managers and agents. Some were only teenagers. Joey McFarland was on hand, of course, and so were Low's rich Middle Eastern and Asian buddies from college, like Al Wazzan and Seet Li Lin.

"in vegas, bring a jacket cos its raining cristal haha!" Seet wrote on Facebook, posting a picture of himself with a jeroboam of the champagne.

As the gambling at Hilton's birthday heated up, the partygoers—Low's Asian clique, minor celebrities from shows like *The Hills*, models, and other rich kids—leaned into the table. These were wealthy folk, many of whom had grown up privileged in Orange County or Santa Monica and formed the core of LA's rich set, but they had never seen anyone quite like Low. He was putting down bigger and bigger bets, hundreds of thousands of dollars on single hands.

Then, in a cascade of bad luck, taking all of ten minutes, he lost $2 million. The stunned entourage couldn't compute the way he parted with money—seemingly without breaking a sweat—and some began to whisper about this guy, and how he acted like the cash wasn't his own.

Rumors swirled. *He's an arms dealer. He's connected to a foreign leader. He's some kind of overseas royalty.* As the next magnum of Cristal arrived, or someone handed out thousands of dollars in chips, questions about Low's provenance flickered momentarily and then faded away.

For all his carefree spending, Low knew that the money wasn't all his to fritter away. In these early stages, he began to focus on how to reward his allies—foremost among them Abu Dhabi executives and the family of Prime Minister Najib Razak—and start building a business that would generate profits. He needed to find a way to sustain his new life.

Chapter 12

How to Spend a Billion

Los Angeles, December 2009

Low was looking for edge. His company, Wynton, was making a $45 million all-cash bid for the L'Ermitage hotel—a $500-a-night, 117-room luxury establishment just off the Sunset Strip in Beverly Hills. But he faced a rival offer from Ian Schrager, the U.S. hotel investor, and Low was looking for a way to swing the deal in his favor. He turned to Mubadala, the Abu Dhabi fund.

Low wrote the executive director of Mubadala's real estate division, asking if anyone at the fund could put in a good word for him with the seller, Tom Barrack Jr., the U.S. real estate billionaire. Khaldoon Al Mubarak, the chief executive of Mubadala, promised to get Ambassador Otaiba to help.

In an email to Barrack Jr., Otaiba put the official weight of Abu Dhabi behind Low's offer, although he did not mention the Malaysian.

"I'm contacting you today to endorse this bid both as the UAE ambassador but also as someone who understands that the full weight of a major investment entity is behind this project," he wrote.

Barrack Jr. replied cordially, noting he had met Otaiba's father thirty years earlier, while a young lawyer. "Mubadala and

Al Mubarak are first class investors and we are honored at their interest," he wrote, promising to see what he could do. The bid went Low's way.

The success of Low was by now important to Abu Dhabi on multiple fronts. Mubadala had recently acquired Viceroy Hotel Group, a hotel-management company, and Low had offered to buy the L'Ermitage and then rebrand it as a Viceroy Hotel. Ambassador Otaiba had made money from his dealings with Low on the Iskandar land project in Malaysia, and he hoped to get in on more deals.

Low knew the scheme would falter unless the money he'd taken was put to work, and he set out to construct a business empire. Years ago, the power of Al Mubarak at Mubadala had inspired Low, and pushed him to create his own sovereign wealth fund. Now the Malaysian, armed with hundreds of millions of dollars, was able to do deals with Mubadala on an equal footing. Al Mubarak did not seem to care where Low was getting his money.

To pay for the L'Ermitage, Low set up a trust account at Shearman & Sterling in the name of Wynton Group, and the law firm represented the company in the purchase. He then sent money into the trust from his Good Star account, the one which had received $700 million in 1MDB cash. Low noted on bank documents that the money was for "STAKE V. H." He was using his tie-up with Viceroy Hotels to give legitimacy to the huge movement of funds. He had made his first major investment, an initial step to build a reputation as a businessman.

As he partied and bought assets, Low needed to pay back the people who had made all this possible: the family of Malaysian Prime Minister Najib Razak. Just as he had misrepresented Prince Turki as an official Saudi envoy, Low was careful to keep the full scope of his actions from Najib. But in return for the long leash Najib had given him, Low needed to make his patron happy.

From the early days of his scheme, Low made sure not to leave the first couple out of the profits. From the IOLTA accounts at Shearman & Sterling, he sent $3 million to Rose Trading, a Hong Kong–based jewelry trading firm that supplied Rosmah. It was only the start of tens of millions of dollars of jewelry that Low would procure for Rosmah, and soon Najib also would begin receiving spoils in the form of political funding.

Beginning in 2010, Low also acquired multi-million-dollar luxury homes in London, Los Angeles, and New York, making them available to Najib and his family. A Low-controlled shell firm acquired a condominium in New York's Park Laurel building, just off Central Park West, for $36 million. But it was Riza Aziz, Rosmah's son, who made the 7,700-square-foot duplex, with floor-to-ceiling windows, his home in New York.

The seller's agent was Raphael De Niro, the son of Robert De Niro (who himself would soon get to know Low and Prime Minister Najib Razak). The younger De Niro worked for high-end property firm Douglas Elliman Real Estate, which, like all U.S. brokers handling hundreds of millions of dollars in property transactions each year—as well as lawyers involved in real estate deals—was not required under American laws to conduct due diligence of clients' finances. In fact, De Niro didn't even need to know the ultimate buyer of a property, and Low purported to be representing Malaysia's prime minister or other rich buyers as he toured apartments and mansions.

By 2010, faceless shell companies, many of them based offshore, accounted for more than half of the hundreds of billions of dollars in high-end U.S. property sales each year—an arrangement that was wholly legal under U.S. law—and Low was becoming adept at hiding his involvement. The agreement to buy the Park Laurel apartment, for instance, was signed by one Low-controlled firm, although it then assigned its rights to another British Virgin Islands–based shell company, which later changed its name.

A Seychelles-incorporated shell company controlled by Low purchased a $17.5-million mansion at 912 North Hillcrest in Beverly Hills in May 2010 as a place for Riza to stay on the West Coast. Known as Pyramid House, for a gold leaf–covered pyramid surrounded by a water feature in the entrance hall, the 11,573-square-foot residence had the feeling of a tropical villa, with a lap pool and semi-open rooms with sweeping views over Los Angeles. While the home underwent a major renovation, Riza often stayed in the L'Ermitage while in Los Angeles. Low, through another entity he controlled, bought an imposing red-brick townhouse for 17 million pounds in the upmarket Belgravia district of London. It was not far from Harrods, one of Rosmah's favorite shops, and the Najib family would stay there on regular trips to the city.

Low was acting as a front for the Najib clan, and eventually Riza would become the owner of all three properties—in London, Los Angeles, and New York—purchasing them from Low with more money stolen from 1MDB. The Malaysian was well on his way to repaying his debt to Najib for allowing him to run the fund. The prime minister did not pry about the origins of the money for these luxurious homes. The involvement of Low, who on paper was behind the purchases, allowed Najib to deny any knowledge of the funds' provenance. He was a figure who permitted the prime minister to keep his hands clean.

Despite purchasing this string of homes, Low began to travel obsessively around the globe, a schedule that fit his inability to focus on the present moment. In a typical three-week period, Low would spend a few days in Kuala Lumpur to meet Prime Minister Najib, and return home for a visit in Penang, before moving on to Singapore and Hong Kong. From there, he'd fly to Shanghai, where he had connections through his grandfather's Chinese clan, before boarding a plane to Abu Dhabi. After a quick trip to London and Paris, perhaps with an excursion to Zurich to explain a weird transfer to Swiss bankers, he'd move on to New York, before finally landing in Los Angeles, and making a gambling trip to Vegas. The tour finished, Low would fly across the Pacific to start all over again. It was a frenetic schedule that most people could not endure.

Tired of leasing planes, Low plunked down $35 million to purchase a Bombardier Global 5000 private aircraft, drawing on the funds at Shearman & Sterling. He lived on the jet more than the many homes he was in the process of acquiring. Outfitted with a bed and mini-office, complete with fax machine and Wi-Fi, he did much of his work from the Bombardier, or tapping away at all hours on his phones while in hotels and restaurants, rather than putting in regular office hours. During busy periods, Low worked until dawn to close a deal, but then missed meetings the next day.

Eight full-time pilots working on shifts, together with half a dozen flight attendants, serviced Low's nonstop travel. He struck the crew as among the most polite ultra-wealthy clients they'd ever met. The catering was eccentric. One request included some of the finest items from the upscale Japanese restaurant Nobu in London as well as one bucket of Kentucky Fried Chicken to wash it all down.

It was an extraordinary life, but Low's demure bearing gave a different impression to those people who met him only fleetingly.

"He seemed like a pretty ordinary fellow," said Joseph Cayre, the billionaire real estate investor who sold him the Bombardier.

Low's scheme was succeeding in fooling many in the United States. Back home, though, the stewards of 1MDB wanted to know what was going on.

Chapter 13

Where's Our Money?

Kuala Lumpur, Malaysia, October 2009

On October 3, 2009, the atmosphere was fraught at a specially convened meeting of 1MDB's board, just as Low and his entourage were drawing attention to themselves in Vegas. The fund had been set up in such a hurry that it did not yet have its own permanent offices. So for this meeting, on a cloudy, humid Saturday, the board gathered in the Royale Bintang Hotel, a four-star hotel in the Mutiara Damansara neighborhood near Kuala Lumpur. Sitting around a table in the executive center, the members of the group supposed to be overseeing the operations of the fund were not happy.

Most disconcerted among them was Mohammed Bakke Salleh, a respected businessman whom Prime Minister Najib Razak had chosen as chairman of the board. Bakke was the epitome of a buttoned-up chartered accountant; he had gotten his training after a degree at the London School of Economics. He dressed in dark suits, often with the same red tie, and wore wire-rimmed spectacles, his bald head framed by graying hair at the side and a neatly trimmed beard, also gray. But his appearance belied a tenacious side, and he had fought his way up the ranks to head Malaysia's largest state-owned agribusiness company. In a land of deep corruption, Bakke had a reputation for doing things by the book, and in the board meeting he was furious.

Why in the hell, he wanted to know, had 1MDB sent $700 million to another company and not the joint venture with Petro-Saudi, as the board had agreed? Shahrol Halmi, the fund's chief executive, tried to reassure Bakke that the money had gone to repay a loan to PetroSaudi. Shahrol was a down-to-earth leader, a geek who enjoyed tech gadgets and cars and was liked by colleagues. Unlike many top executives at 1MDB, Shahrol wasn't a Low associate, but he quickly became addicted to the jet-setting lifestyle. There is no indication he received any payoff, but his life changed in an instant as he went from toiling on IT projects at Accenture to running a multi-billion-dollar fund. Thankful for such a change of station and believing he was carrying out Najib's wishes, he hewed closely to the stories told to him by Low and others, in this case that PetroSaudi was owed the money.

Bakke wasn't so easily duped. Why hadn't the board been informed of this debt in the first place? he demanded. There was no answer. The chairman ordered PetroSaudi to return the money, so it could be invested in the joint venture as agreed.

"The substantial investment of US$1 billion should have merited a more thorough thought and due diligence process," the board recorded blandly in the official minutes from the meeting.

Unbeknownst to the group, the money in question was, as they spoke, being poured into nightclubs, gambling, mansions, and more; it just couldn't be returned like that.

Weeks later, Bakke demanded an independent audit of the oil assets that PetroSaudi was supposed to have put into the joint venture. Keen not to open a can of worms, Low persuaded Najib, as head of the board of advisers, to rule there would be no second valuation of the assets. Disgusted by how he had become entangled in such a mess, Bakke resigned without fanfare from the board a few days later. Another director also wanted to step down, but Najib urged him to hold off for a few weeks, lest it appear the board was suffering an exodus, and he finally left in January.

Low, who hadn't expected such a pushback, scrambled to stop further dissension. After the board had raised concerns, 1MDB's management wrote Patrick Mahony, PetroSaudi's head of investment, to ask for more details. Mahony must have been nervous, because PetroSaudi had conducted scant business before 1MDB came along, and he emailed Low to ask if he should send details.

"No I wouldn't even bother sending it. Keep it simple. I want to give the board as little information as possible until PM clears the air," Low responded.

The prime minister knew 1MDB was secretly fueling his political machinations and was not as legitimate as it appeared. He was allowing an untested twenty-eight-year-old to secretly run operations, lured into the scheme by Low's promises the fund would enhance relationships with the Middle East and bring in investment. For years, Najib's family had used government service to line their own pockets, and Low's involvement in buying jewels for Rosmah and properties for Riza Aziz was more of the same. For these reasons, Najib gave Low a wide berth and remained willfully ignorant about what the young Malaysian was up to, even as reports about his spending in New York reached Malaysia and respected businessmen like Bakke sounded the alarm.

To keep the prime minister's trust, Low set about organizing another state visit to Saudi Arabia in January 2010. Before the visit, he sent an email to the Obaids to stage-manage the trip, asking that Saudi royals use words like "personal," "trust," "friendship," and "bond" in discussions with Najib and Rosmah.

Saudi authorities did better than that, conferring the kingdom's top civilian award on Najib during his visit. It was the kind of honor that went a long way with the prime minister, and it showed that Low had deep connections.

The visit handed Low the ammunition he needed to silence the few 1MDB board members who were continuing to complain in meetings about the missing funds. He told one member that asking too many questions about the deal with PetroSaudi, which he described as a state company, could upset bilateral relations with Saudi Arabia. "We can't insult Saudi Arabia. The PM just got a 21-gun salute on his visit," Low said. The board member backed off.

Low met board members regularly for coffee and let them know he was the prime minister's representative dealing with 1MDB matters. It was vague, and Low's lack of official title was mysterious, but those on the board understood his power came from the top. To many, the blurry contours of his role made him seem even more powerful, and that was something he exploited. To ensure no further scrutiny of his actions, Low solidified his control over the board. To replace one of the vacated seats, he persuaded Najib to appoint a Malaysian Chinese from Penang who was a business partner of his father's. Lodin Wok Kamaruddin, a UMNO party loyalist who was close to Najib, became the new chairman. Low had seen to it that the board was now dominated by Najib loyalists. To put it another way, there was basically no independent oversight of the prime minister, Low, and his allies in 1MDB's management.

With its management hiccups cleared up, 1MDB started to look more legitimate. From its new offices on the eighth floor of Menara IMC, a gleaming skyscraper near the Petronas Towers in Kuala Lumpur, the 1MDB fund's management went about building a business. Chief Executive Shahrol oversaw the hiring of a group of around ten young Malaysians with Ivy League degrees, who were enticed into the job by competitive salaries and the promise of billions of dollars in financing. The pitch was that 1MDB would be a modern kind of fund, like Mubadala in the Middle East, and would transform Malaysia by building new industries, especially green technology. An early plan was to develop a renewable energy corridor in Sarawak, with investment from China and the Middle East, and the young employees set about drawing up presentations and investment plans.

"We genuinely thought that helping a sovereign fund in its start-up stage was a great way to make a difference for the country," said one early staff member.

Working for a big sovereign wealth fund was a prestigious endeavor. But it didn't take long for disillusionment to set in among many of the new hires. The plans for the green-energy business failed to gain traction, and it became clear that none of the senior management had experience running an investment fund. It was as if the bosses didn't really care about the longer-term projects, instead convening in their offices on a mezzanine floor, rarely communicating with regular employees. Everyone knew that Jho Low was the chief decision maker at the fund, but he was almost never around, and for some reason management asked staff to refer to him by a code name, "UC." A joke started going around that it stood for "unsavory character."

Low's focus was on turning a profit with the money he had taken out of the fund, whether through investments in the L'Ermitage hotel or other projects he was hoping to develop with Mubadala. This wasn't a simple bank robbery; he was wagering these businesses would take off, and the profits would easily fill the hole at 1MDB. The fund's operations proper, however, often seemed like an afterthought.

At one point, Nik Faisal Ariff Kamil, an associate of Low's who was head of investment at 1MDB, fretted in a board meeting that there was no cash flow to pay for debt the fund had assumed, not just the $1.4 billion in Islamic bonds but hundreds of millions of dollars more in Malaysian bank loans. These executives started to make ridiculous suggestions. Nik Faisal even proposed that 1MDB buy a Malaysian island to turn into a vacation resort, but the idea was knocked down by the board.

The fund's hallmark development, dubbed Project Wall Street, was a plan to turn Kuala Lumpur into a financial hub to rival Singapore or Hong Kong. The aim was to have Abu Dhabi's Mubadala fund invest billions into the financial center, and 1MDB spent $2 million on a launch party in mid-2010 for the initiative. Low pulled strings to get the crown prince of Abu Dhabi to attend, but when he canceled at the last minute, most of the money for the party was lost, and the financial-center plan made little progress. Kuala Lumpur's stock market and banking sector just weren't important outside the country, and potential investors were hard to find. Still, Low persuaded Najib to grant the fund parcels of vacant city-center land at bargain-basement prices for the project.

Amid the wasted spending and the lack of focus, many of the Ivy League recruits quit after less than a year. More worryingly to many, it became clear the fund's main reason to exist was as a pot of political money to boost Najib's popularity. Even without steady cash flow from operations, 1MDB was starting to channel money as "corporate social responsibility" to help encourage voters to support UMNO, the ruling party.

"We even joked that many of the projects we were assessing were pretend projects to give the company a legitimate front," the 1MDB employee said.

On March 1, 2010, the new board of loyalists met at 1MDB's new offices to discuss how the fund could help Najib's premiership. Even though it still had no viable businesses, Chief Executive Shahrol explained to the board how a new charity arm of

1MDB was planning to pour money into the Malaysian region of Sarawak to coincide with an upcoming visit by Najib. The jungle-covered state, though remote and relatively unpopulated, was crucial to the UMNO party's grip on national power. Lodin, Najib's friend and chairman of the board, responded that getting the support of the "natives"—by which he meant Sarawak's tribal peoples, some of whom still lived in longhouses in the jungle— was crucial. The board agreed without debate to provide more than half a million dollars for school scholarships and housing for the poor, which Najib could promote when he visited.

The prime minister's office staff was tasked with coming up with projects, like funding schools in important voting districts, and 1MDB would provide the finances.

"If we thought it could help the incumbent government pull in some votes, we could propose that," said Oh Ei Sun, Najib's political secretary at the time.

From the start, Najib was obsessed with popularity. Like any old-school Malaysian politician, he saw money—not ideas—as the only way to achieve popularity with voters, and he squeezed 1MDB for funds. A few months after the 1MDB board meeting, Najib told voters before an upcoming local election in Sarawak that he would arrange federal funding for local projects only if the ruling-party candidate won.

"You help me, I help you," a sweating Najib promised in a stump speech before the voting. It was a picture of the rot in Malaysian politics.

Chapter 14

Roll the Presses

Kuala Lumpur, Malaysia, December 2009

Some among Malaysia's elite, hearing whispers about Moham-med Bakke Salleh's resignation, guessed something was not right at 1MDB. Yet the fund's problems remained unknown to the general public, in part because Najib's government controlled the mainstream media. But there was one media tycoon the prime minister could not order around so easily: Tong Kooi Ong, owner of the *Edge*, an English-language weekly business newspaper. The mass-market papers, mostly progovernment, were in Malay or Chinese. The *Edge* catered to the country's business elite.

For years, Tong had been the rebel of Malaysia's business community. The fifty-year-old, with tufts of black hair on either side of his head and a bald skull, preferred open-neck shirts to suits. He once told his wife he had a premonition he would die before fifty, and he needed to live fast before then. He could be bad-tempered with people he considered dimwitted, but he was equally charming, his face often breaking out into an impish smile. It was a combination that riled up the entitled ruling-party elites in Kuala Lumpur.

When Tong heard the rumors about 1MDB, the newspaper-man decided the *Edge* needed to investigate.

In Malaysia, most major papers were subservient to the government. The ruling UMNO party directly owned some of the largest-circulation papers, whose editors slavishly put out puff pieces on politicians and policies. Newspapers had to renew their publishing licenses every year. Given the government's control, even editors at independent newspapers often self-censored.

The arrival of the *Edge*, in the mid-1990s, shook up the industry. Unlike other papers, the *Edge* did not shy away from writing about corruption scandals, which Tong viewed as harmful to Malaysia's economic prospects. He had built his own fortune and was beholden to no one, and that made him a threat.

The sixth of nine children of a Chinese-Malaysian car mechanic, Tong had grown up in the 1960s and 1970s in the gritty Malaysian port town of Klang, not far from Kuala Lumpur. His family scraped together enough to send him to university in Canada, where he eventually earned a master's degree in finance and taught himself computer science. Returning to Malaysia in the 1980s, Tong became a securities analyst at a Malaysian firm before moving to British bank Morgan Grenfell, helping to value companies. But he was ambitious and restless, and by the 1990s he bought his own securities company and soon after acquired a full banking license.

In the clubby world of Malaysian business, Tong was considered a maverick, and he quickly made enemies. By bringing online trading to Malaysia, he undercut other brokers, who came to view him as a dangerous upstart. Foreign fund managers liked Tong, however, and he quickly won a large share of their business in Malaysia. His cocksure manner, obvious intelligence, and contempt for mediocrity irritated financiers who owed their success to years of ties with the establishment.

He also was political—but bet on the wrong horse. Tong befriended Anwar Ibrahim, a charismatic deputy prime minister, sensing he would soon become the nation's top leader. But in the late 1990s Anwar fell out with Prime Minister Mahathir Mohamad, who had ruled Malaysia since 1981. When Anwar fell, jailed on trumped-up charges of sodomizing his male driver (sodomy is illegal in Malaysia), Tong was cast out into the wilderness. Amid rumors that Mahathir would seize his assets, the businessman returned to Canada, transforming himself into a successful property developer in Vancouver. But he could never remain in one place for long, and after Mahathir stepped down in 2003, Tong came back to Malaysia.

Mahathir had forced Tong to sell his bank, but Tong still controlled the *Edge*. The newspaper had built a loyal following. If the press wasn't exactly independent, at least Malaysia wasn't a dictatorship, and the *Edge*'s editors had learned to push the limits of free expression, writing stories on corruption, while maintaining their license. Some topics were off-limits, say, corruption stories about a prime minister. By focusing more on business than politics, its editors had stayed on the right side of the government.

In late 2009, Tong began to hear rumors about 1MDB. From the start, elite Malaysians gossiped about Najib's administration. Malaysian diplomats complained about having to organize Rosmah's shopping trips when she was abroad. More recently, Tong had started to hear more alarming complaints. Bankers told him the Terengganu fund, the predecessor of 1MDB, had sold its Islamic bonds too cheaply. That meant whoever bought the bonds could resell them in the market for a handsome profit. Rumor had it that companies connected to Low had benefited. This kind of trick was common in Asia's capital markets. Now, at cocktail parties in Kuala Lumpur, the talk was of Bakke's abrupt resignation from the fund's board.

Tong was a visionary, not a details man. He could be disorganized, his offices a mess of papers and odd objects, including, for a time, a little-used treadmill. To implement the coverage of

1MDB he leaned on Ho Kay Tat, a veteran journalist who was publisher of the *Edge*. Ho's mane of gray hair, glasses, and eagerness to please in conversation made him seem grandfatherly, even though he was only in his fifties. But his avuncular appearance belied a tenacity to dig for the truth.

Ho had joined the *Edge* in the 1990s, later leaving to become chief executive of the *Star*, a government-aligned newspaper based in Low's home state of Penang. But Ho had been unable to deal with the constant requests to kill negative stories about UMNO-linked companies, and he had jumped at the chance to rejoin the *Edge* as publisher in 2013.

While government mouthpieces like the *Star* and the *New Straits Times* pushed out softball pieces on Najib's administration, the *Edge* under Ho took a critical stance. Backed by Tong, Ho tagged a small team of reporters to start digging. In December 2009, the *Edge* published a story raising questions about 1MDB. Why had Bakke resigned from the board so soon after the fund's inception? Why had the Terengganu Investment Authority sold its bonds so cheaply, despite being a risk-free, state-owned entity? What exactly was the purpose of 1MDB, and what was it doing with the money?

One name that appeared nowhere in the piece: Jho Low. He was nonetheless disturbed by it, and began talking off the record to journalists at the *Edge*, trying to persuade them that 1MDB was a genuine investment vehicle. It would be three years more before the *Edge* began to uncover the truth. For now, Low's secret was safe. In fact, his star was on the rise.

Chapter 15

Welcome to New York

New York, April 2010

The guests, wearing tuxedos and ball gowns, made their way up to the ballroom of the St. Regis Hotel, just off Fifth Avenue in Midtown Manhattan. It was April 16, 2010, a rainy and wind-swept evening, but the mood was ebullient at one of the city's most stylish hotels. Najib and his wife, Rosmah, were in espe-cially good spirits. A few days earlier, President Barack Obama had granted Najib a bilateral meeting on the sidelines of a nuclear-security summit in Washington. Obama, the first black American elected to the U.S. presidency, was a global icon, and Najib sensed an opportunity for a new dawn in relations between the countries.

After the Obama meeting, Low was pulling on his connec-tions to ensure the Malaysian first couple made a splash dur-ing their trip, and the night at the St. Regis was the centerpiece of that effort. The event was hosted by the Business Council for International Understanding, a little-known organization set up under President Dwight Eisenhower to foster ties between world business and political leaders. The night at the St. Regis was to honor Rosmah, on whom the council had decided to bestow its "International Peace and Harmony Award." The award, the council said, was in recognition for work Rosmah had done with children's charities back in Malaysia.

She had set up a children's education organization, but it was financed by public money and critics at home wondered why the Education Ministry didn't just distribute the cash. If the council clearly hadn't done its homework, that was fine with Najib and Rosmah. Awards like this, while essentially meaningless tokens, were crucial to the likes of Rosmah, who detested the whispers about the origins of her money. To trumpet the award, the Malaysian government spent hundreds of thousands of dollars on a double-page advertisement in the *New York Times* to coincide with her visit, congratulating the first lady with a full-page photo of Rosmah and the words "Welcome to New York."

To ensure the St. Regis party's success, Low contacted Sahle Ghebreyesus, the Eritrean-American contact who had arranged the details of Prince Turki's meeting with Najib aboard the *Alfa Nero*. He invited a bevy of Hollywood stars, many of whom would seem unlikely attendees at an award dinner for an Asian politician's wife. The event started at 6.30 p.m. with cocktails and an Islamic fashion show before dinner. Jamie Foxx, the actor and comedian, emceed the proceedings. A number of stars, including Robert De Niro and Charlize Theron, were in attendance, giving the event a buzz. Wearing a traditional Malay sarong and loose-fitting embroidered top, both in a deep yellow color, with a diamond-encrusted bangle around her wrist and sparkling earrings, Rosmah was ecstatic at the attention.

When dinner concluded around 10 p.m., the party really got going. Pop star Leona Lewis sang. Foxx dragged Rosmah up on stage for a flirty rendition of "You've Got a Friend," and he danced with Najib. Later, De Niro, Theron, and others joined Foxx on stage to sing "We Are the World"—one of Low's favorites. "It was like a wedding, bar/bat mitzvah, Sweet 16, quinceanera all rolled up into one," wrote Wendy Brandes, a jewelry designer, who was present. "I was awestruck."

A few months later, De Niro, taking up an invite from Rosmah, traveled to Malaysia on a vacation. Rosmah told local media that she wanted him to see the country for himself, rather than believe any negative stories he had heard. Through Jho Low's extravagant spending, and the expectation, perhaps, of a new source of film financing, Hollywood stars were taking notice of Malaysia. Yet again Low had made himself indispensable. Najib and Rosmah felt like Low could work magic, organizing state visits to the Middle East and, now, attracting the glamor of Hollywood.

Low, however, had an even bigger target, confiding in Ambassador Otaiba that he hoped to deepen Najib's relationship with President Obama. For years, ties between Malaysia and the United States had been lukewarm at best. Former Prime Minister Mahathir Mohamad was confrontational toward the United States, bashing "Western imperialism" and blaming "Jewish" financiers for the Asian financial crisis in the late 1990s. Western governments decried the jailing of Anwar Ibrahim for sodomy as a political vendetta. On an official visit to Kuala Lumpur, Vice President Al Gore urged the "brave people of Malaysia" to push for democracy, infuriating Mahathir. By the time Najib came to power, no sitting U.S. president had visited Malaysia since Lyndon B. Johnson in the 1960s, when the United States was entrenched in the Vietnam War.

At their April 2010 meeting Najib presented himself to Obama as a different political animal. The prime minister was a self-professed Anglophile and talked about deepening democratic reforms. On the face of it, he seemed to be a leader the United States could rely on in the region. He appeared urbane, spoke good English, and made the right noises about Islam, having recently launched a "Global Movement of Moderates," an effort to get Islamic countries around the world to condemn Islamist violence.

President Obama was keen to extricate the United States from costly wars in Iraq and Afghanistan and wanted to shift focus to East Asia, where he was seeking to counterbalance China's influence on the fast-growing economic zone. In a speech in Australia the following year, Obama would underline this pivot to Asia, and Najib, along with the leaders of Indonesia, Japan, South Korea, and Australia, was viewed by the president and his White House advisers as key to the effort.

It was a good start, and Low would do all he could in the years ahead to ensure Najib and the American president got even closer.

Chapter 16

Shitty, Junk Products

Washington, DC, April 2010

As Najib visited New York, the United States was engulfed in political upheaval. The financial crisis, originating in America, had spread to Europe, throwing millions out of work and their homes, causing a deep recession, and inspiring the "Occupy Wall Street" protests. The anger at Wall Street banks, many of which had prospered during the crisis, was palpable.

In late April, Goldman's chief executive, Lloyd Blankfein, tried to stay calm as he answered angry questions from U.S. senators about the Wall Street bank's role in the financial meltdown. Senator Carl Levin, a Democrat from Michigan who headed a Senate subcommittee that had spent eighteen months looking into Goldman's actions, wanted to know why the bank had sold securities backed by toxic subprime mortgages to clients while, at the same time, betting against them. Levin gave example after example of deals that Goldman sold to clients that its bankers described privately in emails as "shitty" and "junk."

"It raises a real ethical issue," Levin said, his demeanor hostile, as he sat opposite Blankfein. In the public gallery, protesters dressed in fake prison jumpsuits held up pink signs with the word "SHAME" and photos of Blankfein's head mounted on sticks.

In the mid-2000s, Wall Street's profits soared due to a boom in the U.S. housing market, as Americans signed up for loans to buy homes with little or even no money down. Banks took these poor-quality mortgages—known as subprime loans—and packaged them into securities, which they sold to big investment funds.

At Goldman, both Blankfein and Gary Cohn, the bank's president, who would go on to serve as President Donald Trump's chief economic adviser, pushed subprime debt products, which the bank continued to market in the run-up to the crisis. But fearing a crash in home prices, with many Americans unable to keep up on their mortgage payments, Goldman itself had bet against the market—a trading strategy that later came to be known as the "Big Short."

When the U.S. housing bubble burst in 2007, these subprime securities blew up. Within a year, losses related to toxic subprime loans toppled Bear Stearns and Lehman Brothers, sparking a full-blown financial crisis. The U.S. government had to step in with a $700 billion bailout for the banks.

The Goldman chief executive, dressed in a gray suit with a maroon tie, tried to parry the angry questioning from Senator Levin, arguing that some clients—big banks and institutional funds—still believed the U.S. housing market was robust in 2007. It was no fault of Goldman's, he said, if those clients desired to acquire securities linked to subprime home loans.

"They wanted to have a security that gave them exposure to the housing market," Blankfein said. "The unfortunate thing is the housing market went south."

Goldman did not operate retail bank branches, and few Americans knew much about investment banks, whose clients are largely companies, governments, pension funds, high-net-worth individuals, and other banks. But Blankfein was becoming the poster boy for financial sector greed. The collapse of the housing market had left many Americans destitute. Goldman's profit, by contrast, soared to a record $13.4 billion in 2009. Senator John McCain, a Republican from Arizona, asked Blankfein to tell the room his bonus for the year. Visibly ill at ease, the chief executive stuttered, before responding: it was $9 million.

The 140-year-old bank was on the defensive. The U.S. Securities and Exchange Commission, which enforces securities laws and regulates the industry, was suing Goldman for withholding information from a German bank to which it sold a subprime mortgage product. A young French trader at Goldman named Fabrice Tourre, who referred to himself in emails as "Fabulous Fab," had talked about selling the product, known as Abacus, to "widows and orphans." Three months after Blankfein's appearance in Congress, Goldman settled with the SEC for $550 million, the largest-ever penalty paid in a civil case by a Wall Street firm. It apologized for giving "incomplete information" to its client, but did not admit wrongdoing.

Senator Levin later asked for a criminal investigation of Goldman, but the U.S. Justice Department decided not to pursue charges, adding to a sense that Wall Street bankers walked away scot-free from the crisis they created. Even though no senior Goldman executives were sanctioned, however, banks were under scrutiny like never before. In 2010, Congress passed the Dodd-Frank Act, a sweeping series of laws brought in as a response to the financial crisis.

The Volcker Rule, proposed by former Federal Reserve chairman Paul Volcker, restricted banks from speculative trading that did not benefit their customers. The idea was this kind of activity—say, betting on risky subprime securities—destabilized the financial system and hurt ordinary savers and home owners. Banks would fight a rearguard action in Congress: The rule was watered down, permitting certain investments, and took years to come into effect. But Wall Street banks had to stop acting like hedge funds, which make proprietary investments using money from rich individuals, and look after their clients' interests, whether a small home owner or a multinational corporation.

These new restrictions, coupled with an anemic U.S. economy, low interest rates, and a weak stock market, led Blankfein to double down on his push into emerging markets. China continued to grow at double-digit rates, and the economies of Brazil, Russia—even small Malaysia—were humming along. In a speech later in 2010, as Goldman licked its wounds from the damage the crisis had done to its reputation, Blankfein said the biggest opportunity for the bank was to be "Goldman Sachs in more places."

In 2010, as Goldman looked to increase its business in emerging markets, a thirty-seven-year-old Italian banker named Andrea Vella arrived in Hong Kong. A former engineering student, Vella had short-cropped, graying hair, a sturdy build, and a pugnacious face. He was a persuasive and confident banker who colleagues believed could convince anyone of his perspective on just about anything. Vella was also a product-structuring specialist—an expert on complicated derivatives—just the kind Goldman was hoping to sell in places like Malaysia.

Vella had developed a reputation among some colleagues for focusing on unsophisticated clients who would, without question, pay huge fees for the bank's expertise. A year after Vella joined Goldman's London office in 2007, he began overseeing the bank's relationship with the Libyan Investment Authority, a new sovereign wealth fund set up by Muammar Qaddafi's government.

On a simple level, derivatives are financial products whose value is linked to an underlying set of assets. Derivatives can help businesses smooth out price fluctuations. For example, if a company wants to protect itself from a fall in a commodity price, it could buy a kind of derivative called a forward contract, which allows it to sell at a fixed price in the future. As the subprime crisis exhibited, derivatives could also be dangerous by allowing investors to make big, debt-fueled bets on the direction prices were headed, in this case mortgage-backed securities. That was fine when a wager paid off, but could cause a cascade of losses if markets moved in an unexpected direction.

Vella's Libyan clients wanted to accumulate a stake in U.S. banks, as Middle Eastern funds were doing in the chaos of the financial crisis. But the managers of the fund didn't really understand derivatives. Vella urged a junior colleague, who handled the Libya relationship on the ground, to go heavy on marketing. "Often they don't know what they want or need, we need to interpret their confused words and show them the right things. Focus on that," Vella emailed the colleague.

Goldman designed a complex derivative, backed by shares in Citigroup and other companies. The derivatives were structured so the Libyan authority would profit handsomely if Citigroup's shares went up, but with significantly more downside risk. As the financial crisis deepened, the shares fell and the Libyan authority eventually lost more than $1 billion. The authority later sued Goldman, unsuccessfully, in a London court, claiming its executives didn't understand what they had bought. Goldman didn't reveal how much it made taking the other side of the trade, but the Libyan authority claimed it was more than $200 million.

George Jabbour, a banker for Goldman who was fired during the financial crisis after raising concerns internally about the Libyan deal, was among a number of former colleagues who said Vella was ruthless in the amount of money he charged "stupid" clients.

"The only way you have profit is by having a markup. With a hedge fund that knows what's going on, how can you make money?" Jabbour said.

After the Libyan debacle, Vella came out to Hong Kong in 2010 to head up the investment bank's structured-finance business in Asia. He soon teamed up with another one of Goldman's most ambitious Asian-based bankers: Dr. Tim Leissner.

Goldman's emerging-markets focus had been a boon for Leissner. Suddenly, Malaysia was no longer an obscure market in the eyes of the bank's New York bosses. Since advising the predecessor fund for 1MDB, the German banker had been looking for ways to get Goldman a fat fee by helping the fund raise money or buy assets. There was no immediate deal on the horizon—the initial fund-raising was handled by Malaysian banks—but Leissner was laying the groundwork for Goldman to be in pole position among its Wall Street rivals.

In the summer of 2010, he organized for the twenty-five-year-old daughter of Malaysia's ambassador to the United States, a close ally of Najib, to undertake a short internship at Goldman Sachs in Singapore. He also began a short-lived love affair with her, a relationship that was widely talked about inside the bank. The internship was risky because of the potential for running afoul of the U.S. Foreign Corrupt Practices Act of 1977, which bans companies from paying bribes of any kind to overseas officials to win business, but she nevertheless completed her stint in the Singapore office of the bank. Few people outside the bank knew about it, and, if there was anything improper about the internship, no action was taken against Goldman.

Only weeks later, 1MDB agreed to pay Goldman $1 million to advise it on plans to purchase a hydroelectric dam in Sarawak, the rainforest-covered state whose chief minister, Taib Mahmud, had been ripped off by Low. The money was peanuts, like the fee Leissner had generated for advising on the formation of the Terengganu Investment Authority. In the end, Goldman got nothing as the deal never happened. But there was promise of more.

In the meantime, Leissner concentrated on deepening his connections in Sarawak. The German banker, in 2009, had conducted a relationship with Taib's niece. Leissner even told colleagues he had taken the Muslim name "Salahuddin" as part of his conversion to Islam ahead of a planned marriage that never materialized. In the end the pair split up, but Goldman's Malaysia business rolled on uninterrupted.

Even though the dam project foundered, Goldman saw other opportunites in Sarawak. The state government was seeking cash to develop renewable energy projects and a palm-oil exporting hub. It wanted to raise money through an international bond issuance, and Leissner took the potential business to Hong Kong, Goldman's regional headquarters. There, Andrea Vella began working out how to raise the capital.

The Sarawak government sold $800 million in bonds, but rather than line up investors—typically big mutual funds or pension funds—Goldman bought the entire issue itself, only later looking for willing buyers. Vella had Goldman make the purchases through a trading desk known as the Principal Funding and Investing Group. The PFI desk, which designs complex fund-raisings for clients, was involved in some of Goldman's most profitable deals, including insurance swaps with American International Group during the subprime crisis.

These arcane trades had wagered on a fall in home prices, helping the PFI desk to pocket about $2 billion. A Goldman banker named Toby Watson, a derivatives specialist, was sent out to Asia after the crisis to open an outpost of the PFI desk in Hong Kong—part of Blankfein's emerging-markets strategy. The desk had borrowed around $20 billion from other banks before the crisis, locking in super-cheap rates, and was trawling for ways to deploy this huge cash pile in Asia. The desk would make money if it could find investments that paid out more than the PFI desk's interest costs on the money.

The bank effectively cut a check to Sarawak, allowing the state government to get its hands on the cash immediately and without having to go through a road show to attract investors. In return, Goldman got the bonds for cheap and was later able to sell them to investors. By the time Goldman had offloaded the entire issue to institutional investors—mutual and pension funds—it made a profit of $50 million on the deal. That was significantly higher than the normal $1 million fee that Asian, U.S., and European banks charged for selling bonds for governments in the region—work that was considered easy and risk free, in part because governments are less likely to default than companies.

The huge profit was a coup for Goldman. But the deal also caught the attention of Global Witness, an international watchdog, which questioned why a major Wall Street bank was dealing with a government known for corruption and environmental crimes. In a report, Global Witness claimed some of the contracts funded by the bonds were going to Chief Minister Taib's relatives, which might have explained why the government wanted the money so quickly and was willing to overpay.

The transaction in Sarawak was the first time Leissner, the relationship banker, had joined forces with Vella, the derivatives whiz, to deliver a major amount of money to a client, quietly and fast, while making large profits for Goldman. It was a formula that would be central to Goldman's future relationship with 1MDB.

As he worked on other projects, Leissner continued to keep up with Jho Low, hoping Goldman could advise on a major 1MDB acquisition. But Low's mind was elsewhere. His Hollywood connections had impressed Najib and Rosmah. Now he moved to turn them into a business opportunity.

Chapter 17

My Good Friend, Leo

Johannesburg, South Africa, July 2010

The deep house music was pulsating in the VIP area of Taboo, one of Johannesburg's top nightclubs. The South African financial capital, in the midst of hosting the soccer World Cup finals, thronged with visitors, and the nightclub was heaving. At the club's gold-themed main bar, perched on a designer transparent plastic high stool, Aimee Sadie was enjoying the evening. A few drinks in, the black-haired television personality and entrepreneur was surprised when a friendly American in a suit approached her. It was Joey McFarland, the talent booker and friend of Paris Hilton.

"Would you like to join us in the VIP? Leonardo DiCaprio is there and he's been eyeing you," McFarland told Sadie.

Thrilled to be asked, she accompanied McFarland, slipping behind the velvet rope of the VIP section at the back of the club, where DiCaprio and his crew were hanging out. The actor was dressed down, wearing tracksuit pants and a baseball cap, and he was lounging on the sofa and smoking a huge cigar. McFarland, who said he worked with DiCaprio, introduced the star to Sadie, and they shook hands. But the actor seemed half dazed, sprawling on the couch, and he made little conversation. Others danced and helped themselves from a drinks table, where there was vodka, Red Bull, cranberry juice, and Chivas Regal.

A few days earlier, Low had made the arrangements for the VIP section, introducing himself as a businessman from Malaysia. To the club's owner, he seemed eager to part with a spectacular amount of money. During the evening, as the group sat around chatting and dancing, McFarland asked Sadie to join them on a three-day safari in Kruger National Park, before watching the World Cup final back in Johannesburg. Around midnight McFarland, Low, and the others headed back to their suites at the luxury Westcliff Hotel, a smattering of buildings perched on a wooded hillside. As the group departed, McFarland asked for Sadie's number and he called her from the hotel to ask if she wanted to join the after-party. She politely declined. Despite the attraction of DiCaprio's presence, this group and their massive security detail seemed a little strange, just sitting there in a joyless corner, she thought.

In the few months McFarland had known Low—since their first meeting in Whistler—the pair had become fast friends. But it was a hierarchical relationship. Low began calling the Kentuckian "McCookie," a play on McFarland's sweet tooth, and treated him as a younger brother, even though McFarland was about a decade older. In his work as a talent booker, the American had developed an extensive phone book, and he helped Low with favors, including throwing a party for "Fat Eric," his Malaysian associate, featuring Playboy Playmates.

Low and McFarland also had started to talk seriously about building a Hollywood movie production business, along with Riza Aziz, the stepson of Prime Minister Najib, and for that they needed to get closer to big-name actors and directors. In early 2010, Riza tapped Low's connection with Jamie Foxx, whose manager began to introduce the Malaysian prime minister's stepson around Los Angeles, telling industry bigwigs about Asian investors with $400 million to make movies.

With that kind of cash, and with Foxx as a friend, it wasn't hard to open doors, and Riza secured a meeting with Avi Lerner, an independent producer whose Millennium Films had just made *Righteous Kill* with Al Pacino and Robert De Niro. They talked about financing a film together, possibly starring Foxx and Bruce Willis. That project went nowhere, but a few weeks later Joe Gatta, an executive at Millennium, met Riza and McFarland and persuaded them to build their own film company. As the trio—Riza, Low, and McFarland—planned their next move, they knew they had one trump card: their budding relationship with DiCaprio, one of the most bankable stars on the planet.

DiCaprio didn't really need the favors, the chartered plane ride to South Africa, or a box at the soccer World Cup finals. He'd been a household name since the early 1990s, and like many celebrities, he saw those kinds of freebies as an entitlement. How Low differed from other Hollywood hangers-on, though, was the sheer scale of his wealth and his willingness to spend it. There are lots of wannabe producers out there, but none threw money around like Low.

For Foxx and Hilton, who already were wealthy by any normal standard, Low offered juicy fees to emcee or appear at events. In DiCaprio's case, the Malaysian dangled the possibility of independence from the marquee Hollywood studios. Although he was Hollywood royalty and owned a production company, Appian Way, DiCaprio still had to bow to the will of powerful studio executives, and this power dynamic had been laid bare in his faltering plans to make *The Wolf of Wall Street*.

In 2007, DiCaprio won a bidding war with Brad Pitt for the rights to the memoir of Jordan Belfort, whose firm, Stratton Oakmont, had marketed penny stocks to mom-and-pop and institutional investors in the 1980s and 1990s, defrauding them of tens of millions of dollars. For a while, Belfort succeeded and hosted wild parties in his Long Island offices, featuring cocaine and prostitutes. At one party, his team famously played a game that involved throwing Velcro-suited midgets against a giant, sticky target (a story that inspired Low to hire Oompa Loompas for his 2012 birthday celebration). In 2004, Belfort was sentenced to four years in jail for securities fraud, and ordered to repay investors, but he went free after only twenty-two months, and began penning a memoir.

The result was *The Wolf of Wall Street*, a partially fictionalized tale, which prosecutors said aggrandized Belfort's role at the firm and diminished the damage inflicted on his victims. Even the title was a stretch: Belfort's firm wasn't in the city limits, based miles from Manhattan, and he wasn't widely referred to as "the Wolf of Wall Street." But Belfort intrigued DiCaprio, who had made *Catch Me If You Can*, about master impersonator Frank Abagnale Jr., and, at this time in 2010, was about to sign on to play Jay Gatsby in Baz Luhrmann's *The Great Gatsby*.

Hollywood was obsessed with greedy male financiers—from *Wall Street* in the 1980s to *American Psycho* and *Boiler Room*—and audiences have lapped up such depictions of financiers run amok. But the script that Terence Winter, a writer on *The Sopranos*, carved out of Belfort's memoir took such depictions to a new level—it was full of unadorned debauchery, to the extent that studio executives at Warner Bros., which was developing the film, got cold feet and pulled the plug in 2008. They figured audiences wouldn't go to see an R-rated film in sufficient numbers to earn back the $100 million it would take to produce.

Martin Scorsese, the legendary film director who had worked with DiCaprio on a number of projects, was frustrated. Even though he was at the apex of his career—recently clinching his first directing Oscar for *The Departed*—he could not control the studios. He'd spent five months annotating Winter's script in preparation for filming and grumbled to people in the industry that it was wasted time. In the midst of this stalemate, Jho Low entered DiCaprio's orbit. The Malaysian's money offered an alternative solution, one that could provide DiCaprio and Scorsese with the Hollywood holy grail: boundless financing coupled with unfettered artistic control.

In September 2010, Riza Aziz and Joey McFarland set up Red Granite Productions (it would later change its name to Red Granite Pictures), operating at first out of a suite of rooms in the L'Ermitage hotel in Beverly Hills. Aziz was appointed chairman, and McFarland became vice chairman. As per his habit, Low took no official title. He left the day-to-day running of the firm to others. He was the secret money. The firm soon announced it had hired a number of executives from Millennium Films, including Joe Gatta, to head production. From day one, there was a furtiveness about finances. McFarland informed staff that Low was an investor, but that the Malaysian, Riza, and McFarland would stay in the background.

"That's why we'd hire someone like you," McFarland told one of the Red Granite executives.

A few months later, Red Granite's offices were ready, in the same low-rise building on the Sunset Strip where DiCaprio's production company, Appian Way, was located. It wasn't a coincidence. "They chose to be in Leo's building because they wanted to be close to him and be in business with him," the Red Granite executive said.

The plan was to coproduce *The Wolf of Wall Street*, and Red Granite bought the film rights to Jordan Belfort's memoir for $1 million. Suddenly, Low was no longer just a guy who threw flashy parties. Through McFarland and Aziz, he was a player in Hollywood.

Chapter 18

Two-Million-Euro Bottle Parade

Saint-Tropez, France, July 2010

It was Fleet Week in Saint-Tropez, and the world's superyachts vied for berthing space at the town's marina. In July and August, the resort on the French Riviera, centered around a warren-like medieval old town of ochre-colored houses and old churches, is heaving with the world's richest people. They flock to the town for parties on yachts and in the town's bars and the daytime carousing at the clubs on nearby Pampelonne beach.

Tourists walking along the Quai Jean Jaurès gawp at the yachts backed up right next to a line of cafés. It's an annual display of concentrated wealth unsurpassed anywhere, as crews of young deckhands run around polishing balustrades, while onlookers try to see who is on board. For many, these boats represent the pinnacle of success. Yet the real parties of Saint-Tropez happen far from the tourist hordes. While regular folk get caught in horrendous traffic jams trying to reach town, located on the end of the peninsula, the pampered set are ferried in on motorized skiffs. The hottest nights take place on yachts out at sea, or in the town's exclusive clubs, where A-list celebrities mingle with billionaires.

The most illustrious of all is Les Caves du Roy, a fixture on the world party scene since the 1960s. Every inch of the club, situated in the basement of the Hotel Byblos, just a few hundred meters back from the port, is covered in gold. There are golden columns, which end in waves of fluting, a parody of the Corinthian style meant to evoke champagne bursting from a bottle. The dance floor is golden, as are the tables on which are perched gold leaf–covered cocktail bowls. Here, late on July 22, not even two weeks since the World Cup final in South Africa, Jho Low was engaged in a bidding war.

He'd sailed into town a few days earlier, with Paris Hilton still in tow, on the *Tatoosh*, a 303-foot, ten-cabin superyacht, complete with swimming pool and helicopter pad, owned by Microsoft cofounder Paul Allen. These were the days of bottle parades, an invention by clubs to get "whales" to spend even more money by ordering multiple magnums—or even jeroboams—of champagne. If the order was big enough, bottle girls—usually models earning extra cash—would bring out the champagne with sparklers attached, as the DJ cut the music and lauded the buyer. Back in New York, Low's spending had helped popularize these parades.

Even by the usual standards, this bottle parade tonight was going to be unseemly. Dressed in a black polo shirt with a checkered collar and gray slacks, a Rolex on his arm, Low had become entangled in a battle with Winston Fisher, whose family were in New York real estate, to see who was willing to pay the most for Cristal champagne. A year earlier, before Low got his hands on serious money, he had lost out in this exact venue during a similar bidding war with a Belgian billionaire of Pakistani descent. Not this time.

As the revelers looked on in awe, with an emcee overseeing the escalating war of affluence, Low and Fisher matched each other as the bids mounted. With no signs the Malaysian would bow out, Fisher caved. As the bill was announced over the stereo system, revelers in the club couldn't believe what had occurred. Low had just spent 2 million euros on champagne—an amount of alcohol that the whole club couldn't possibly finish off in a week of drinking.

As the frantic staff produced bottle after bottle of champagne—including jeroboams and methuselahs—Low's coterie, which included wealthy Russians, Arabs, and Kazakhstanis, cheered with pleasure. Paris Hilton, wearing a short blue dress with polka dots, blue pendant earrings, and pink nail polish, got up on a table near a gold column and began opening a bottle, spraying the contents over Low and others. A ruddy-faced and sweat-damped Low was photographed with his head laying on Hilton's shoulder.

Days later the pair was in another club, with yet another bottle parade. As the champagne came out with sparklers attached, the theme music from *Rocky* and *Star Wars* blaring, Low took control. Handed a microphone, he directed waiters to ensure everyone in the club got a bottle. "Saudi Arabia in the hoouuussse," he yelled, as Hilton danced and embraced him from behind. She was so drunk that other partygoers had to support her. Both Hilton and Low, who sported a white fedora, were drenched in champagne, as alarmed-looking security guards tried to make space around them.

As one Kuwaiti friend put it, Low excelled at making people feel like they were included in the most exclusive of circles. But amid all the revelry, he was also hard to know, more like a compère. The friend came to believe he was taking part in a charade of wealth, rather than genuinely having fun.

"It felt fake and as if we were just there to go through the motions and entertain and look cool as a group," he said.

The spectacle in Saint-Tropez garnered widespread paparazzi coverage, and gossip writers speculated Low was Hilton's latest boyfriend. Although he appeared intimate with Hilton at the parties, he told friends they were never physically involved. Instead, another woman had captured his imagination.

The Rolls-Royce rolled up at Dubai's Atlantis, the Palm, a towering hotel located on one the city's islands, a series of man-made landmasses that from the air look like palm fronds in the sea. The main building was framed around a gigantic Arabian-style arch, with multiple pools and 360-degree views of the Persian Gulf. It's a decadent place, and Low, a few months after his French vacation, had taken over part of the resort's private beach for an elaborate ceremony. Accompanying him in the Rolls was Elva Hsiao, a thirty-one-year-old Taiwanese pop star. Wearing white pants, a light blue shirt, and slip-on leather shoes without socks, Low escorted Hsiao, also dressed informally in a striped skirt and sandals, from the car. They stood hugging around the waist, as Low pointed out candles that had been set up on the beach in the shape of a gigantic heart. A light display behind the candles spelled out their names.

Low then led Hsiao to a long dining table, bedecked with flowers and more candles, and placed on a raised platform, behind which the planners had erected an intricately carved screen. As they began to dine on a multicourse tasting menu, a blonde musician in a blue evening dress played a harp set up next to the table, later switching to a jewel-encrusted violin. Hsiao looked nervous and began to giggle. Low slipped his arm around her in a stiff embrace. There was little conversation.

It was time for the grand finale. Suddenly, a helicopter hovered into view. As it neared the beach, two men parachuted out, each wearing a smart tuxedo and bow tie. Landing on the beach, inside the heart made of candles, the men unhooked their parachutes and strode up to the table. Smiling, they presented Hsiao with a box. Inside was a Chopard necklace holding a round pendant made from diamonds and gold. After dinner, the pair watched a special fireworks display, set off from a boat anchored off the island.

It was a gaudy, laughably clichéd exhibition of love, and as the ostentation piled up, Hsiao wiped a tear from her eye. The event had reportedly cost more than $1 million to stage, and it was a date, not even a marriage proposal.

As it turned out, Low already had a girlfriend, a woman called Jesselynn Chuan Teik Ying, whose father owned a seafood restaurant back in Penang. Low often flew her out to the United States, but he told McFarland, who was increasingly acting as a kind of catchall fixer for Low, to keep her away from the partying. Instead, she would be sequestered in a hotel or one of Low's apartments, accompanied by the other females in his inner circle, women like Catherine Tan, a former Vegas croupier who organized Low's schedule, and Jasmine Loo, 1MDB's legal counsel. Back in Malaysia, visitors to Low's Kuala Lumpur apartment noticed Chuan acted deferentially, serving drinks on bended knee. While Low treated her respectfully in public, he was also in the habit of making gifts of luxury cars and jewelry to other women, and paying for models to mill around at parties in hotel suites, clubs, and on yachts.

It was clear to Low's friends that he was cheating on Chuan, as he began to rub up against more famous individuals like Elva Hsiao. Chuan found out about Hsiao—she came across a book the Taiwanese singer had gifted Low—but decided not to break things off. Chuan, too, seemed taken with the glitzy change of station Low now afforded. At one point, she showed friends back in Penang a new watch, a gift from Low she said once had belonged to the singer Usher.

Low told friends he was torn by the duplicity in his life, between maintaining a girlfriend and the other women. His relationship with Chuan had been on and off for years. But he wasn't a typical playboy. Some of the models whom Low regaled with Cartier jewelry or gambling chips were astonished he never hit on them. Far more than sex, it seemed, he craved recognition, whether from women or Hollywood stars, and he sought to create spectacles that reinforced his power and prestige.

Extreme by any standard measure, the Dubai episode was merely a foreshadowing of what was to come. Low already was one of the most unhinged spenders anyone had encountered, but he was about to switch it up a gear.

If his spending was winning him friends in Hollywood, others were perplexed by the way Low drew attention to himself. For many of Low's business associates, his showy displays of wealth were hard to swallow. It was as if the same compulsive nature that made his scheme take off—Low's ability to procure the biggest and best of anything, be it a yacht or a Hollywood star—was also his Achilles' heel. By 2010, Otaiba, the UAE ambassador to Washington, was becoming unnerved by Low's public antics.

"He really needs to calm down and stop partying so much," Otaiba complained in an August 4, 2010, email to a friend.

Like many of Low's contacts, Ambassador Otaiba wanted to keep his dealings with the Malaysian discreet. When Low asked Otaiba to act as a reference to help him open a private bank account with Goldman, the ambassador wondered in an email to Shaher Awartani, his business partner, whether such a letter would be "considered liable." Low had told Awartani that banks were starting to question the hundreds of millions of dollars flowing through his accounts.

Ultimately, Goldman rejected Low's request to open a private wealth account at the bank, which required at least $10 million in deposits, because it was unable to ascertain his source of funds. This was a private wealth-management business, far removed from Leissner and Ng, who worked for the investment banking arm, but that didn't stop the pair from lobbying for Goldman to take Low on as a private client. When the bank turned him down, Leissner and Ng realized they would have to be even more careful to keep Low's role at 1MDB a secret from compliance officers, according to a U.S. Department of Justice filing.

Prime Minister Najib Razak, too, believed Low needed a more serious image. Low told Awartani his "boss"—meaning Najib—had suggested Low join several prominent government advisory boards to rebrand himself as a credible businessman.

Back in Penang, where the *New York Post* article about Low's clubbing habits had raised eyebrows, Larry Low was furious and ordered a damage-control strategy for his son. After his French vacation in the summer of 2010, Low flew back to Penang, and, dressing in a conservative black suit with a light blue tie, gave a lengthy interview to a local English-language newspaper, the *Star*.

He spun a web of fiction, telling the reporters that he had started Wynton, his private investment vehicle, with $25 million in capital from his rich friends from Harrow and Wharton, and that the firm's assets now stood in excess of $1 billion. He attempted to pass off the nightclub spending covered by the *New York Post* as really that of his rich Middle Eastern friends, describing himself as merely a "concierge service" who catered to their whims.

"I come from a fairly okay family but nowhere as close to the prominence and wealth levels of the people I usually spend time with, who also are my very good friends," he told the *Star*. His business success was "attributable to being at the right place and right time and meeting the right people, coupled with a trusting relationship."

At home, Low knew he couldn't get away with the story he told abroad: that he came from a billionaire family. Now his stories were starting to collide into one another. Any potential investor overseas who heard Low boast that he was from old money in Asia need only have perused the *Star*'s interview, easily available online, to know something was wrong. But no one, it seemed, bothered to do even this cursory research. As for the spending at Les Caves du Roy, Low contended it was his group, not him, that had purchased the champagne.

"We all work very hard," he said. "I am not an excessive person but I do have my breaks for relaxation with friends."

In private, Low shrugged off the media coverage of his parties, as if his reckless behavior was of no import. "I am not stupid. I know the issues with media and I am dealing with it," he told Patrick Mahony of PetroSaudi in a BlackBerry message. With so much cash in his pocket, and a bevy of celebrity friends, Low was starting to believe he would never get caught.

Some of Low's allies were not so easily placated. There was dissension among the conspirators.

Chapter 19

"Keep Your Nonsense to Yourself"

Montreux, Switzerland, October 2010

Perched on a hill on the shores of Lake Geneva, Clinique La Prairie is considered one of the world's preeminent medical centers and spas. Located in the Swiss town of Montreux, the clinic's original mansion, constructed in the Swiss-chalet style with a widely projecting roof, is surrounded by a French formal garden and a collection of elegant modern buildings. From the rooms, guests have unobstructed views of Lake Geneva, framed by towering snow-topped Alpine peaks. Founded in 1931 by a professor named Paul Niehans, whose pioneering "cellular therapy" soon attracted the rich and famous, including Charlie Chaplin, the clinic's website described itself as "the expert in longevity."

In October 2010, Low checked into the clinic for a respite. Owing to his unwholesome lifestyle—a predilection for alcohol-fueled late nights, buckets of KFC chicken, and nonstop travel—Low knew he was out of shape. He stopped short of regular exercise, but was happy to buy expensive juice cleanses that came with a glass straw, and was now seeking out the most cutting-edge treatment money could buy—and that meant Clinique La Prairie.

Mortality and aging cast a shadow across everyone's life, but the überwealthy have a better chance of cheating death. For

$30,000, the clinic offered a weeklong revitalization program during which patients were fed an extract derived from the livers of fetuses of black sheep. The process supposedly helped to revitalize dormant cells. This wasn't the first time Low had checked into a high-end medical spa, hoping, perhaps, for a brief escape from the stresses of his scheme. He'd been feeling a little under the weather and on this occasion was undergoing sinus surgery to help his breathing. But even here, surrounded by the world's top doctors, business was calling.

A few days after Low checked into the clinic, Goldman's Tim Leissner arrived to discuss possible investments. The German banker saw how much money 1MDB supposedly had put into the joint venture with PetroSaudi and was looking for ways for Goldman to get a piece of the action. Until now, the fund had mainly raised money from Malaysian bank loans and local debt sales, but Leissner was taking steps to position Goldman to win the lucrative business of helping 1MDB tap vastly larger international capital markets.

Having evidently brushed aside his earlier misgivings about Low, Leissner was now cozying up to the Malaysian, hoping to get his bank involved in the billion-dollar flows emanating from this fund. Leissner had a problem, though. Goldman's private bank in Switzerland had turned down Low's request to open an account due to concerns over the origin of his funds. Yet the German knew Low was front and center at 1MDB, even though he played a strange behind-the-scenes role, including hosting meetings at locations such as Clinique La Prairie rather than the 1MDB fund's offices in Kuala Lumpur. Leissner would have to find a way to navigate these issues and keep Goldman involved in the fund's business.

So far, Low had diverted most of the money meant for the 1MDB-PetroSaudi joint venture. He'd paid off the family of Najib Razak with real estate and promises of funding for Red

Granite. The prime minister would soon start receiving hundreds of millions of dollars in political funds. Mahony and Obaid, as well as Prince Turki, also had received their cuts. But some of the 1MDB money did eventually go to buy two aging oil drill ships, which the joint venture leased to Venezuela's state oil company. This business wasn't going to generate enough profits to fill the hole of the diverted funds, and so the principals sought out a bigger investment.

Patrick Mahony, the investment director of PetroSaudi, also was visiting Low in the clinic. In the Malaysian's private room, Mahony discussed with Leissner and Low the possibility of investing in a U.S. oil refinery. To do so, however, would require another infusion of cash into the fund. Mahony wanted Low to get Najib to agree for 1MDB to invest even more state money into the joint venture. Leissner suggested bringing TPG, a large California-based private-equity firm, into the deal. The head of TPG in Asia, Tim Dattels, was a former Goldman banker and close friend of Leissner.

The refinery acquisition did not happen, and neither did the TPG investment, but Low and Mahony continued to strategize about other possible deals. Even in the absence of a firm plan for their next moves, Low persuaded Najib to invest more money in the joint venture, arguing it was necessary to keep Prince Turki happy and ensure friendly ties with Saudi Arabia. Evidently pleased with the benefits his family derived from 1MDB, the prime minister gave the green light to send even more government cash to the PetroSaudi joint venture.

In 1MDB documents pertaining to the new lending, Najib argued it was valid "in consideration of the government relationship between the Kingdom of Saudi Arabia and Malaysia." On July 24, 2010, in a meeting of 1MDB's board, one member questioned whether the prime minister was backing this further investment. Chief Executive Shahrol Halmi replied that Najib was fully on board. In the end, 1MDB sent over a further $800 million, almost doubling the amount the fund had pumped into the joint venture.

The 1MDB fund, like most schemes, needed to be continually fed with fresh funds. It wasn't just that Low was spending so much money; he also had to find cash to pay off an ever-increasing group of people involved in or with knowledge of the fund's doings, among them Taib Mahmud, the Sarawak chief minister. Taib felt duped by Low in the early deals involving the Iskandar land and was demanding a payback. To pacify Taib, Low persuaded PetroSaudi to use some of the fresh 1MDB cash to buy out one of the Chief Minister's companies at a rich price.

With the new cash infusion into the joint venture, the perpetrators went looking for investments to generate profit that would pay 1MDB back. But they seemed to understimate that regenerating nearly $2 billion was no easy task. The group agreed Low would persuade Prime Minister Najib to write off hundreds of millions of dollars of 1MDB's investment as a loss. Low acted as if this was make-believe money, debt that Najib could erase with a magic wand, without any cost to taxpayers or society. The Malaysian had promised Mahony that they only needed to pay back $1 billion.

"Jho agreed that when we repay the $1b, we dissolve the venture and walk away," Mahony wrote, perhaps in a moment of wishful thinking, to Tarek Obaid in an email on August 7, 2010.

But the plan for the oil refinery was a long shot, and unlikely, even if it did come off, to make enough profit to fill a $1 billion hole. Mahony had another strategy ready: to throw Low under the bus.

In the email, Mahony suggested a plan. Obaid should tell the prime minister that PetroSaudi had a bunch of deals in the pipeline, but lost out to rivals because Low had been distracted by partying. "I think saying delays have cost us helps us because we can then blame them for the losses later," he wrote.

The prime minister knew 1MDB was being used partly as a political slush fund and that Low was making his family very comfortable. But Najib did not realize the size of the financial losses at the center of the fund, and Mahony urged Obaid to hide the problem from him.

"I think the PM thinks we are making good investments," he wrote.

When Low got wind of the fact that Obaid had been in contact directly with the prime minister, he was apoplectic.

"We all know best how to manage our ends. If anyone starts to think they can 'openly' express or deal direct with my end, that is when issues will start," Low snapped to Mahony in a BlackBerry message on August 8, 2010.

The Malaysian said that he would never directly contact Prince Turki, the co-owner of PetroSaudi, and had even stopped Rosmah from doing so.

"We will never go around you," Mahony promised in his reply, but he admonished Low.

"Do work on the party thing as it can hurt us all. Last thing we need is publicity given what we are doing. . . . Just keep your nonsense to yourself and out of the news. Doesn't help that I see you partying again last night and dj keeps yelling 'malaysia' . . ."

PetroSaudi and Low were caught in an increasingly unhappy marriage.

Troubles continued to pile up. Back in Kuala Lumpur, many of the fund's bright employees had left, disconcerted by the lack of progress on deals. The PetroSaudi joint venture had achieved little, and plans for a new financial center were going nowhere. Those who remained, led by Chief Executive Shahrol, wondered why 1MDB had so little to show for the billions of dollars in investment. But they questioned little, taking comfort from Prime Minister Najib's involvement.

The fund's management in Kuala Lumpur was looking to post its first-ever financial results, for the year to March 31, 2010, but late into the year the accounts still hadn't been released. Ernst & Young, 1MDB's accountants, did not agree with how the fund's management was attempting to book profits. The fund's interest costs, coupled with a lack of significant investments, meant it was heading for a net loss.

To avoid this, the fund's management wanted to undertake some tricky accounting. The idea was to turn 1MDB's investments in the joint venture with PetroSaudi into loans due in 2020, effectively kicking the can down the road. If it worked, the fund could promise future profits—and gain years before it actually had to produce them. Perhaps fearful of the whole scheme unraveling, Low and PetroSaudi had agreed to turn the initial $1 billion investment into a loan of $1.2 billion, and 1MDB wanted to book the difference as profit.

Ernst & Young didn't like it one bit. Its auditors were skeptical of the loan's value, and they told the fund they had concerns about whether the joint venture would ever be able to pay back the money. Ernst & Young wasn't going to risk its reputation by signing off on these accounts. Time ticked on without any financial statements coming out. The 1MDB board began to fret, noting in its minutes that the fund was "perceived as a secretive cloak-and-dagger setup with sinister motives to benefit cronies and not the Malaysian people." It recommended spending more money on charity, and advertising the fact widely—along with another drastic step.

To get around the auditor problem, why not just get rid of Ernst & Young and find another auditor? To keep investors and markets happy, accounts of big companies need to be audited by one of the "Big Four"—Ernst & Young, KPMG, Deloitte Touche, and PricewaterhouseCoopers. The problem with the system is that clients pay for the auditing services, and when Ernst & Young made trouble, the fund could go looking for a replacement.

So 1MDB's management turned to KPMG. The firm also had concerns about what was going on at the fund, but they were willing to take on the job as long as 1MDB could guarantee that the business with PetroSaudi was sanctioned by governments in both countries. PetroSaudi was a private company, with a Saudi prince holding only a half share, while 1MDB was controlled by a young Malaysian who held no official positions. But with official sanction, KPMG was willing to move ahead with its audit.

"At the very least, KPMG requires a document to confirm that PSI is related to the Saudi royal family," 1MDB's board noted in September 2010, referring to PetroSaudi.

The participants provided a document, playing up Prince Turki's role in the company, and, on September 16, Prime Minister Najib signed a directive to remove Ernst & Young as the fund's auditors. The board noted Ernst & Young's "unprofessional conduct" even though the firm simply had been doing its job. The fund promptly hired KPMG, whose auditors allowed 1MDB to book the value of the loan to PetroSaudi and keep the cash spigots open.

Eventually, KPMG signed off on the accounts for the financial year to March 31, 2010, but was worried enough to cover itself with an "emphasis of matter" paragraph, a section of an audited account meant to underline a potential future problem to investors. The auditor noted that 1MDB's management "believes" that PetroSaudi was in good financial standing. For anyone following closely, this was a very lukewarm approval of the fund's financial stability.

There was one person, though, who didn't need to comb through 1MDB's financials to sense a fraud. And that person was Jordan Belfort.

Chapter 20

Belfort Smells a Scam

Cannes, France, May 2011

On the beach just off La Croisette, Cannes's most iconic street, Kanye West and Jamie Foxx were performing a rendition of their hit "Gold Digger." "Whad'up France," yelled West, who was dressed in a white suit, as a crowd of celebrities and film-industry executives watched from a cordoned-off part of the French Riviera town's main beach. Earlier, Pharrell Williams had opened the night with a twenty-minute set under an opulent display of fireworks. In the crowd, Leonardo DiCaprio, swimwear model Kate Upton, and Bradley Cooper danced. Among the guests was disgraced investor turned best-selling author Jordan Belfort, and the onetime "Wolf of Wall Street" could not believe what he was seeing.

This was the biggest party of the week-long Cannes Film Festival, and it was a multi-million-dollar coming-out event for Red Granite. A few days earlier, the fledgling firm had made a big announcement. It had reached an agreement to adapt Belfort's memoir into a movie. Leonardo DiCaprio would star as Belfort, with Martin Scorsese directing—quite a coup for a new outfit in the industry like Red Granite. To celebrate, the company had flown Belfort out with his girlfriend, Anne, for the party.

As with 1MDB, Low never took a formal position at Red Granite and stayed out of day-to-day operations, but he was a behind-the-scenes force. He organized a first batch of funding for the film company in April 2011, a wire transfer of $1.17 million from Good Star, the Seychelles company he controlled, to Red Granite's account at City National Bank in Los Angeles. The notation on the wire transfer referred to "INVESTOR ADVANCES." It had then embarked on its first modest production, the $10 million comedy *Friends with Kids* starring an ensemble cast including Kristen Wiig and Jon Hamm, the rights to which Red Granite had acquired from another studio.

Some in Hollywood were already asking questions about Red Granite. *Sure, people come out of nowhere in Hollywood. But who the hell are Riza Aziz and Joey McFarland?* The staggering amount of money an unknown firm had paid for this launch party stirred disbelief. The rumor was that West alone earned $1 million to perform. The rapper peppered his stage banter with weirdly positive statements including: "Red Granite will change the way films are made forever."

"People thought the company was a real enigma," said Scott Roxborough, a reporter for the *Hollywood Reporter* who attended. "A huge party, with so much money and no real films under their belt, seemed very suspicious."

Himself no stranger to fraud, Jordan Belfort thought something wasn't right about this setup. The event must have cost at least $3 million, Belfort calculated, as he nibbled on canapés and watched the A-list entertainment. *And the movie hadn't even gone into production!*

"This is a fucking scam—anybody who does this has stolen money," Belfort told Anne, as the music thumped. "You wouldn't spend money you worked for like that."

A few months later, Low would offer Belfort $500,000 to attend an event in Las Vegas with DiCaprio. Red Granite had paid him handsomely for the rights to his memoir. But Belfort was starting to distrust this group. Eager to stay out of trouble, focusing instead on his new career as a writer and motivational speaker, Belfort turned them down, but DiCaprio and his costar Margot Robbie went along.

"Leo got sucked in," Belfort later told Swiss journalist Katharina Bart. "Leo's an honest guy. But I met these guys, and said to Anne, 'These guys are fucking criminals.'

"I was like, 'I don't need these fucking people.' I knew it, it was so obvious."

For a week during the film festival, Low and Red Granite each had a superyacht moored in the Mediterranean waters just off Cannes, Low's slightly more impressive than that occupied by Riza Aziz, the Malaysian prime minister's stepson. As well as the film company's launch, Low had arranged for Pharrell to record a number of songs in a makeshift recording studio on his yacht. Not content with setting up a major Hollywood film company, Low also wanted to launch himself into music ventures.

A few months earlier, Low had arranged for legendary music producer Jimmy Iovine, cofounder of Interscope, to throw a Grammys after-party on the roof of L'Ermitage. Interscope wasn't hosting its own party, and so Low approached Iovine with an offer to organize one for him.

The cream of the music world came out for it. Lady Gaga, Snoop Dogg, and Dr. Dre performed to a crowd that included Beyoncé and Jay-Z, as well as Busta Rhymes, Nicole Scherzinger, Eminem, and others. Low's usual group was there, too: Jamie Foxx and Paris Hilton among them. Under Arabian-style tents, DiCaprio, wearing an Irish cap and smoking a cigar, chatted with Bar Refaeli, his model girlfriend. Low brought along Elva Hsiao, the Taiwanese pop star he had feted in Dubai. The *New York Post*, referring to Low as a billionaire, speculated the

event must have cost him $500,000. To Low, it was an invest-
ment, as he continued to build his name around town.

Low wasted no time after the party to leverage his new
contacts. He took steps to form a music-production company
called Red Spring and set about hiring the best musical talent
to help produce an album for Elva Hsiao. She was big in the
Chinese-speaking world, but Low wanted to make her a star in
the United States. He agreed to pay $3 million to Pharrell to
come up with three songs for Hsiao, and to appear in the music
videos with her. He also reached terms with Alicia Keys and her
hip-hop producer husband, Swizz Beatz, paying them $4 mil-
lion to oversee the album and the launch of Hsiao's career in the
United States. Despite Low setting aside a $12 million budget,
she never made it.

Swizz Beatz, whose real name was Kasseem Dean, became
one of Low's closest allies and would remain with him even
when things started going awry. Born and raised in the Bronx to
an Eritrean father and a Puerto Rican mother, Swizz Beatz had
worked on tracks for DMX, Jay-Z, Drake, and Beyoncé, among
others. He was intensely ambitious, with a goal of becoming a
business mogul, not just a record producer, and he saw potential
in his connection with Low. ("The sky's not the limit, it's just a
view," he liked to say.) Reebok hired him as a creative executive,
an attempt to gain credibility in the hip-hop world. Before he
met Low, however, Swizz Beatz's business endeavors had pretty
much been limited to celebrity endorsements; Low represented
a source of funding to take his career to the next level. What's
more, Swizz Beatz owed hundreds of thousands of dollars to the
Internal Revenue Service for unpaid taxes. The IRS put liens on
his accounts.

The producer became Low's conduit into the music world.
As part of the production deal, Swizz Beatz, rapper Lil Jon, and
Jho Low recorded a song entitled "V" at a studio in the Palms

Casino Resort in Las Vegas, a kind of party anthem. Low's contribution was to repeat the words "very hot" over and over in the background. It was never commercially released.

Swizz Beatz and Alicia Keys entered Low's trusted circle, attending his end-of-year ski holidays with Joey McFarland and Riza Aziz, Jasmine Loo of 1MDB, and other close associates. The producer was a collector of modern art, including paintings by Jean-Michel Basquiat, and he acted as Low's cultural tutor, schooling him on galleries and auctions. The Malaysian began to wear a cap with "Basquiat" written on the front, and talked of building his own collection.

To make *The Wolf of Wall Street*, Low knew he was going to need access to a bigger pot of money. Red Granite had agreed to pay DiCaprio and Scorsese multiple millions each for the movie, and added to the costs of production, the overall budget was set to top $100 million. By this point, the summer of 2011, Low and his allies had taken control of almost $2 billion from 1MDB, but much of that had been spent on mansions, hotels, gambling, and partying, as well as to pay off conspirators. Low needed new deals, both to plug the hole at 1MDB and to give him the financial muscle to dominate in Hollywood.

His relations with PetroSaudi fraying, the Malaysian looked around for other partners. Distracted and always on the move, he didn't seem willing to put in the legwork to pull off a complicated acquisition, such as the plan to buy the U.S. oil refinery that Patrick Mahony had pushed. He lacked Mahony's banking skills and had no ability to value companies in the oil-and-gas sector. Low wanted to quickly flip assets and forge alliances with partners who could help him make a fast dollar.

Around this time Low read a news story about a battle to take over a group of hotels that included London's famed Claridge's. One of the bidding groups included a wealthy British property magnate called Robert Tchenguiz. The fifty-year-old had salt-and-pepper hair, which descended in waves to his shoulders, and he was often seen in white shirts with a few buttons undone. Talking in a deep, gravelly voice, Tchenguiz hailed from an Iraqi Jewish family that had moved to Iran and later settled in London after being driven out during the Islamic Revolution. He was always involved in some property deal or another, and his latest was a heated contest with the Barclays brothers, among Britain's wealthiest individuals, for control of Coroin Limited, which owned Claridge's. For his bid, Tchenguiz had teamed up with a Middle Eastern fund called Aabar Investments.

It was just the kind of acquisition that appealed to Low: a swanky hotel at the center of London's Mayfair district. The involvement of Aabar was also an attraction. The fund was controlled by the International Petroleum Investment Company, or IPIC, a $70 billion sovereign wealth fund owned by the government of Abu Dhabi. Low had done business with Mubadala of Abu Dhabi, but he had yet to make contacts at IPIC or Aabar. The IPIC fund's managing director, a wealthy Arab businessman named Khadem Al Qubaisi, had a reputation among financiers who did business with him for demanding kickbacks from deals. In the wake of the financial crisis, IPIC had been snapping up stakes in Western companies—Barclays Bank, Daimler-Benz, Virgin Galactic—and Al Qubaisi had become a powerful figure in the emirate.

Low wanted in on the deal, and he got to know Tchenguiz through a wealth adviser they both knew. At first Tchenguiz did not consider Low a serious investor. Who had heard of Wynton, after all? But then, during discussions over the deal for Claridge's, Low provided a letter from 1MDB stating it would provide up to 1 billion pounds in financing for the acquisition.

"We didn't know 1MDB was a bullshit thing," Tchenguiz told friends later. It appeared to be a government subsidiary, just like Aabar. "That's why we went partners with him."

To show his seriousness, Low signed a check on the spot for 50 million pounds, which he said could be used to start building a stake in Coroin. In the end, the shareholders of Coroin decided against the Wynton-Aabar offer. Still, it wasn't a wasted exercise; through the deal making, Low had made a new connection with Aabar's chief executive, Mohamed Badawy Al Husseiny, a U.S. citizen of Kenyan origin.

A former accountant who went by "Mo" to friends, Al Husseiny wore sharp suits and expensive watches. He was short and balding but fit, with a penchant for the "Insanity" workout routine, an interval training set that burned one thousand calories an hour. He was Al Qubaisi's right-hand man in Aabar and was known mostly for his obedience to the "boss." Low began to invite Al Husseiny to his star-studded parties, and the Aabar chief executive took to Low's exclusive social milieu, boasting to friends about the celebrities he was meeting.

If Low had started cultivating famous friends to quell some kind of lingering insecurity—or even for the sheer hell of it—he also came to realize it was good business. Many of his prospective partners were wowed by Low's familiarity with DiCaprio, Hilton, and others. His Hollywood friends gave him an edge over other investors looking for Middle East tie-ups. It wasn't long before Low and Al Husseiny worked out a way for the entities they controlled to work together. In June 2011, Low brokered a deal for Aabar to acquire a stake in a Malaysian bank, RHB, for which it paid $2.7 billion. Soon after, the bank's stock price fell sharply, and Aabar was stuck with paper losses of hundreds of millions of dollars.

Undeterred, 1MDB and Aabar then set up a joint venture of their own—a fund intended to invest in commodity markets—and the first deal was for a stake in a Mongolian coal mine. That investment also performed badly when coal prices crashed as China's economy slowed. No matter: Low and Al Husseiny personally prospered from the deal by arranging a multi-million-dollar fee from the seller as a reward for bringing in Aabar and 1MDB.

When he found out about the losses, Al Qubaisi, the IPIC chief, was livid, and, once again, Low needed another deal to placate an angry partner. To make it up, Low was hoping to involve his new Abu Dhabi friends in his biggest scheme yet, one that would leech even more cash out of 1MDB, helping to pay for DiCaprio, Scorsese, and the production budget of *The Wolf of Wall Street*.

With his ambitious new collaborators, Low was moving on from 1MDB's original partner, PetroSaudi. But there was a dangerous divide at the company, one that threatened to bring the whole house of cards crashing down.

Chapter 21

Bitter Severance

London, April 2011

The bar in the Connaught, a five-star hotel in London's Mayfair district, was an apt place for Xavier Justo, an employee of PetroSaudi, to be discussing his severance deal with Patrick Mahony. The place reeked of money, from the dark leather sofas to the Cubist-inspired wood paneling and a Wedgewood-like molded plaster ceiling. Justo, a muscled and extensively tattooed Mediterranean-looking man in his midforties, who at six feet six inches tall towered over most people, repeated his demand for 6.5 million Swiss francs.

As head of PetroSaudi's London office, Justo had worked on deals involving the oil drill ships that the PetroSaudi–1MDB joint venture acquired. Tarek Obaid, the firm's chief executive, was an old friend, and he had promised Justo millions of dollars for opening the London office. But the money had never materialized, and Justo had even been left to personally cover some company expenses. He was there at the Connaught to try to get his money.

Fearing a problem, Mahony was keen to settle, but he haggled. The pair talked for some time, with Tarek Obaid on the phone with Mahony at one point, and left the Connaught agreeing on 5 million Swiss francs.

But Obaid later sought to lower the amount further. As Obaid saw it, he had been good to Justo, and now his friend was being disloyal. Justo was a Swiss citizen, born to Spanish immigrants, who had gotten to know Obaid in the 1990s. After working for a Swiss private bank, Obaid had set up businesses with Prince Turki, looking to pave the way for foreign investors in Saudi Arabia. He took a desk at a financial services company in Geneva partly owned by Justo. The pair became close despite the decade difference in their ages.

Justo owned a share in a Geneva nightclub called the Platinum Club, but it made little money. When Obaid set up Petro-Saudi, he persuaded his friend to become director of a number of the new firm's affiliates. Initially, Justo had little to do— PetroSaudi's operations were more or less nonexistent—and he went traveling in Asia. Obaid called him in 2010 with an offer: PetroSaudi had come into a lot of money, and he wanted Justo to become director of the firm's London office.

Offered a starting salary of 400,000 pounds per year, with the chance to make millions, Justo moved to London and ran PetroSaudi's sleek new offices in Curzon Street, only a five-minute walk from the Connaught. Justo helped with the only real business the 1MDB-PetroSaudi joint venture ever conducted—two drill ships, acquired by the company and then leased to Venezuela's national oil company—and was often on the plane to Caracas. But his relations with Obaid soon deteriorated, as his young friend seemed paranoid and arrogant after the 1MDB deal, while at the same time failing to deliver the proposed millions.

Seemingly intoxicated by the extent of his newfound wealth, Obaid began flying to Saudi Arabia and elsewhere in the Middle East on private jets and, like Low, renting yachts in the South of France. His brother suggested setting up a family office to manage all the money. To some observers, Obaid started to act erratically. He always had been a hypochondriac, complaining of vague illnesses, and after the money started flowing he wrote to the Mayo Clinic in the United States to get a full medical check-up, despite being in his midthirties. He began to party incessantly and put on weight. People who knew him said he flew into frequent rages.

Patrick Mahony also began to spend. His wife was pregnant with their first child, and in November 2009 Mahony signed a deal to buy a 6.2-million-pound town house overlooking a private park in London's Ladbroke Square. He talked with his private banker at J.P. Morgan about getting an Amex Black card, the kind used by celebrities and billionaires. Only thirty-two years old, he worried about one of his sisters being jealous over his growing success and the lifestyle that came with it.

Observing all this, Justo, though he didn't know the full details of what had happened at PetroSaudi, sensed he was not getting treated fairly. He believed Obaid was stiffing him by not fully paying his salary, as well as failing to reimburse travel and other costs. Adding insult to injury, Justo had to perform what he considered menial work, including organizing for Obaid and Jho Low to get exclusive credit cards from a Dubai bank. Fed up, in the spring of 2011, he decided to quit. But he wasn't just going to walk away.

"Due to our history, and all the projects I've taken part in over the years, I think an amicable separation is the best way for me to leave PetroSaudi and the other companies," he wrote Obaid in an email. "I'll wait for your confirmation that our collaboration is over from today, and that I'm to leave the office, and also that you will let me know how to get my severance pay."

"You're a smart ass. It's one thing to be a big mouth but now you've blown everything up. Another word from you on that, and we're finished," Obaid replied.

The Connaught meeting was a last-ditch attempt to reach

terms. But Obaid insisted the amount agreed on in the bar be reduced again, this time to 4 million francs. It was a fateful decision. Justo received the 4 million Swiss francs in a severance agreement with PetroSaudi, but he felt short-changed by 2.5 million Swiss francs.

In the ensuing weeks, Obaid went around telling mutual friends that Justo was a loser who owed everything to Petro-Saudi. Justo was furious when he heard the talk, so he came up with another plan. He knew something was not right about PetroSaudi's relationship with 1MDB, so he set about obtaining proof. To gain leverage in his dispute, Justo arranged to get ahold of a copy of PetroSaudi's computer servers from a PetroSaudi IT person. Amid the more than 140 gigabytes of data, including some 448,000 emails, documents, and other official papers, were details of the fraud that had transpired.

He wouldn't do anything with the servers for more than two years, but when he did, it would cost Obaid and Mahony more than a few million Swiss francs.

As the drama unfolded in Europe, Low, unaware, was a continent away—busy shopping for a New York penthouse fit for a billionaire. And he was trying out a new story to explain his riches: family wealth.

Chapter 22

Penthouse with a View

New York, March 2011

Surrounded by an entourage of security, models, and friends, Low took in the views from penthouse 76B in the Time Warner Center on the southwest corner of Central Park. With trees and lawns filling the floor-to-wall windows to the east, and the Hudson River stretching out to the west, the apartment boasted unfettered views of virtually the entire island of Manhattan. The 4,825-square-foot unit, with three bedrooms, a library, and a fish tank hanging from the ceiling in the "Great Room," had once been the home of Jay-Z and Beyoncé, who rented it for $40,000 per month.

As Low toured the apartment in the spring of 2011 he claimed to realtors to be picking up the place for a group of investors. To a member of the condominium board, however, Low purported to represent the prime minister of Malaysia. But it was really for him. The next year, he would transfer ownership of the Park Laurel apartment and his mansions in Los Angeles and London to Riza Aziz, Najib's stepson. The Time Warner penthouse, however, was his crown jewel, the residence that matched his aspirations to build a reputation in the United States as a movie mogul and serious investor.

The acquisition of penthouse 76B was secured in June for

$30.5 million in cash, one of the highest prices for the building and a price tag that made it among the most expensive apartments in the United States. With questions bubbling in the media about the source of his funds, Low took even greater precautions than in the past to mask his involvement. Over the years, Low had come up with creative reasons to justify his expenditures. Either rich Arab friends were paying, or he merely represented a group of investors or Malaysia's prime minister. As it became difficult to deny his involvement, Low came to rely more on another explanation that he first had tried out on his Wharton and Harrow friends: The money issued from his grandfather, and Low simply was investing the family's billions.

To make the story seem true, he needed to wash hundreds of millions of dollars through the bank accounts of family members, notably his father, Larry. Thin, with a narrow mustache and neatly parted hair, Larry Low was seen as a likable party guy back in Penang—though allegations he had cheated a former business partner trailed him. To send huge amounts of cash to his father, Low had to find a bank that wouldn't dig too deeply.

Until this point, Low had managed to skirt banks' compliance departments, but it was hard work. With Deutsche Bank and Coutts, he was constantly forced to invent fake investment agreements to justify weighty movements of cash, and even had to fly to Zurich to explain deals. Low's ability to get this far was in part a result of the failings of compliance efforts at major financial institutions. Banks made money through letting transactions happen—not putting up roadblocks—and compliance officers were often pressured to turn a blind eye. But operating on this scale, Low was finding it harder and harder to hoodwink compliance.

The primary U.S. law against money laundering is the Bank Secrecy Act of 1970, which requires institutions to keep records of financial transactions and report suspicious activity. A 1986 law made it illegal for banks to take part in, or cover up, money laundering. The PATRIOT Act of 2001, aimed at snuffing out terrorism financing after the September 11 attacks, forced banks to set up compliance programs and enhance due diligence on customers. And it allowed harsher financial penalties against banks that failed to stop shady transfers. By the late 2000s, though, banks were making too much money in the housing bubble to lose sleep over compliance. Few punishments were meted out and, as a result, banks and regulators didn't enforce these regulations all that stringently. More often than not, compliance departments were a weak appendage of a bank's ecosystem, isolated under legal affairs.

The subprime crisis, starting in 2007, changed the picture. U.S. regulators had been caught napping, and the collapse of Lehman Brothers and Bear Stearns, under the weight of bad mortgage loans, led to tighter scrutiny of banks' actions. That extended to anti–money laundering, as Treasury and the Justice Department began to hand out heftier punishments to transgressors. Wachovia Bank, in early 2010, agreed to pay $160 million in penalties for failing to report $8 billion in dodgy transfers. Around this time, the Justice Department was building its case against J.P. Morgan, where Bernie Madoff held his accounts, eventually leading to a record $2 billion fine under the Bank Secrecy Act. These actions were forcing Wall Street and major global banks in Europe and Japan to get their act together on compliance.

What Low needed was a smaller bank, one that would be dependent on his business and took compliance even less seriously than Wall Street behemoths. He found it in a struggling Swiss bank called BSI, which was owned by Italian insurance group Assicurazioni Generali. Ironically, the bank had refused to handle the original PetroSaudi deal because of concerns over Low's role. But from late 2010, he started opening dozens of individual and corporate accounts at BSI's small Singapore branch. One of them, on June 28, 2011, was credited with $55 million from the Swiss account of Good Star at Coutts. On the same day, Low sent $54.75 million from that account to one that Larry Low had recently opened, also with BSI in Singapore. From there, only hours later, $30 million was sent to Switzerland, digitally moving to Asia and back on the same day, landing in the account of another Low-controlled company at Rothschild Bank in Zurich.

This was layering, the process of hiding money's origins through a complex maze of transactions—a crucial instrument in the money launderer's tool kit. In this case, Rothschild's compliance department could only see money coming from Larry Low to Jho Low. By this simple process, Low created the impression of inherited money, flowing down through the generations.

But BSI bankers could investigate under the hood, and should have alerted authorities to the needless back-and-forth transactions between Low and his father. The likes of Coutts and Rothschild had failed to catch Low, but they had asked questions. Now Low was testing BSI's willingness to look the other way, a tryout the bank passed with flying colors, opening the doors to more lucrative business. The bank would become a crucial element in the plumbing of the 1MDB scheme as its scale escalated in the years ahead.

From Rothschild, Low sent $27 million to one of his IOLTA accounts at Shearman, the U.S. law firm. Since 2009, Low had relied on these lawyer trust accounts for his myriad purchases, drawing on them to pay for gambling, parties, and yacht rentals, as well as to purchase multiple properties. Back then, Low had sent money directly to the IOLTA accounts from Good Star. Now Low was taking greater precautions, sending money in a circuitous fashion into his lawyer accounts.

These accounts were used to fund the purchase of the Time

Warner penthouse, finalized in June 2011, as well as to pay Douglas Elliman a brokerage fee of $1.2 million. A Seychelles company, with 1MDB employee Seet Li Lin as a signatory, was the initial purchaser of the Time Warner penthouse, but it assigned its rights to yet another shell firm controlled by Low.

A notice to the Time Warner condominium board identified Larry Low as the occupant of the apartment, an attempt to buttress the image of a billionaire family. But it was Low who would live there, a suitably grandiose base in New York for one of the world's newest billionaires.

Chapter 23

Switzerland of the East

Singapore, December 2009

How BSI came to be Low's bank of choice started with a fight. Back in late 2009, Hanspeter Brunner was angry with his employer, Coutts International, the Zurich-based foreign arm of the three-hundred-year-old British private bank, which has offices on the Strand and counts Queen Elizabeth among its clients. Brunner, a private banker in his fifties with short-cropped hair and a ruddy complexion, the consequence of a lifelong appreciation for vintage red wine, had taken a banking internship at age fifteen in his native Switzerland rather than finishing high school and attending university. He spent a quarter century at Credit Suisse, where he learned the ropes of private banking, the industry of investing money for individuals with more than $1 million in liquid assets.

By the 1990s, private banks were looking to expand in Asia, an area of fast economic growth, and Brunner moved to head Coutts's business in Singapore. The Southeast Asian city-state of five million people, located on a tropical island near the equator, was positioning itself as the "Switzerland of the East," complete with banking secrecy laws modeled on Switzerland's.

For a while, business flourished as Asia's economies powered ahead, generating scores of new millionaires. After the Asian financial crisis took hold in the late 1990s, slashing the stock holdings of rich Asians, Brunner was recalled to Switzerland to head the bank's international business. But he had developed a taste for the lifestyle in Asia, with its servants and drivers, and he was back in Singapore by 2006, residing in a modern apartment with a pool and outdoor whirlpool bath within walking distance of the city's botanical gardens. In the other direction was Orchard Road, a shopping-and-entertainment hub with restaurants and bars. The remuneration was another attraction: Brunner earned more than 1 million Swiss francs a year, with more in bonuses, received stipends for a driver and multiple free business-class flights home, and enjoyed tax rates of only 15 percent.

But he also had a problem. The global financial crisis had forced the British government to bail out the Royal Bank of Scotland, Coutts International's parent company. Now state controlled, RBS set about cutting bonuses at Coutts and offering deferred payments in bonds instead of cash. Brunner was incensed. Senior management demanded his return to Switzerland. Hooked on the perks of living in Asia, and with another card up his sleeve, he declined to do so.

For a year, Brunner had been holding talks with senior executives at BSI. Founded in the nineteenth century in the Italian-speaking part of Switzerland, BSI had thrived for generations in a similar fashion to all Swiss banks: aiding wealthy Europeans and Americans who wanted to hide their cash in private accounts and evade the payment of taxes at home. For decades, rich Americans, Germans, French, and Italians would come to see their bankers in Switzerland, sometimes lugging suitcases of cash on the train to Geneva, Zurich, or, in BSI's case, the bank's headquarters in a 1700s colonnaded mansion in the picturesque Alpine town of Lugano. Switzerland's stringent bank secrecy laws, which made it illegal for banks to divulge information about their clients, protected the business.

By the mid-2000s, however, European nations and the United States had lost patience with Switzerland and began to pressure the country to hand over information on tax cheats. The European Union and Switzerland signed a treaty that forced Swiss banks to divulge information on accounts held by citizens of other European nations or withhold a tax on customers who wished to remain anonymous. Surrounded by EU nations on all sides, and dependent on open-border trade with its neighbors, Swiss politicians had no choice but to agree to this compromise. European clients began to look for other places to stash their money. Under this regulatory onslaught, the business model of small Swiss banks like BSI was imperiled.

BSI had opened a Singapore office in 2005, but it had failed to make headway in Asia against better-known rivals like UBS and Credit Suisse. Brunner knew this and he hatched an audacious plan that would change BSI's fortunes overnight. In late 2009 he reached an agreement with Alfredo Gysi, the bank's Lugano-based chief executive, to jump ship with more than one hundred Coutts employees, who were enticed by promises of salaries that were 20 to 40 percent higher and guaranteed bonuses for three years. The bank suddenly had over $2 billion in new customer money, more than tripling its assets under management in Asia, with Brunner as the new regional chief. "It was a marriage of convenience," said Kevin Swampillai, a Malaysian banker who was among those who left Coutts for BSI.

Before the exodus, some Coutts bankers feared they might lose account holders who didn't want to shift their assets to BSI. Among the most nervous was Yak Yew Chee, a Singaporean banker in his fifties, who had a very important client: Jho Low. Yak was the private banker at Coutts for Larry Low, helping to invest the Penang resident's modest fortune. In 2006, just after Low had graduated from Wharton, Larry asked Yak to open an account for his son at Coutts in Singapore.

Yak, who had spiky, thinning hair, graying at the sides, and often wore sunglasses, was a domineering personality who cowed coworkers. Often dismissive of others' views, he would complain to subordinates that women weren't cut out to become bankers, as they demanded time off for maternity leave. But he was tolerated by his bosses because he aced the only metric that counts in private banking: He brought in clients. The key to his success was a burgeoning relationship with Larry's son, Jho Low.

In mid-2009, Low told Yak he would be helping a Malaysian sovereign wealth fund called 1MDB invest money. The idea was preposterous—*why would a state fund need to work through someone so young, and for what ends would it require the services of a bank specializing in private wealth of individuals?*—but Yak agreed to help. He opened an account for Good Star at Coutts, and he kept the firm's records. It was this account that ultimately received more than $1 billion in 1MDB money, forcing Low to make up a story to compliance staff at Coutts that Good Star had an investment agreement with the Malaysian fund. Yak knew Good Star was controlled by Low, who explained that he was engaged in super-secretive "government-to-government" business—a line the banker swallowed without query.

Low had found his perfect banker—tough but unquestioning— and when Yak told him of his decision to move to BSI, a more obscure institution than Coutts, he decided to move his accounts over. Ecstatic at his accomplishment, Brunner boasted to a Bloomberg journalist about his plans to triple BSI's assets under management in Asia in just five years.

Yak already had proven pliable, and Low sensed BSI would not create trouble for him, especially if he helped turn Brunner's dream into a reality by channeling billions of dollars to the bank. It was part of a system Low was developing to identify institutions with weak governance, and use that to his advantage. A few years later, he would ask a New York art dealer in an email to recommend him a lender with a "quick and relaxed [know your customer] process." BSI would prove to be the ultimate example of this—a bank whose management, in the search for profit, asked few probing questions.

From late 2010, Low relayed instructions to Yak, now a managing director at BSI, to open a series of accounts in his name and those of scores of shell companies. There was an "onboarding" procedure—a checklist of simple *know-your-customer* bullet points that included items such as passport details, legal convictions, and the source of a customer's money. Low came up clean. It was at this point that he began laying the groundwork for his tale of family wealth. The June 2011 transfer of $55 million— some of which was used for the Time Warner purchase—was a test to see if BSI compliance staff would buy the story that this was family money. It worked and Low began to send gushers of cash into his BSI accounts.

The 1MDB fund also opened a slew of accounts with BSI— accounts which would receive billions of dollars in funds in the years ahead. The bank's compliance queried why a Malaysian sovereign fund would need a Swiss bank account. So, to ensure the buy-in of senior management at BSI, Low took precautions. He arranged for Yak to set up a meeting in Lugano between senior 1MDB officials, including Chief Executive Shahrol Halmi, and BSI's top management.

It was yet another sign of Low's total control over the fund. The Malaysian executives flew to Switzerland, telling Brunner, BSI's chief executive, Gysi, and others to expect billions of dollars in business from the sovereign wealth fund. Low's ability to arrange such gatherings gave him an aura of respectability, and, despite his lack of a formal role at the fund, senior bankers like Gysi and Brunner stopped asking questions.

Yak was feted as BSI's star banker.

"I wanted to personally thank you for your immense contribution not only to our new Asia business, but to BSI Group as a whole," Gysi, the chief executive, wrote Yak.

His connection to Low made him exceedingly rich; Yak began to take home around $5 million a year in salary and bonuses, more than five times his previous earnings, binding him to Low, the money and adulation too alluring to turn down. The bosses, too, began to reap the benefits of the relationship, as BSI became a force to be reckoned with in Singapore and globally. Brunner enjoyed hosting parties at his $7 million, 2,500-square-foot colonial-era town house in Singapore, close to his old apartment. The two-story whitewashed building had been restored and furnished in the opulent style of a Chinese mandarin, with terra-cotta horses, statues of Chinese gods, and deep Persian carpets.

According to Kevin Swampillai, who became BSI's head of wealth management in Singapore, it was a "lame duck" management team that cared only about salaries, allowing lower-ranking bankers to act however they pleased. One of those given free rein was Yeo Jiawei.

Chapter 24

Brazen Sky

Singapore, December 2011

With pointed eyebrows, pronounced cheeks, and a thick head of hair, Yeo Jiawei, a twenty-eight-year-old Chinese Singaporean banker at BSI, gave off a boyish air. But Yeo had become an expert in a dark corner of the global financial system. At BSI he was a "wealth manager," but his real expertise lay in an intricate knowledge of ways to help elite customers reduce tax bills. The bank's bread and butter—like many private banks in Singapore—was devising such strategies, largely for rich Indian and Southeast Asian clients. One method Yeo employed was to wash clients' money through investment funds in faraway places.

Yeo's skills were perfectly suited to one of BSI's star clients: Jho Low. Low wanted a way to send money through multiple accounts to keep its origins secret, and Yeo had promised to deliver.

Instead of dealing with mundane tax evasion, Low told Yeo he would have a new assignment: secret government work. Like many people who brushed up against the Malaysian, Yeo was intrigued and flattered. He set about doing what Low wanted. In December 2011, Yeo set up a meeting in Singapore with José Renato Carvalho Pinto, a Brazilian relationship manager at Amicorp Group, a small financial firm. Yeo described to Pinto how

BSI was doing work involving Malaysian and Middle Eastern investment funds and needed Amicorp to set up a series of fund structures. Pinto was interested.

Amicorp was cofounded by a Dutch financier named Toine Knipping, who had worked for years as a financier in Curaçao, a sun-swept Caribbean island that was formerly a colony of the Netherlands, before settling in Singapore. Knipping had an eclectic curriculum vitae: He'd worked for a Venezuelan bank, held an interest in a South African aloe vera drinks company, and authored a book on ethical investing. One of his main areas of expertise was Curaçao, which in the 1970s and 1980s emerged as a major offshore center. It also got a name as a transshipment point for drugs from South America to enter the United States and a haven to stash dirty cash, regularly landing Curaçao on the U.S. State Department's list of "Major Money Laundering Countries."

Knipping's company helped hedge funds and other financial firms run their day-to-day business—calculating the value of investments, for instance, or clearing trades. But like many smaller trust companies, Amicorp did a bit of everything, and this included administering small investment funds in Curaçao that were often used by rich Asians to discreetly move money around.

In the meeting, Yeo explained how BSI needed Amicorp's help to set up an investment-fund structure for Malaysian fund 1MDB, and Pinto got to work. The first transaction, for $100 million, went from a BSI account controlled by 1MDB into an Amicorp-administered mutual fund in Curaçao. But it wasn't a usual mutual fund, the kind in which a manager pools cash from mom-and-pop investors, using it to buy stocks and bonds. Sure, this entity, Enterprise Emerging Market Fund, took cash from multiple investors. But the structure masked one major difference from a plain-vanilla mutual fund: It also comprised segregated portfolios that took cash from only one client, before "investing" in another asset.

It was simply a way to wash a client's money through what looked like a mutual fund. In other words, cash coming out the other side appeared to be a transfer from a mutual fund. This was exactly what happened with the $100 million, which Enterprise Emerging Market Fund promptly sent to a shell company controlled by Fat Eric, Low's associate and, increasingly, an important nominee for his many companies. Yeo never made clear the business reason for the transfer. It was unclear why a state fund such as 1MDB would use such secretive financial structures, but Pinto didn't pry, as BSI had vouched for 1MDB. As Kevin Swampillai, Yeo's boss, put it: "There was only a semblance of compliance at these funds." In the next couple of years, Amicorp would set up $1.5 billion of such structures for 1MDB, Low, and his family.

Here was a legal, if highly questionable, way to disguise money flows. In the earlier stages, Low had been content to send cash straight from Good Star to his U.S. law-trust accounts with Shearman & Sterling or, more recently, into his accounts at BSI. But the media spotlight on his partying, and the compliance hassles, were making him more paranoid. By using an intermediary step like the Curaçao fund, Low hoped to cover over any footprints.

Yeo had delivered and Low began to trust him. As he moved deeper into Low's orbit, Yeo's self-regard for his own skills grew, and he expressed disdain for bankers at BSI who didn't deal directly with such powerful clients. Like BSI itself, Yeo had proven himself an amenable fit for Jho Low, and Low would soon turn to the young banker again.

The 1MDB fund still had to account for the $1.8 billion it claimed to have lent to PetroSaudi. Of this, Low and his conspirators had taken the lion's share, and now he needed Yeo to help make the debt go away. Earlier, the fund's executives had attempted to get Tim Leissner of Goldman to find a bank that would value the oil drill ships—about the only asset PetroSaudi had acquired with 1MDB's money—at an inflated price of $1 billion. The idea was for 1MDB to take over those assets and, in return, write down the debt. Although he likely did not know the full picture, Leissner got Lazard, the U.S. investment bank, to take a look at the drill ships, but it couldn't come up with a valuation anywhere near high enough to make this plan work.

Instead, Yeo got to work on a convoluted set of transactions that was pure financial trickery. Essentially, 1MDB would swap a large portion of its debt for a stake in a PetroSaudi subsidiary that owned the drill ships, even though they were worth nothing like the $1.8 billion that 1MDB was owed. Yeo then arranged for 1MDB to sell that stake to Bridge Partners International, which was controlled by a Hong Kong financier named Lobo Lee.

A long-distance triathlete, who was middle-aged but kept fit cycling Hong Kong's mountainous terrain, Lee was just another one of the many small-time fund managers in the Caribbean, Hong Kong, Bangkok, and Singapore who created arcane structures for a fee, without querying the need for such complexity. By remaining ignorant of the full terms, they were the cogs that allowed the money-laundering machine to keep humming along.

Instead of paying in cash, Bridge Partners set up a Cayman Islands investment fund, effectively giving 1MDB units in the fund in return for the stake. The fund, called Bridge Global, had only one client—1MDB—and hadn't even registered with authorities in the Cayman Islands for permission to make investments. Magically, 1MDB now claimed in its financial statements the Bridge Global investment was worth $2.3 billion—a profit of $500 million on the money it had lent to PetroSaudi. The 1MDB fund set up a new subsidiary called Brazen Sky, which

opened a bank account with BSI to hold the units. It was nothing but a facade: There was no cash there, only fund units, supposedly the profits from selling a stake in two almost-worthless
oil drill ships.

On paper, however, 1MDB could claim it had made a profit,
and Low conspired to get it past auditors. Pressed by accountants at KPMG, Yeo gave the impression the Bridge Global fund
units were backed by cash. The financial engineering had helped
disguise the truth, and KPMG carried on with its audit. But the
problem hadn't gone away, and the firm's accountants would not
prove that easy to con the following year.

Yeo must have known what BSI was doing was ropy, and so
he set up a scheme with his boss, Kevin Swampillai, to profit
himself. The 1MDB fund had agreed to pay $4 million annually
to Bridge Global and $12 million to BSI for helping set up the
Cayman Islands arrangement. But Yeo was managing the process and Lobo Lee didn't know the full details, so Yeo persuaded
the Hong Kong fund manager to settle for $500,000, and Yeo
and Swampillai funneled off millions of dollars to their personal
accounts.

The seemingly massive amount now in 1MDB's Brazen
Sky account at BSI worried Hanspeter Brunner, the bank's
chief executive in the region. BSI's Singapore branch suddenly
appeared to have billions of dollars in new deposits, and Brunner
feared the Monetary Authority of Singapore, Singapore's central
bank, would want an explanation. After a period of fast growth
in its private banking industry, the city-state was facing pressure
to do more to impede money laundering.

Singapore's private banking industry was booming, managing $1 trillion in assets, a third of Switzerland's total, but still
making it one of the largest offshore centers on the planet. The
city-state already had a reputation as a place for corrupt Indo-
nesians, Chinese, and Malaysians to hide money. Now, it was

6666666666666

attracting more European and U.S. clients trying to escape the increased scrutiny from Western regulators, who were fed up with tax cheats. The Financial Action Task Force, the Paris-based group which sets anti-money-laundering standards, recently had singled Singapore out for failing to prosecute more dirty-money cases.

So Brunner later set up a meeting with Singapore's central bank, during which he gave a presentation on Brazen Sky and the bank's other 1MDB-related business. But he did not go into detail, instead giving a simple overview and stressing this was the business of an official Malaysian government fund.

Brunner's stewardship of BSI would cost him and imperil the bank's very existence. But Low, at least for now, had overcome another complication, and was readying for the next phase of his scheme. This time, Tim Leissner of Goldman wouldn't miss out.

Chapter 25

Goldman and the Sheikh (The Second Heist)

Abu Dhabi, March 2012

In early March, Tim Leissner flew into Abu Dhabi, the humid Persian Gulf emirate, for a rare meeting with one of the world's richest people: Sheikh Mansour Bin Zayed. As one of nineteen children of the founder of the UAE, the sheikh was worth an estimated $40 billion, and perhaps best known for his ownership of Manchester City Football Club. His grandparents' generation had been born penniless, living as date farmers, camel rearers, and pearl fishermen, but the discovery of oil in the late 1950s had changed their fortunes.

Obtaining a sit-down meeting with Sheikh Mansour was almost unheard of, even for the most heavyweight investors. The sheikh's power derived not only from his personal fortune, but also his role as chairman of the International Petroleum Investment Company, a $70 billion sovereign wealth fund. IPIC, financed by huge amounts of debt, recently had become a global investment force—it had even taken a stake in Barclays Bank of the UK during the financial crisis.

Wall Street bankers were often seen sniffing for deals at IPIC, which was in the process of building a futuristic modern headquarters, a series of domino-thin skyscrapers, one shorter than the next, which would offer panoramic views of Abu Dhabi's main island and the expanse of the Persian Gulf. But few had met Sheikh Mansour.

Leissner was among the chosen, thanks to Low's newfound closeness with Khadem Al Qubaisi, an aide to the sheikh. In a few days, the Goldman banker would be boasting to colleagues in Asia about his unparalleled access in the Middle East, although he was careful not to play up Low's role in making this happen. But right now, he needed to get the sheikh to agree to a deal that could change his fortunes. He was on the cusp of winning the mega-1MDB business, for which he had spent years laying the groundwork.

In his meeting with the sheikh, Leissner was accompanied by Low and Roger Ng, who also had traveled to the emirate. After pleasantries, the group got down to discussing the outlines of the deal. The Wall Street bank was preparing to sell a total of $3.5 billion in bonds for the 1MDB fund to finance the purchase of coal-fired power plants in Malaysia and overseas. The plan was for 1MDB to package these facilities, as well as some new plants, into one company and IPO the shares on Malaysia's stock exchange. The listing could earn 1MDB around $5 billion, as the power plants put under one entity would be worth a lot more.

The problem was that 1MDB had never issued a U.S. dollar bond to international investors, and it had no credit rating. So, Goldman was suggesting it ask IPIC—a sovereign entity with a strong credit rating—to guarantee the issue. That would put investors at ease, giving them confidence that 1MDB would be able to repay the debt whatever the circumstances. In return for its guarantee, IPIC would acquire the rights to buy a stake in the listed power company at a favorable price.

This was Low's latest blueprint for 1MDB, a way for the fund to enter the power-generation business, make some money, and, hopefully, paper over losses. But there were many oddities in the plan. Why would a Malaysian state fund seek a guarantee from a similar fund of another country? Why didn't Malaysia's government just offer a sovereign guarantee for the debt? Indeed, Leissner's colleagues at Goldman's Middle Eastern headquarters in Dubai, who did regular business with IPIC, found the idea preposterous and declined to get involved. Even IPIC's own finance director raised questions about why IPIC would put itself at risk over another fund's business—one with no track record, at that—but was outranked.

But Leissner and Ng knew what was really going on. A month earlier, they had met with Low in London and discussed how, in order to get the guarantee from IPIC, they would need to pay bribes to officials in Malaysia and Abu Dhabi. Together with Andrea Vella, the banker in Hong Kong who would be structuring the bonds, they agreed to keep this information from Goldman committees that would review the transaction, according to a Justice Department filing. (A lawyer for Vella denied his client had any knowledge of, or involvement in, any bribes or fraud, and noted that he did not receive any of the missing 1MDB funds. He also denied that Vella ever discussed 1MDB business with Jho Low.)

The sheikh, a youthful forty-one-year-old with a toothy grin, had the final say at IPIC. After Leissner and Low made their presentations, Sheikh Mansour gave the go-ahead. The proposal for IPIC to guarantee the Malaysian fund's bonds may have looked strange, but it was an artificial construct, purely aimed at creating an excuse to divert more than a billion dollars from 1MDB.

Low had put the scheme together with Al Qubaisi, who was also the managing director of IPIC. They had gotten to know each other on the failed Claridge's bid, and Low had brokered a deal for Aabar, an IPIC subsidiary, to buy a Malaysian bank. That deal had lost money for Al Qubaisi, but now Low was about to repay him many times over.

And IPIC's guarantee was the linchpin of the plan.

With gelled-back hair and a bodybuilder's physique, the result of two hours a day pumping iron, the forty-year-old Al Qubaisi was a striking figure. The Al Qubaisi family had married into the ruling Al Nahyans a generation earlier, a family tie that had helped his career. After working for the Abu Dhabi Investment Authority, the emirate's most well-known and largest sovereign wealth fund, he had become managing director of IPIC in 2007, but his real power lay as Sheikh Mansour's trusted dealmaker.

There was another attraction to Al Qubaisi: He had a reputation for taking kickbacks on deals, making him incredibly rich. Low had spent hundreds of millions on parties, mansions, and trophy investments like the L'Ermitage hotel, not to mention secret payments to his coconspirators. Yet he craved greater riches: He wasn't happy with a smattering of low-profile deals in real estate. He wanted to become a genuine mogul. *The Wolf of Wall Street* was slated to kick off filming in the second half of 2012, and Low still didn't have financing in place. He needed more cash, and he sensed Al Qubaisi could deliver it—for a price.

Through his relationship with Sheikh Mansour, Al Qubaisi was one of the most powerful men in the emirate. Even in the brash and showy UAE, Al Qubaisi struck bankers as an unparalleled egoist, traveling with a retinue of Egyptian security guards and embossing his initials—KAQ—on cigars, drink coasters, boxes of tissues, and even his collection of high-end cars worth tens of millions of euros, which he kept in a storage facility in Geneva and at his villas in the South of France.

In Abu Dhabi, Al Qubaisi wore the traditional emirati cloak and head covering, and had a family home, a sprawling villa, where his wife and four children lived. But like many rich emiratis, he conducted a different life overseas. At his villa on the Côte d'Azur, with Bugattis and Ferraris parked outside, he partied with models, and he had a younger Moroccan wife in Paris. When abroad, he traded in traditional emirati dress for tight-fitting T-shirts, including one with a montage of images of Al Pacino's Tony Montana from the 1983 film *Scarface*. Once, when an executive showed up to Al Qubaisi's mansion in France to discuss business, he answered the door wearing a skimpy swimsuit, while women in bikinis lingered in the background.

The sheikh oversaw IPIC, and he liked to have the final say on major deals, like this burgeoning business with 1MDB. But he also delegated incredible powers to Al Qubaisi, who had the ability to green-light acquisitions without board approval. With a single execution of his wide, sharp signature, he could okay a multi-billion-dollar deal on behalf of the fund.

"Khadem was the only man in the world who you could call with a $10 billion deal and he'd just say 'yay' or 'nay.' He thought he was God," said one financier.

In return, Al Qubaisi ensured that Sheikh Mansour remained flush with funds to pay for a lifestyle that required vast expenditures: salaries for dozens of staff, the cost of maintaining houses, boats, cars, and planes around the globe. IPIC had been founded in 1984 to invest in oil-related companies, but with Al Qubaisi at its helm, the fund and its subsidiary, Aabar Investments, had engaged in a spending spree, most famously its bailout alongside Qatar of Barclays in 2008, which saved the bank from a government takeover, but also the acquisitions of minority stakes in Daimler-Benz, UniCredit, Virgin Galactic, and other companies—all of them major deals.

The boundaries between IPIC, a state fund, and the sheikh's personal business empire were not always sharply drawn. In the case of the Barclays acquisition, for instance, British regulators believed Sheikh Mansour was putting in the money, when in fact the funds came from IPIC. Although he had not invested any personal cash, Barclays issued warrants to the sheikh as part of the deal, allowing him to buy shares in the bank at a low price. He eventually made more than $1 billion in profit—at no risk to his own funds.

Aabar's books contained a tangle of transactions with companies tied to Sheikh Mansour, involving land and loans in the billions of dollars. In addition to his day job, Al Qubaisi oversaw these private businesses, and his privileged position, close to the Al Nahyans, gave him free rein to feather his own nest. In a 2009 lawsuit filed in the United States, two businessmen claimed Al Qubaisi had asked for $300 million in kickbacks during a failed bid to take over the Four Seasons hotel chain. (The plaintiffs later withdrew the suit.)

Behind his brash demeanor, Al Qubaisi had a problem. Unlike ADIA, which could rely on payments from the state's oil profits, IPIC was fueled mainly by debt. By 2012, it had $19 billion in borrowings, and only the Abu Dhabi government's 100 percent ownership ensured its debt was awarded investment-grade credit ratings. The fund's image as a major investor, in fact, was partly a mirage. After the crisis, when Al Qubaisi saw an opportunity to buy stakes in big Western companies and banks, he turned to Wall Street for financing.

Goldman Sachs, Morgan Stanley, and others made huge profits arranging derivatives financing for IPIC—just another naive emerging-market sovereign wealth fund—helping to make up for subdued markets and economies in the West.

But it was becoming harder for Al Qubaisi to raise money from Wall Street. In 2011, the de facto ruler of the UAE, Sheikh Mansour's brother, Mohammed Bin Zayed, had ordered all debt issuances to go through a central authority to avoid a repeat of the Dubai debt crisis, in which state entities overborrowed and had to be bailed out by the UAE government to the tune of $20 billion. As he was searching for new ways to keep the cash flowing, Al Qubaisi came into contact with Jho Low, who boasted he could sign multi-billion-dollar deals involving the 1MDB fund.

Like Al Qubaisi, Low was a young, unaccountable figure who, through relations with the truly powerful, controlled billions of dollars. Low had brokered Aabar's investment in RHB, the Malaysian bank, which had lost money, but his latest proposal would more than make up for that debacle. IPIC agreed to guarantee the 1MDB bonds, and Goldman set about arranging the issue.

Chapter 26

Bilking the State

New York, March 2012

At Goldman's global headquarters at 200 West Street in downtown Manhattan, a forty-four-story skyscraper on the Hudson, completed just after the financial crisis, senior bankers were growing concerned over this business in faraway Malaysia. But the unorthodox dealmaking had a powerful supporter: President Gary Cohn.

Bald with a pointed skull, and furrows across his brow, the fifty-one-year-old banker was a formidable presence. He was aggressive and blunt, a personality forged on Goldman's trading floors, where he had launched his career alongside Lloyd Blankfein. When his friend rose to chief executive, Cohn had taken the number two job and had remained a loyal lieutenant, helping defend the company's precrisis bet against the housing market. Now, with Western economic activity subdued, Cohn was spearheading a drive to do more deals with sovereign wealth funds in emerging markets. And that led him to throw his support behind a potentially lucrative line of business that Leissner and Andrea Vella were developing in Malaysia.

Cohn had set up a special cross-divisional unit to make money from sovereign wealth funds—co-investing with them in private-equity deals, devising hedging strategies, or simply raising capital. This business line was colloquially termed "monetizing the state" inside Goldman and was a major focus inside the bank. Cohn started to travel regularly to Southeast Asia, where he had high-level meetings about co-investing with Singapore's powerful Temasek Holdings investment fund. He viewed 1MDB very much in this vein, although the fund shared almost no similarities with Temasek, a professionally run entity.

The backing of a domineering and powerful personality like Cohn afforded significant cover to those involved in the 1MDB business and drowned out the voices of those who were uncomfortable with the plans to raise billions of dollars for the fund. David Ryan, president of Goldman in Asia, was among those urging caution. He had visited 1MDB's staff in Malaysia and came away with concerns over its plans to take on so much debt, and the inexperience of its management, none of whom seemed to have overseen multi-billion-dollar investments before.

The potential deal wound its way through five Goldman committees that look at financial and legal risk. One of the main points of debate was the role of Jho Low, whose exact position baffled some Goldman executives. One Goldman executive, in an email to colleagues on March 27, acknowledged Low was a "1MDB Operator or intermediary in Malaysia." But in conversations with Goldman staff around the same time, Leissner denied Low was involved in the deal. Such middlemen were considered highly risky at American banks because of the possibility they were receiving bribes, a violation of the Foreign Corrupt Practices Act that could lead to a big fine.

Low's plan was for 1MDB to sell the bonds quickly and secretively via a private placement. Typically, most companies issuing bonds prefer to do so through a public issuance, in which the bank arranging the deal canvasses a wide range of investors. Through this process, called book building, banks with access to a large network of investors can reduce a company's cost of funds. Investors in a private placement, by contrast—typically big institutions like pension funds or hedge funds—demand higher returns. The advantage is that companies can raise money quickly and without getting credit ratings from big agencies like Moody's and Standard & Poor's. The process also involved much less scrutiny, just how Low liked it.

The 1MDB fund had agreed to pay $2.7 billion for power plants owned by Malaysian billionaire Ananda Krishnan's Tanjong Energy Holdings, the first of a series of acquisitions it planned to make in the sector. To give the deal a veneer of authenticity, 1MDB needed an independent valuation of the plants. Leissner stepped in, asking Lazard if it could oblige. The U.S. bank agreed to take a look, but its bankers crunched the numbers and couldn't figure out why 1MDB was willing to pay $2.7 billion for the suite of plants, which were located in Malaysia, as well as Egypt, Bangladesh, Pakistan, and the UAE.

The deal seemed favorable to Tanjong, especially given that its power-sale agreement with the Malaysian state would soon run out, handing the government leverage to achieve a bargain price. Lazard believed the whole deal smelled of political corruption. It was common in Malaysia for the government to award sweetheart deals to companies in return for kickbacks and political financing; that was what Lazard thought was going on, and so it pulled out.

With no other choice, Goldman instead became an adviser to 1MDB on the purchase, as well as helping the fund raise the capital. The bank provided a valuation range that justified 1MDB paying $2.7 billion for the plants.

Leissner was at his most charming as he tried to cajole members of 1MDB's board of directors to accept Goldman's terms for selling the bonds. Sitting opposite the Goldman banker in a room at the fund's downtown Kuala Lumpur offices, just a few weeks after Leissner's meeting in Abu Dhabi, some of the board members looked skeptical. Goldman was preparing to launch what it internally dubbed Project Magnolia, a plan to sell $1.75 billion in ten-year bonds for the 1MDB fund. But some board members were alarmed by what Leissner had informed them: Goldman would likely make $190 million from its part in the deal, or 11 percent of the bond's value. This was an outrageous sum, even more than Goldman had made on the Sarawak transaction the year before, and way above the normal fee of $1 million for such work.

The banker defended Goldman's profit by pointing out that 1MDB would make big returns in a future IPO of the power assets, all without putting down any money of its own.

"Look at your number, not at our number," he said cajolingly.

Working together with Andrea Vella in Hong Kong, Leissner had arranged for a rerun of the Sarawak bond. As last time, the PFI trading desk would buy the entire issue, using its massive capital, and later find investors. That meant Goldman would be taking on all the risk and 1MDB would get the money quickly. Despite some questions, the board, filled mainly with Najib loyalists, was ultimately a rubber stamp, and it wasn't going to mount a serious attempt to stop this plan in its tracks.

Even at Goldman, some bankers, including David Ryan, considered the bank's likely profit excessive. Alex Turnbull, a Hong Kong–based Goldman banker whose father, Malcolm Turnbull, would later become Australia's prime minister, also raised concerns internally. Turnbull wasn't involved in the deal, but he knew how bond markets worked, and he sent an email to colleagues expressing disbelief about Goldman's profits. The email led to a reprimand from Goldman's compliance department, while Turnbull's boss told him to keep his mouth shut if he ever wanted to get promoted. He left the bank almost two years later for reasons unrelated to 1MDB.

Internally, Leissner, backed by Vella, defended the returns as commensurate with the risk Goldman was taking by buying the entire $1.75 billion in bonds. The 1MDB fund was paying most of its fee to Goldman by selling the bonds at a discount, and the bank would make its money if they could find investors willing to pay a higher price. But the face value—that is, the undiscounted price—was still high enough to yield 6 percent annually to an investor, a high return given the guarantee from IPIC, and an inviting proposition at a time when rates in Western economies and Japan were hovering close to zero. In fact, Goldman already had lined up mutual funds in South Korea, China, and the Philippines to buy the bonds. The sale was handled quietly, and one Goldman employee was told to keep all correspondence about the bond off email. If word got out Goldman already had buyers, its profits would not seem justified.

There was another reason Goldman didn't need to worry. Tanjong, the seller of the power plants, had itself agreed to subscribe to a "significant" portion of the offering, according to the prospectus, a document Goldman bankers had drawn up to detail the bond for investors. The 1MDB fund had paid Tanjong a favorable price for its assets, and now the company itself was getting bonds with an attractive yield. In return, companies linked to Ananda Krishnan secretly made donations of $170 million to 1MDB's charity arm. Soon after, in its financial accounts, the fund was forced to "impair"—or write off—$400 million of the value of the plants on its books, an admission it had overpaid. Lazard had been right to mistrust the high valuation of Tanjong's assets, but Goldman missed what was going on.

Goldman's internal committees, set up to catch fraud, had failed in their job. An agenda for a committee of senior bankers in Hong Kong convened to discuss the deal noted "potential media and political scrutiny" of Goldman's colossal profits. They gave the green light anyway. Those arguing in favor of the deal cited the imprimatur of Malaysia's government and the role of Prime Minister Najib in 1MDB. But there was another—unspoken—reason to make this happen. The profits would make this one of Goldman's biggest paydays of the year.

The stewards of Goldman, only a few years after the mortgage meltdown and promises of more upright behavior, were once again failing to uphold principles. The whole notion of "monetizing the state"—in countries without rule of law and sophisticated investors—risked costing taxpayers in poor places for the benefit of Wall Street. Goldman already had gotten entangled in a bad situation with the Libyan Investment Authority. Now the bank appeared to be overcharging a client in Malaysia whose willingness to pay above the odds was illogical.

A series of red flags—from the involvement of Jho Low, to the unusual decision to obtain a guarantee from the fund of another country, to 1MDB's willingness to overpay for the power plants—were all overlooked.

In May, Tim Leissner was late for a dinner at a Chinese restaurant in Singapore's ION Orchard, a futuristic shopping center that looked as if it had been designed by an understudy of Frank Gehry. As he entered, Leissner saw that the other guests sat around a circular banquet table. The group included 1MDB executives, Jho Low, and Roger Ng, as well as Yak Yew Chee of BSI and compliance officers from the Swiss bank. Leissner was annoyed to be there and told participants he could not stay for long. This was not an official gathering, and Leissner realized he should not have come.

Low had put the attendees together in an attempt to overcome an obstacle. The plan was for Goldman, on May 21, 2012, to deposit the proceeds from the $1.75 billion bond into the bank account of 1MDB's energy subsidiary. Just a day later, $576 million of that amount was to move on to the BSI bank account of a British Virgin Islands company called Aabar Investments Ltd.

But BSI's own compliance department wanted to know why 1MDB was planning to transfer such a huge sum into their small bank. Leissner was there to smooth things over, but he seemed nervous. After some general talk about the bond, the German banker excused himself and left. BSI's senior management, including Yak, nonetheless used his presence at the meeting, and the involvement of Goldman, to overcome the compliance department's concerns. This was a senior representative of Wall Street's best-known bank, after all.

They could not have known that Leissner, after discussions with Low, had made a monumental decision. No longer would he simply hide Low's involvement from Goldman, allowing bribes to be paid and the scheme to roll on. Instead, according to Department of Justice filings, along with Roger Ng, he was about to receive tens of millions of dollars in bribes himself. After three years of dallying with Low, Leissner had crossed the Rubicon and there was no way back.

Compliance had good reason to be wary. Aabar Investments Ltd. was meant to look like Aabar Investments PJS, a subsidiary of IPIC. 1MDB would later claim, in its audited financial statements, that the $576 million transfer was part of a payment to compensate the Abu Dhabi fund for its guarantee of the bond.

But this was an imitation firm, set up two months earlier, and the directors of the look-alike Aabar were Al Qubaisi and Al Husseiny, the chairman and chief executive of the real fund. It was as if the chief executive of General Electric, or another blue-chip American firm, had set up a fake company to look like General Electric to engage in off-the-books fraudulent behavior, while still enjoying the cover of a well-known name.

It was a move straight out of Jho Low's playbook. When he was just starting out, Low had set up look-alike companies to make it appear he had the backing of Middle Eastern sovereign wealth funds. This time, the stakes were much higher. It was a ruse, devised by Jho Low and Al Qubaisi, to take more money from 1MDB.

As a further level of security, the pair had arranged for the money to flow via Switzerland-based Falcon Private Bank, which Aabar had bought from American insurance conglomerate AIG.

Al Qubaisi had snapped it up when AIG was in trouble during the financial crisis and renamed it Falcon Bank, after the Gulf's famous hunting bird. Switzerland was under pressure from the United States to clamp down on money laundering, but Al Qubaisi had control of his own Swiss bank. Consequently, Falcon's bankers raised no red alerts, despite huge flows of money that would normally have tripped compliance alarms.

Five months later, Goldman launched Project Maximus, buying another $1.75 billion in bonds to finance 1MDB's acquisition of power plants from the Malaysian casino-and-plantations conglomerate Genting Group. Again, the fund paid a high price, and, like Tanjong, Genting made payments to a Najib-linked charity. This time, $790.3 million disappeared into the look-alike Aabar.

David Ryan, president of Goldman's Asia operations, argued to lower the fee on the second bond, given how easy it had been to sell the first round. But he was overruled by senior executives, including Gary Cohn. While Goldman was working on the deal, Ryan was effectively sidelined; the bank brought in a veteran banker, Mark Schwartz, a proponent of the 1MDB business, as chairman in Asia, a post senior to Ryan's. Goldman earned a little less than the first deal, making $114 million—still an enormous windfall.

For bringing in the business, Leissner was paid a salary and bonuses in 2012 of more than $10 million, making him one of the bank's top-remunerated employees. But that was just the tip of the iceberg. Unknown to his bosses at Goldman, and three months after the first bond, millions of dollars began to flow into a British Virgin Islands shell company controlled by Leissner, some of which he shared with Roger Ng, according to Department of Justice filings. Millions of dollars more moved through Leissner's shell company to pay bribes to 1MDB officials. Over the next two years, more than $200 million in 1MDB money, raised by Goldman, would flow through accounts controlled by Leissner and his relatives.

He could have taken his hefty Goldman salary and dis-
avowed knowledge of the bribery carried out by Low and others.
Perhaps he would have gotten away with it, as many Wall Street
bankers do in countries far from headquarters. But he decided to
take a risk by becoming a direct accomplice in the fraud, rather
than just greasing its wheels. He had seen the kind of life Low
was leading, and he must have thought that a mere $10 million
wasn't going to cut it, not if he wanted to buy super yachts and
host parties himself. Soon he would be doing just that.

In October, Toby Watson, head of Goldman's PFI desk in
Asia, made partner. It was a good year also for Blankfein, Goldman's CEO, who was paid $21 million, still well off his precrisis
record of $68 million, in 2007, but a major payday nonetheless.
Blankfein had developed other lines of business for Goldman,
delivering a $7.5 billion profit that year. But the developments
in Malaysia signified a big strategic win for the chief executive.
The business was so important, in fact, that Blankfein welcomed
Low and Al Husseiny of Aabar in December 2012 for a private
meeting at Goldman's headquarters in Manhattan. Leissner
didn't want to shout from the rooftops about it, though, instead
acting as if the bonds were a secret. When a senior Goldman
colleague in the region circulated the profits internally, he testily
asked for the information to be kept tight.

As the colleague put it: "There was a real sense you didn't
want to draw attention to this."

Jho Low had executed his second major heist. Unlike the first
phase in 2009, with PetroSaudi as his partner, the Malaysian
had laid out this plan in minute detail. Three years earlier, Low
had sought to do a big sovereign-wealth deal, put himself in
the middle of the money flows, and perhaps earn a broker fee.
Events moved quickly, and the conspirators saw their chance to
take money.

This time around, Low carefully laid the groundwork. Instead of an unknown Saudi company as a partner, he had roped in IPIC, one of the largest sovereign wealth funds on the planet. Al Qubaisi was an infinitely more powerful figure than Prince Turki, a layabout seventh son of the Saudi king. Back in 2009, Low's excuses about the money flows varied, as if he were making them up on the fly. The Malaysian also took a huge risk, sending the cash to a Seychelles company he had set up. This time, Low and Al Qubaisi took much greater precautions, sending cash to a company that looked like an Abu Dhabi sovereign wealth fund and was controlled by Al Qubaisi.

Known to only a handful of insiders at the time, the money fanned out from the look-alike Aabar to a small set of beneficiaries connected to the deal. In total $1.4 billion was diverted. Here was the capital needed to make *The Wolf of Wall Street*, to pay off Malaysian voters, and to finance ever-more-exuberant parties and gambling.

Al Qubaisi was rewarded handsomely for his role. Soon after 1MDB raised its second bond and funds flowed to the look-alike Aabar, a stream of money—eventually totaling more than $400 million—moved to an account controlled by Al Qubaisi's company, Vasco Investment Services, at Edmond de Rothschild bank in Luxembourg. From here, Al Qubaisi would buy mansions in the United States, on both coasts, but he also was careful to ensure his patron, Sheikh Mansour, was taken care of.

As the Goldman bonds came together, engineers from the shipbuilding firm Lürssen in Bremen, Germany, were putting the final touches to *Topaz*, Sheikh Mansour's 482-foot yacht, which cost more than $500 million and was as large as a floating hotel, with two helicopter pads and eight decks. Al Qubaisi handled the financing for the *Topaz*, raising a large loan from Deutsche Bank that required payments of 6.4 million euros a month—a considerable outlay. One of the first payments Al

Qubaisi made from Vasco, after receiving money from 1MDB, was a 6.4 million euro transfer to Deutsche Bank—an installment on the *Topaz* loan. He'd later pay a total of $166 million of the payments with funds from Vasco.

In late April, as Goldman prepared 1MDB's first bond issue, some one hundred thousand anticorruption protesters poured out into the streets of Kuala Lumpur. From the sky, the city center was awash in yellow—the color of the demonstrator's T-shirts. For some time, anger among regular middle-class folk—teachers, office workers, lawyers, students—about everyday corruption had been rising.

The demonstrators brandished antigraft signboards; some called for electoral reform. Others held up caricatures of Rosmah, who had become the symbol of Prime Minister Najib's kleptocratic regime. How had she paid for her jewels? people wanted to know. As the swell of protesters tried to make their way to Independence Square, a grassy area at the heart of the city, riot police blocked their way. Late in the afternoon, as the marchers pushed forward, security forces met them with tear gas and water cannons.

Suddenly, a police officer drove a vehicle into a group of demonstrators, injuring two people. The crowd reacted violently, dragging the officer out and turning the car upside down, before smashing in its windows. Scores of protesters were injured, some severely, over the next few hours. The battle lines had been drawn for elections, due the following year.

The protesters knew nothing of what Low had carried out at 1MDB. But corruption in Malaysia already was eating away at the nation's social fabric, from vote buying by UMNO, the ruling party, at election time to the regular backhanded payments by businesses to win government contracts. While middle-class Malaysians dealt with stagnating wages, Malaysia's elite was accruing greater wealth, and it was fueling discontent.

In 2006, a group of opposition politicians, lawyers, and

anticorruption activists had started a movement called "Bersih"—the Malay word meant "clean"—seeking reforms to ensure fair elections. In 2007 and 2011 Bersih protesters, wearing trademark yellow T-shirts, had taken to the streets, clashing with police. But nothing had changed, and the Bersih organizers had called this protest as a last-ditch attempt to ensure clean elections, which were due to be held in mid-2013.

They hoped this demonstration, the largest democratic protest in Malaysia's history, would force the government to listen. Instead, it ended in rancor and division.

Yet it was so much worse than the public knew. Low had taken graft to new levels, risking Malaysia's financial stability. The 1MDB fund's debt stood at a whopping $7 billion, and it had few assets to show for the huge borrowings. Most of the money had been diverted, and the fund had crashed to a $30 million net loss in its latest financial year. But most of these details were kept secret. It was even hard to get a copy of the fund's financial report.

Prime Minister Najib had envisioned 1MDB as a way to create jobs, and as a slush fund to build his popularity with all Malaysians. Instead, it had become a cesspit of graft. With his popularity sinking, Najib soon would double down on his bet on Low, backing the 1MDB fund's push to take on even more debt in a bid to win the upcoming elections. His actions would send 1MDB even deeper into a death spiral.

Low hoped the planned IPO of 1MDB's power assets would stabilize the fund, and hide the growing thefts—a risky strategy, to say the least. But the Malaysian didn't dwell much on the future. This was only government money, after all, and he still had the confidence of Najib, who had the power to write off debt.

From another perspective, Low had replenished his stock of capital and now had the firepower to push ahead with constructing a Hollywood empire. He was on the cusp of entering the most reckless period of his young life.

PART III

EMPIRE

Chapter 27

Making Busta His Bitch

Aboard the Serene, *French Riviera, July 2012*

As the helicopter approached the landing pad, nestled in the bow of the 440-foot superyacht *Serene*, Jho Low was in high spirits. He was about to fly off to Monaco with an entourage of women for a shopping excursion to settle his nerves, before coming back to host his most significant party to date. He had reason to celebrate: The thirty-year-old's new company, a Hong Kong outfit called Jynwel Capital, had just acquired a stake in EMI Music Publishing, whose hit-making writers included Kanye West, Beyoncé, Usher, Alicia Keys, and Pharrell Williams. On top of the EMI acquisition, Red Granite, the film company started by Low, Riza Aziz, and Joey McFarland, was set to begin filming work on *The Wolf of Wall Street.* Low, who had once been rejected for a personal bank account at Goldman in Switzerland, could now lay claim to being an entertainment mogul, and he wanted to make a splash.

The *Serene*, with fifteen guest cabins and dozens of crew members, was a floating pleasure palace, whose centerpiece was a huge whirlpool bath and bar on the top deck. Features included a sauna, a partially covered swimming pool, a lounge with a grand piano, and a twisting marble staircase connecting the multiple levels of the boat. When anchored, decks on hydraulic arms opened out over the water, permitting guests to dine al fresco.

Low required the most sumptuous backdrop for the night's party, and Noah Tepperberg and Jason Strauss were on hand as always to oblige. The owners of the Marquee nightclub had taken care of the details. The $330 million yacht, the ninth largest in the world when it was completed in 2011, belonged to Russian billionaire Yuri Shefler, whose businesses included Stoli vodka. Tepperberg and Strauss also flew out models from the United States, the glamorous nightclub hosts whom Low demanded at every party. Danny Abeckaser, the club promoter and actor, brought along a group that included Leonardo DiCaprio, who was preparing to start filming *The Wolf of Wall Street* the following month. DiCaprio was known as a method actor, said to inhabit his characters' minds even when off set. The actor's hard-partying ways had been a tabloid fixture for years, so presumably it was not difficult for him to channel Jordan Belfort as he prepared for his next big role. And with Jho Low paying for the excesses, as he had done for years now, life and art began to fuse, even before the filming began.

While Low and his entourage shopped in Monaco, Tepperberg and Strauss ensured everything was in place. Workers were putting the finishing touches to a stage on the boat for the night's performances. The guest list included some of the world's best-known pop stars—Kanye West, Rihanna, Chris Brown, Ludacris—as well as actors and members of Middle Eastern royal families.

The $2.2 billion acquisition of EMI, finalized a month earlier, was led by Sony Music Holdings, the Estate of Michael Jackson, and U.S. private equity giant Blackstone Group. Low's Jynwel Capital had invested alongside Mubadala, the Abu Dhabi fund run by Khaldoon Al Mubarak. His share, just over $100 million, was by far his most legitimate-looking deal to date. Low had set up Jynwel with his brother, Szen, and told financiers it was his "family office," investing his grandfather's billions. His partners in the EMI deal had fallen for it.

Low's share, in truth, was financed by the 1MDB bonds that Goldman had sold for the fund. To hide the origin of the money, Low used an old trick, getting his associate Fat Eric to set up an offshore shell company called Blackstone Asia Real Estate Partners. This firm was designed to look like a bonafide subsidiary of the Blackstone Group but was controlled by Fat Eric, who worked for Low. On official documents, it would appear that Fat Eric owned scores of shell companies and assets, permitting Low to keep his involvement secret.

By now Low had siphoned off more than $1 billion of the 1MDB money generated by the bonds sold by Goldman Sachs. With the help of IPIC managing director Khadem Al Qubaisi, Low had secured control of the cash, which was sitting in a shell company that looked like a subsidiary of IPIC. The money was supposedly to compensate IPIC for guaranteeing 1MDB's bonds, but it was now Low's to do with as he pleased. Looking for a way to fund his EMI stake, Low arranged for hundreds of millions of dollars to move to a Standard Chartered bank account of the look-alike Blackstone. To hide its traces, much of the money flowed through Amicorp-administered funds in Curaçao. From the money in the fake Blackstone account, Low financed Jynwel's stake in EMI, as well as paying off Al Qubaisi, Jasmine Loo, the 1MDB legal counsel, and others.

Soon after, Low became nonexecutive chairman, Asia, for EMI Music Publishing and joined the firm's advisory board. In an instant, the position at EMI gave him serious credentials in the music industry, elevating him from the status of a simple rich party boy and gambler. This was his big play. A media empire would generate profits to pay money back to 1MDB. In the first two stages of the heist, Low had simply taken about $3 billion—and spent wildly.

Now, he was aiming to build a real business, with actual profits. Low had started Red Granite in 2010, but *The Wolf of Wall Street* would put the production company on the map. The film, coupled with the EMI deal, would, Low hoped, put to rest some of the questions that dogged him regarding his business interests and the source of his wealth.

As Low arrived back on the boat with his shopping bags, the atmosphere was buzzing. Low was worried the gossip columnists, out in force around Saint-Tropez in the summer, would catch wind of what was going on.

"Noah—need to manage press carefully," he wrote to Tepperberg. "Sony boss sent me an email and know abt all the performances! Haha. I hope press doesn't know yet."

The stars began to arrive on the *Serene*. Kate Upton, the American model, made a dramatic entrance on a helicopter. Amid a shower of sparklers, Low presented her with Hermès Birkin bags worth tens of thousands of dollars. Low told friends he craved the company of beautiful women, especially models, as if they validated his importance. In an intimate setting, he remained a reserved character, often at a loss for what to say— he was not even especially charming—but he reveled in being the center of female attention.

There was a more practical element to the showmanship. As well as the stars, a number of Middle Eastern royals, including a Dubai prince, had come on board for the party. These royals had all the money in the world, but even they could not access the kind of crowd Low was able to muster—and the Malaysian understood that this was his edge. By delivering Hollywood to them, he was gaining prestige for himself with these powerful Middle Eastern figures—and, he hoped, opening the door to future deals.

Growing up on the Malaysian island of Penang, Jho Low was a smart student and a smooth talker with a keen awareness of his social status. In 1994, aged 13, Low persuaded his new friends at Chung Ling, a school in Penang, to vote him a class monitor.

Founded by British colonialists in 1786, Penang's capital, George Town, came to be dominated by Chinese immigrants, including Low's grandfather, who arrived in the 1960s from China via Thailand. Low's father, Larry, made millions through his investment in a garment company, allowing him to send Low and his siblings to private schools overseas. *Courtesy of Alex Frangos*

In 1998, Jho Low left Malaysia to study at the prestigious Harrow School in England, where he joined Newlands house. This expensive education was part of a plan by Larry Low to vault his youngest child into the realm of the world's wealthiest people. At Harrow, Jho Low's school friends included the children of Middle Eastern and Asian royal families.

At the Wharton School, Low befriended some of the richest students, many from important Middle Eastern families, who would prove useful to him later in life. With his father's money, he also began to host extravagant parties. In November 2001, Low, then a sophomore, threw a party at Shampoo, one of Philadelphia's top nightclubs, earning the nickname "Asian Great Gatsby."

You are cordially invited to a celebration in honor of:

Jho Low's Birthday

Saturday November 3, 2001 at Shampoo Nightclub
9:30pm - 2:00am. No guests will be admitted after 11:15pm

*** Complimentary premium open bar all night ***

Shuttle busses from International House (37th & Chestnut Street) will depart continuously from 9:30pm - 11:00pm. Return trips begin at 12:30am.

Each guest must present an invitation and identification at the bus and the nightclub to be admitted. Fashionable attire is a must. No jeans or sneakers.

Shampoo is located between 7th & 8th on Willow Street

As a student in London, Low got to know Riza Aziz, the stepson of Malaysian Deputy Prime Minister Najib Razak. Hailing from Malaysia's foremost political dynasty, Najib and his second wife, Rosmah Mansor (Riza's mother), were extremely powerful. After graduating from Wharton, Low deepened his ties to Najib and Rosmah, using his connections to bring Middle Eastern investment to Malaysia. *Getty Images*

Rosmah Mansor was born to a middle-class family but grew up on the grounds of a royal palace and had the taste to match. Low knew that his way to power in Malaysia ran through Rosmah, and he set about procuring jewels and other luxuries for her. *Getty Images*

In 2009 Najib became Malaysia's prime minister. Low soon persuaded him to set up a sovereign wealth fund, known as 1Malaysia Development Berhad. Najib saw 1MDB as the way to modernize Malaysia, and to further bolster the country's image with allies such as President Barack Obama. *Getty Images*

Although Low took no formal role at the 1MDB fund, he made all the major decisions, working through proxies. His most trusted allies included Casey Tang Keng Chee, 1MBD's executive director, and legal counsel Jasmine Loo Ai Swan. In the wake of allegations of fraud at the fund, Tang and Loo went on the run. *Bank Negara Malaysia*

WANTED BY
BANK NEGARA MALAYSIA

Bank Negara Malaysia is looking for the following individuals to assist investigation under the Exchange Control Act 1953.

Casey Tang Keng Chee
IC: 650207-10-6975
Address:
No. 112, Jalan S/1-89G
Taman Seri Endah,
57000 Kuala Lumpur

Jasmine Loo Ai Swan
IC: 730613-14-5160
Address:
25, Jalan Seri Beringin 2
Damansara Heights, 50480
Kuala Lumpur

Members of the public who have any information on the whereabouts of the individuals above may contact Bank Negara Malaysia at 03-26988044 ext. 8554 / 7610 or lodge a report at the nearest police station.

* No rewards offered on the information provided for the above

In October 2009, 1MDB invested $1 billion in a joint venture with PetroSaudi International, which was co-owned by Prince Turki Bin Abdullah Al Saud, a son of Saudi Arabia's king. The idea was to invest in oil exploration, but hundreds of millions of 1MDB's money instead moved to a shell company in the Seychelles controlled by Low, who made sure to pay off his co-conspirators. *Getty Images*

Patrick Mahony, a former Goldman banker who was PetroSaudi's director of investment, helped Low structure the deal with 1MDB. Fluent in French and English, Mahony had attended international school in Geneva, and was considered brash by many business associates.

Xavier Justo was tasked to run PetroSaudi's London office, but he left in April 2011 after falling out with the firm's founders over pay. After he resigned, Justo arranged to get ahold of a copy of PetroSaudi's email servers, 140 gigabytes of information, including emails between Low, Mahony, and others that painted a picture of what had transpired at the company. It was a fateful decision that later landed Justo in a Thai jail and had his new wife, Laura, battling for his release. *Xavier Justo*

Low came to rely on powerful friends such as Yousef Al Otaiba, a young adviser to the crown prince of the United Arab Emirates. Otaiba introduced Low to executives from Mubadala, a sovereign wealth fund, which invested in Malaysia and did deals with Low. In return, Low made sure that Otaiba received millions of dollars. *Getty Images*

Khadem Al Qubaisi, the managing director of the International Petroleum Investment Company, or IPIC, became a close ally of Low. Known for his love of luxury cars, Al Qubaisi agreed for IPIC to guarantee $3.5 billion in bonds that the 1MDB fund was issuing via Goldman Sachs to fund the purchase of power plants. But the guarantee was just a ruse for Low and Al Qubaisi to funnel billions more out of 1MDB. *Getty Images*

Al Qubaisi's patron in the gulf was Sheikh Mansour Bin Zayed Al Nahyan, who hailed from the UAE's ruling family and was one of the world's richest people. Better known for his ownership of Manchester City Football Club, Sheikh Mansour gave Al Qubaisi cover to run IPIC and to feather his own nest. In return, Al Qubaisi ensured the sheikh had ample funds to pay for staff, houses, cars, and boats around the world. *Getty Images*

Goldman Sachs banker Tim Leissner got to know Jho Low in 2009. In 2012 and 2013 Goldman netted nearly $600 million by selling three bonds for the 1MDB fund, and Leissner, paid millions in bonuses, later married model Kimora Lee Simmons. *Getty Images*

As far back as college, Low had been a big gambler. But after his first big haul in late 2009, he became the largest "whale" any casino manager had encountered, often spending days at the tables in Las Vegas. He thought nothing of losing millions of dollars in a hand, stunning onlookers. On one occasion, he dropped $50,000 in chips on the floor, only recovering them when a friend pointed it out.

Tired of leasing planes, Low spent $35 million of the money he took from 1MDB to purchase a Bombardier Global 5000 private jet. He lived on the jet, which was outfitted with a bed and mini-office, more than the many homes he acquired. In a typical three-week period, Low would crisscross the globe, from Malaysia to Abu Dhabi, Zurich, London, New York, and Vegas, before starting over again.

Most of Low's partying, in casinos and nightclubs, took place behind closed doors. But as he accrued wealth and status, he made an effort to ingratiate himself with New York society. In October 2014, he was honored at a charity gala on Wall Street, congratulated here by model Gigi Hadid. *Getty Images*

One night, after recording a track at Jungle Studios in Manhattan, Low relaxed with Swizz Beatz, a friend and hip-hop producer. Low recently had acquired his stake in the music label EMI, and when one of the label's artists, Busta Rhymes, walked into the studio, Low called out to Busta, "I own you. You're my bitch!"

In early 2013, with elections approaching in Malaysia, Low drove Busta Rhymes around his home state of Penang, where the rapper performed a concert financed by Low. *Ooi Keng Eng*

At Wharton, Low had fantasized about Paris Hilton, the reality star and model, and by 2010 he had befriended her. Gossip columns speculated this mysterious Asian was Hilton's new boyfriend. In fact, he paid her hundreds of thousands of dollars in appearance fees to attend his events. *GoffPhotos.com*

With 1MDB money, Low financed Red Granite Pictures, a production company founded by Riza Aziz (right), the stepson of Prime Minister Najib, and Joey McFarland (left), a former talent booker. Almost overnight McFarland became a top Hollywood producer. Even Swizz Beatz (center) got his first acting role, a bit part in Red Granite's *Dumb and Dumber To.*

Red Granite's coup was buying the rights to *The Wolf of Wall Street*, which released in December 2013. Low spent three years courting its star, Leonardo DiCaprio, inviting him to parties and presenting him with lavish gifts. For DiCaprio, Red Granite offered independence from the big studios. *Getty Images*

Low had a girlfriend back in Malaysia, but he also wooed Australian supermodel Miranda Kerr. Low met Kerr at a Korean restaurant in New York in early 2014. The Malaysian lavished her with millions of dollars in jewelry and they vacationed together on Low's yacht in the Mediterranean. *Getty Images*

Low bought this townhouse in London's exclusive Belgravia neighborhood, then transferred ownership to Riza Aziz. The home, costing 17 million pounds, served as a pied-à-terre for Prime Minister Najib and his wife, Rosmah Mansor, on their many trips to London. *Tom Wright*

In June 2011, Low paid $30.5 million for a penthouse in New York's Time Warner Center. The 4,825-square-foot unit, with three bedrooms, a library, and a hanging fish tank, offered panoramic views of Central Park. Low made the apartment his base in New York. *Getty Images*

In 2013 Low began to collect art. To celebrate Najib's election victory, Low bought *Dustheads*, a 1982 masterpiece by Jean-Michel Basquiat. He paid $48.8 million for the work, a record for the artist, in a heated bidding war at Christie's in New York. In all he amassed art worth more than $300 million, including priceless works by Monet and van Gogh. *Getty Images*

In spring 2014, Low took delivery of the *Equanimity*, a $250 million yacht that could accommodate twenty-six guests. With its Asian-inspired interior constructed out of wood, bamboo, marble, and gold leaf, the boat helped Low stand out from the merely wealthy. As his scheme began to implode, Low used the yacht as a bolt hole. *Associated Press*

Ho Kay Tat, publisher of the *Edge*, a Malaysian weekly, drove the early coverage of the 1MDB scandal. In 2015, the *Edge*, along with the *Sarawak Report*, got ahold of PetroSaudi documents from Xavier Justo and published a series of damning stories. Prime Minister Najib suspended the *Edge*'s publication license and had Ho detained for a night in July 2015. Here Ho greets journalists after his release. *The Malaysian Insider*

In June 2015, Thai police arrested Xavier Justo on charges of attempting to black-mail PetroSaudi. One of his first visitors in a Bangkok jail was a former British policeman called Paul Finnigan, who was working with PetroSaudi. Finnigan promised to get Justo out by December if he pleaded guilty, according to a later criminal complaint. Justo did as he was told, but in August a Thai judge sentenced him to three years in prison. *Royal Thai Police*

Prime Minister Najib's kleptocratic regime sparked protests from ordinary Malaysians. A group known as Bersih, the Malay word for "clean," organized large demonstrations in 2015 and 2016 calling for Najib to step down over the 1MDB scandal. Here, protesters hold up caricatures (from left to right) of Riza Aziz, Rosmah Mansor, Najib, and Low. *Getty Images*

In July 2016, U.S. Attorney General Loretta Lynch announced the Justice Department was moving forward with a civil lawsuit, seeking to seize $1 billion in assets bought with money stolen from 1MDB. The assets included Low's Time Warner Center apartment, the proceeds from *The Wolf of Wall Street*, as well as multiple other homes, his stake in EMI Music Publishing, and more. The lawsuit referred to Najib as "Malaysian Official 1." *U.S. Department of Justice*

Punctuated by Kanye West's performance, the party raged until deep into the morning. The rap star was there with Kim Kardashian, his girlfriend, whose every move was noted by the press corps. Some gossip columnists did get wind of the party, focusing on the presence of West and Kardashian, as well as that of Chris Brown and Rihanna, who spent hours in conversation that evening despite his physical abuse of her three years earlier. Some newspapers even wrongly reported that Brown had rented the *Serene*. Low stayed out of the press. He could no longer afford the scrutiny of his dealings that press coverage would entail. No matter: Everything about the party was meant to indicate that Low had arrived. He could be content with the secret life of a powerful billionaire.

As the party ratcheted down, most of the revelers left the boat, but a couple of dozen, including Low, his brother, Szen, DiCaprio, the nightclub owners, and the "bottle girls," stayed on. At 6 a.m., as the party finally fizzled, the superyacht pulled anchor and began to sail toward Portofino, the holiday destination on the Italian Riviera.

While he was paying for their services, Low had always been polite with movie and music stars, but now the power balance began to shift. In April 2013, less than a year after the EMI deal, Low was hanging out in Jungle City Studios, in Manhattan's Chelsea neighborhood, a place where Jay-Z, Rihanna, Nicki Minaj, and countless other stars had cut tracks. Low was there to record his own song for fun, his version of the soulful ballad "Void of a Legend."

The song had been written by Antoniette Costa, a singer who recently had begun to date Joey McFarland. Low loved singing but had a tuneless, high-pitched voice, and it took eight hours, and judicious use of Auto-Tune, for Costa, working with a studio producer, to get an acceptable version in the can.

As Low sang, friends, including McFarland and Swizz Beatz, came in and out of the recording booth. It was well into the evening when Busta Rhymes and Pharrell Williams, longtime clients of Jungle City, dropped by the studio where Low was now relaxing, a little inebriated.

"Yo!" Low called out to Busta Rhymes, ecstatic to see him. "I own you. You're my bitch!"

The comment, meant to be taken lightly—a playful reference to Low's EMI purchase—went over like a lead balloon. Busta Rhymes, a thickset rapper, actor, and record producer, looked put out but stifled any remark, while Pharrell tried to cover up the embarrassment with small talk. Low was trying to act like a mogul, but he was awkward, an imposter who for all his money didn't quite fit the bill.

Chapter 28

All the Wealth in the World

New York, August 2012

On a Saturday in late August, Joey McFarland was sitting in his producer's chair in Manhattan's financial district. The neighborhood, quiet on a Saturday, had been taken over by the production of *The Wolf of Wall Street*. Martin Scorsese was directing a scene with Leonardo DiCaprio, as Jordan Belfort, and Cristin Milioti, playing the role of Belfort's first wife. Sitting a block from the actual Wall Street, it was hard for McFarland to fathom how he got there. Less than three years after meeting Low in Whistler, and with basically zero film experience, here he was producing a movie with the biggest director and actor on the planet.

Of all the people swept into his orbit, Jho Low helped change McFarland's situation more than anyone's. At forty years old, McFarland had gone from a minor talent booker to a top-flight film producer. McFarland and his Red Granite partner Riza Aziz, the stepson of Malaysian Prime Minister Najib Razak, had not undertaken any apprenticeship in filmmaking—and had released only one film, *Friends with Kids*—but they were now rubbing shoulders with professionals who had served for decades in the industry. For Scorsese and DiCaprio, these interlopers were a godsend; not only did they control seemingly limitless cash, but they also permitted the pair boundless artistic freedom. When

Scorsese wanted to crash a real white Lamborghini in the opening scenes of the movie—an event from Jordan Belfort's life—he
was able to get Red Granite to foot the bill, even though most producers would have insisted on a replica for such purposes. As the
money men, McFarland and Aziz's presence on set was tolerated.

Back in Los Angeles, McFarland lived in a one-bedroom
place in West Hollywood. Embarrassed by such a modest abode,
he avoided inviting his movie star friends over. Now McFarland
was residing in the Time Warner penthouse in New York with
Jho Low. Moreover, McFarland had established himself as one
of the Malaysian's closest friends. The pair became inseparable,
traveling to the spa together, to Las Vegas to gamble, and on ski
trips in the United States and Europe.

McFarland began to rewrite his life story, airbrushing out
his talent-booking past. Hung up about his lack of experience,
McFarland told interviewers that he'd been in and out of the
film world for years and, prior to that, had worked in private
equity. He made no mention of the gyros restaurant in Cincinnati. Film-industry professionals, including those working for
Red Granite, considered him a parvenu.

Despite his humble origins, McFarland had become the face
of Red Granite. Riza was shy, and was not in the office much,
preferring to play or watch tennis, while the American enjoyed
the limelight. Low stayed off the set, worried about attracting
press coverage. After earlier telling Red Granite employees that
Low was the financier, McFarland now took to saying the money
came from the Middle East.

Low had taken pains to ensure this fiction might stand up to
some scrutiny. Red Granite Capital, a company owned by Riza Aziz,
had received more than $200 million from the bonds arranged by
Goldman. This money had initially moved into a shell company
controlled by Al Qubaisi of IPIC and his employee, Mohamed Al
Husseiny. As filming began, Al Husseiny began to hang around

the Red Granite offices and attend screenings, as if he represented the money behind the production. The cash received by Red Granite Capital went to finance *The Wolf of Wall Street*, as well as to pay for Riza's acquisition of properties in Los Angeles, New York, and London from Low—the bulk of the homes Low had acquired two years earlier. In public, the Red Granite executives were coy about financing. McFarland refused to tell a reporter from the *Hollywood Reporter* about funding, while Riza vaguely explained that money came from investors in the Middle East and Asia.

Although he kept his name out of the press and avoided the set, Low continued to deepen his relationship with DiCaprio as filming progressed. At one point during production, the Malaysian spent more than a week at the Venetian in Las Vegas, accompanied at times by DiCaprio, Riza, and McFarland. He told friends he liked the quietness of the gambling floor, where cell phones are prohibited, as it allowed him to escape. The paid-for gambling excursions also helped reel in the actor.

The Red Granite executives were hoping for a long-running collaboration. In the fall of 2012, McFarland had dinner at Le Bernardin, a top French restaurant in Manhattan, with DiCaprio and South Korean director Park Chan-wook to discuss another possible film project. Low, Riza, and McFarland also began to mimic aspects of DiCaprio's lifestyle. An avid collector of movie posters, the actor introduced Riza to Ralph DeLuca, a New Jersey–based dealer in film memorabilia, and the Red Granite principals began to use money taken from the 1MDB funds to acquire millions of dollars in collectibles from him. In October 2012, Riza paid DeLuca the huge sum of $1.2 million for an original film poster for Fritz Lang's 1927 silent film *Metropolis*, which he hung in his private office at Red Granite.

McFarland wanted to go one better. "What is the greatest poster in [the] world that is obtainable?" McFarland asked DeLuca in an email. Over the next eighteen months, McFarland and Aziz would arrange to buy more than seventy items from DeLuca at a cost of over $4 million, plastering the walls of the Red Granite offices and Riza's Park Laurel condominium in New York with posters. McFarland sent DeLuca and Riza lists of posters he wanted to collect.

"I have decided—I have to own these. Its [*sic*] a must. Not to mention a 1000 others... Can't sleep—obsessing," he wrote.

"Hahaha now you feel my pain!! Mwahahahaha—$$$$," Riza replied.

"I'm obsessing over posters... we are such neurotic obsessive creatures...WE HAVE TO OWN THEM ALL," McFarland retorted.

As DiCaprio got closer to Low and McFarland, the friends even went to view mansions together. On September 20, 2012, the actor forwarded a confidentiality agreement from his broker at Sotheby's to McFarland. The agreement gave the signer the right to view a property situated on 658 Nimes Road in Bel-Air that was on the market for a staggering $150 million. The owner was a Saudi sheikh. Not wanting the publicity, Low used McFarland as a front, and the American signed as the prospective buyer.

Low and McFarland toured the property, one of the most expensive in the United States, comprising multiple houses clustered around a central driveway on 40,000 square feet of land, with more than twenty-eight bedrooms and more than thirty bathrooms, in addition to an infinity pool with views over Los Angeles, a gym, a spa, and a cinema.

Despite almost three years of incessant acquisitions, Low was not sated. He'd offloaded his Hollywood mansion to Riza Aziz and now was looking for a palace fit for a billionaire. Like William Randolph Hearst, whose castle at San Simeon in California remains a symbol of the excess of the early twentieth century, Low yearned for the most opulent property conceivable.

In the end, Low did not make the acquisition. He bid $80 million for the property, but the Saudi sheikh rejected the offer.

There were some things—although not many—that even Low could not afford.

On November 17, 2012, Low and Riza entered the Monkey Bar in the Hotel Elysée in Midtown Manhattan, an establishment with red-leather sofas and booths that created an old-vibe Hollywood feel. The place, owned by *Vanity Fair* editor Graydon Carter, was popular with Midtown lawyers and bankers, as well as movie and media types. As glasses of champagne were handed around, the Red Granite principals mingled with Hollywood A-listers, from DiCaprio and Daniel Day Lewis to Harvey Keitel and Steven Spielberg.

The guests had assembled for Martin Scorsese, who was turning seventy. He was deep in the filming of *The Wolf of Wall Street*, which had been pushed off schedule by Hurricane Sandy in late October. He'd been told only a few close friends were attending his birthday celebration, but there were some 120 people in the bar, which had been rented out for the evening. The celebration included a montage of blooper clips from Scorsese movies, a four-course meal, and a champagne toast to the director.

As a birthday gift, Low had sent Scorsese a Polish-language version of the movie poster for *Cabaret*. In an old-fashioned typewritten note, Scorsese later thanked Low "for the amazing gifts!" The "very rare" Polish-language poster "made my 70th all the more special."

This period was the high-water mark of Low's influence in Hollywood. Only two weeks earlier, Low had hosted his own birthday party, the circus-themed extravaganza that would go down in Las Vegas lore as the most expensive private party ever held (the details of which opened this book). The evening featured an indoor Ferris wheel, circus performers, and a who's who of Hollywood—not to mention Britney Spears emerging from a fake birthday cake. All of Low's contacts attended, not just the stars like DiCaprio, but also Tim Leissner, Al Husseiny, and other Low business associates. Almost everyone who had played a role in facilitating Low's triumph was on hand to celebrate with him. Low arranged for every aspect of the event to be paid from the 1MDB bonds, and the amounts were staggering. For an evening's work, Swizz Beatz, Low's producer friend and husband of Alicia Keys, received $800,000 from a shell company funded from the stolen money.

This was peak Jho Low. The filming of *The Wolf of Wall Street* was nearly over, he was at the height of his powers, and the celebrations were so frequent they practically blurred together. A few days after the Vegas party, Low, Aziz, and McFarland presented DiCaprio with an unforgettable present for his thirty-eighth birthday on November 11. There was buzz around *The Wolf of Wall Street*—DiCaprio had been delivering some elec-trifying scenes, and photos were leaking online. The producers talked about the possibility of him finally winning an Oscar.

As a gift, they managed to secure Marlon Brando's best actor statuette from the 1954 film *On the Waterfront*—a nod to DiCaprio that he was overdue for one himself. Years ear-lier, the statuette had gone missing from Brando's Hollywood home, and despite an Academy bylaw that prohibits the sale of Oscars, it had ended up with DeLuca, who charged $600,000 for it. DiCaprio was intrigued by Brando, whose progressive politics led him to reject another Oscar in 1973 in protest at the depiction of Native Americans in film. DiCaprio, too, had become politi-cally outspoken, campaigning for the land rights of indigenous people in North America over corporate interests, and drawing attention to how climate change was endangering their way of life.

Over Christmas that year, McFarland had a hamper of cav-iar from Petrossian, a favorite of Scorsese's, sent to the director and his wife's town house on the Upper East Side of Manhattan, and he spent $2,245 of company money on a bottle of Cristal Rose champagne for Scorsese at the *Wolf of Wall Street* wrap party held at Marquee, the New York nightclub owned by Tepperberg and

Strauss of the Strategic Group. Despite the producer's lavish gift, when Scorcese passed McFarland in the lobby of the Time Warner building, the director didn't seem to recognize him. As he did for all his films, Scorsese sent key chains to everyone as his wrap gift.

Whatever the men's personal dynamic, even before filming was finished, Riza and McFarland were attending readings with Scorsese for *The Irishman*, a film project involving Robert De Niro that was next on the director's slate, and Red Granite was attempting to line up DiCaprio to headline a remake of *Papillon*, the 1970s Steve McQueen hit movie.

Still, after this season of celebration, as filming wrapped up toward the end of December, Low and DiCaprio hadn't had their fill of partying. The Malaysian had one more treat for the cast and other friends.

A Boeing 747-400 can hold around six hundred passengers, but the VIP-configured model Low had chartered, with plush reclining seats, was a more spacious alternative for the forty or so people who boarded in Los Angeles at the end of December. Atlas Air rented these kinds of planes to professional sports teams or Saudi princes. The cost of chartering such an aircraft was in the tens of thousands of dollars—*per hour*. The guests included Jamie Foxx, Kevin Connolly, Jonah Hill, Leonardo DiCaprio, and a handful of models. On the plane, Low and McFarland were as inseparable as ever.

The group was heading to Sydney, Australia, where they spent a couple of days partying on yachts, gambling, and eating. On one yacht, DiCaprio, a black baseball cap turned backward, took a shot at DJing, while Foxx, dressed in a buttoned-up white shirt and black jacket, danced. Beautiful women in short black dresses milled around the dance floor. One rich Thai friend of Low's, Chavayos Rattakul, posted a picture on his Instagram of gambling chips on the floor of the Star, a casino overlooking Sydney's Darling harbor. "A good way to waste a million dollar," he wrote in the caption. In the casino complex a Marquee nightclub recently had opened, owned by Tepperberg and Strauss. For the group's New Year's Eve celebration in the club, Low had ordered ice baths to be filled with scores of bottles of Cristal champagne. "Showtime!!!!!!!!!!!!" Swizz Beatz wrote on Instagram.

After the stroke of midnight, the group got back on the Boeing 747-400 for a fifteen-hour flight to Las Vegas. After crossing the international dateline and being picked up by stretch limousines, the partygoers made for LAVO, a nightclub also co-owned by Tepperberg and Strauss—ready for yet another New Year's countdown. Perhaps in an effort to sustain the group for a few more hours of partying, Low ordered buckets of KFC chicken. Dressed in a red shirt with black pants and sports sneakers, Low at one point took a swig of champagne directly from the bottle. Someone put on a fake panda head. As midnight approached for the second time that day, models danced on the bar, holding champagne bottles lit with sparklers.

The KFC was popular, but nobody really drank the champagne, preferring to spray it around the room, as if they had finally had their fill after years. "Only JL can manage this for double countdowns 2013," Chavayos boasted.

Jamie Foxx, who by now had known Low for three years, was no stranger to outrageous parties. He'd been there for Low's birthday in Las Vegas only two months earlier. But even he was excited by the self-gratification of the past few days. He told British talk show host Jonathan Ross about the party, but like almost everyone who knew Low well, he kept the Malaysian's name out of the story, sensing he didn't need the publicity.

"I got a friend, you know he got some money, and he flew me, Leonardo DiCaprio, Jonah Hill and some other cats, and we flew to Australia right. And we did the countdown in Australia, then jumped back on a plane and then did the countdown in Vegas. That's crazy! That was nuts!"

Chapter 29

Mystique of the Orient

Singapore, November 2012

Low's focus on partying might have made him appear carefree, but his attitude belied turmoil behind the scenes. Just days after his birthday extravaganza in Las Vegas, Jho Low faced a road-block. He was trying to send $110 million from his BSI account in Singapore to a trust he controlled at another bank, Roths-child in Zurich, to finance the purchase of a mansion on Ori-ole Drive in the Bird Streets area of the Hollywood Hills. After the Saudi sheikh rejected Low's offer for the Nimes property, Low had agreed to pay $39 million for a Mexican-style home, double the previous record for a house in the Hollywood Hills, a trendy enclave near Red Granite's Sunset Strip offices and close to DiCaprio's place. Low planned to spend millions more to tear down the older home and construct a white-themed modernis-tic mansion, with eighteen thousand square feet of living space, two swimming pools, and a go-cart track in the basement.

But compliance executives at the Swiss bank BSI—finally—were causing problems. Ahead of the intended transfer, Low's BSI account had received the money from Good Star, his Seychelles company, before he sent it to his father, Larry, who then routed it back to Low, all within the same day. As with his purchase of the Time Warner penthouse, the purpose of these circuitous transactions was to make Rothschild bankers believe Low had received the money from his father. By then putting it into a trust at Rothschild, Low was attempting to make it appear as if the Bird Streets mansion was part of the Low family's estate, held in trust for future generations. He did the same with many assets.

BSI's compliance department could see behind the scenes. In an email, a banker charged with rooting out fraud at BSI wrote to Yak Yew Chee and other senior managers that the frenetic movement of cash—from Good Star, to Low, to his father, and back to Low—was "nebulous to say the least and not acceptable in Compliance's view." The family wealth story was facing some scrutiny.

Low was determined to find a way around the compliance officers, whose concerns had been relayed to him by Yak. In the predawn hours of the night, he began to type furiously. In an email to BSI management, Low explained that the money he wanted to transfer to Switzerland originally had been a gift he sent to his father. The money, Low explained, was a mark of respect to his elders—a cornerstone of Confucianism. "When good wealth creation is generated, as a matter of cultural respect and good fortune that arises from respect, we always give our parents the proceeds. This is part of our custom and culture." In the email, Low explained that, per custom, it was up to the elders in question to decide what to do with the gift.

"In this case, my father receives it as a token of gesture, respect and appreciation and decides to give it back to me for me to then subsequently provide a portion for the benefit of my family trust."

He then chided the Swiss bankers for their cultural naïveté: "I hope this clarifies as this is culturally sensitive and it would be taboo and bad luck otherwise and our family is very particular about respect of the elderly and being appreciative to family."

This bastardized picture of Chinese culture in no way adequately explained the need for such shady transfers. But Low had another card to play—he knew BSI had become dependent on his business and, faced with the prospect of losing it, would go to lengths to keep the money flowing. "I hope I do not need to keep explaining the same matter over and over again as our time is better spent generating wealth so that the AUM [Assets Under Management] in BSI Bank can be increased as opposed to providing answers for questions which have already been provided for previously. I fully understand and respect the requirement of compliance, but one should not be over burdening your customers [especially] when they have been addressed in the past." At 2:10 a.m. on November 7, Low clicked send, firing off the email to a number of top BSI managers in Singapore.

Ordinary folk often get questioned by their banks for small transfers of money. But billionaires are not ordinary. By this point, Low already was by far the biggest client that BSI had anywhere in the world, and he was making a lot of people in the bank richer than they ever could have hoped. He was referred to as "Big Boss" in the bank's Singapore offices, and senior BSI executives would join him for parties in Las Vegas and on yachts. The bank's senior executives would do all they could to keep Low's business.

Within days of Low's email, BSI's top executives approved the $110 million transfer. "Intra family transfers are not always going to be logical," a senior BSI banker wrote in response to the compliance officer's concerns.

Days later, though, bankers at Rothschild, where the money ended up, wanted more details about the origins of so much cash. Low realized they would not be as easy to fool as BSI, and so, on November 20, he wrote Yak requesting he send a letter to a senior Rothschild banker vouching for the source of funds. Low himself drew up the letter, which stressed BSI had known the Low family for years and had "extensive compliance procedures." The contents made it appear the money came from Larry Low, even though the original source of funds was Good Star and 1MDB.

By this time, Yak was entirely in Low's pocket. He had begun to let other clients drop, and spent 90 percent of his time on Low's account, following him around the world on private jets and attending his yacht parties. As Yak seemingly became addicted to the money and jet-set lifestyle, Low was able to get him to do almost anything he asked. Alarmed, a female subordinate of Yak's advised him to ensure proper compliance procedures were met.

"If you guys are so scared, then don't be private bankers. Private bankers must take some risks. If not, go back and breastfeed your children," he retorted angrily.

Yak secretly signed and sent the letter to Rothschild on BSI's official letterhead, without getting approval from his managers and legal department, as dictated by the bank's compliance procedures. The letter assuaged any concerns Rothschild's bankers had harbored. Low, it appeared, was succeeding in blotting out the past and, with Yak's help, embellishing the story that he had grown up with billions. But Yak had stepped over the gray line that in private banking divides the merely unseemly from the illegal. It was a misstep for which Yak would pay, and a sign of the risks Low was running.

As the fear of detection consumed him, Low's attempts at subterfuge could appear almost comical. He set up a Gmail account under the name of Eric Tan, his associate known as "Fat Eric," and began to use it, trying to hide his involvement in deals. When he wanted to open an account with the Aabar-controlled Falcon Bank, Low used the "Eric Tan" Gmail to set up an appointment with a Swiss banker in Kuala Lumpur. The banker, the head of Falcon's Singapore office, flew to Kuala Lumpur to meet Tan, but was picked up at night from the lobby of his hotel by Low. The Malaysian took the banker to a residence, where he revealed his true identity, but asked him to continue to refer to him as Eric Tan in public and email exchanges. Low began to use the "Eric Tan" Gmail address for most correspondence, and many of the shell companies and bank accounts from this point on—like Blackstone—would be opened by the real Eric Tan, who hung around mainly for the partying and the payoffs, likely unaware of the risks he was taking on Low's behalf.

What was Low thinking? Like Yak, he seemed to have crossed another line. Beyond shady transfers and misrepresentation of business deals, he had now taken to conducting business behind a false name and even misrepresenting his identity in person. Low's behavior might seem like evidence of desperation, but he had proven himself a survivor. He'd overcome the early challenges to his scheme from 1MDB board members, and the fighting with PetroSaudi, as well as questions from auditors and the media attention on his partying. He was acquiring companies, financing films, and building on the image of a successful businessman. But there was never any rest; just getting the money moving was a constant battle. And now he had another debt to pay: He had to get Najib reelected.

Chapter 30

"681 American Pies" (The Third Heist)

Penang, Malaysia, April 2013

On a sweltering day in George Town, the capital of Penang, an island off the northwest coast of Malaysia, onlookers in the historic district would have been treated to a curious sight. Back home to help campaign for Malaysia's upcoming national elections, Jho Low was building up a sweat peddling Busta Rhymes around in a rickshaw. In another rickshaw, a friend was taking care of Swizz Beatz. Dressed in baggy cargo pants and desert boots, with a gold chain, Busta Rhymes took in the attractions of Low's hometown, including the Edwardian Baroque arcades of the early twentieth-century City Hall, before heading to a local canteen with his entourage for a lunch of Penang *kway teow* noodles and sodas—the kind of down-to-earth food Low liked. By the time he got to lunch, the Malaysian was tired and his blue "1Malaysia" polo shirt was covered in sweat patches.

The next day, Busta Rhymes performed in concert, alongside Swizz Beatz and Redfoo of the music duo LMFAO, at a local Chinese-language school. The crowd of eighty thousand people, all wearing free 1MALAYSIA T-shirts, had gotten the tickets to the show for a nominal donation. Low had organized and financed the concert, occuring just two weeks before Malaysia's general election. It wasn't a coincidence. The "1Malaysia" concept was Prime Minister Najib's banner initiative meant to attract Malaysians of all ethnicities.

"There were no political speeches," Low lamely told a television interview. "There was obviously the push by both the organizers and some of the entertainers, of course, for unity, peace, and prosperity."

These were the last-gasp efforts by Low to swing the elections in Penang, a state which had turned to the opposition in the previous polls and was a prime focus of Najib's campaigning. To win back the state would be the ultimate coup for the prime minister. Low made arrangements for local restaurants, festooned in 1MALAYSIA banners, to hand out free food for weeks. The 1Malaysia Penang Welfare Club, set up by Low, paid for South Korean pop star Psy, whose song "Gangnam Style" was a surprise global hit, to give another concert. The club also took over a ballroom and gave out checks for hundreds of thousands of dollars each to local charities. The 1MDB fund, meanwhile, spent $400 million buying up land in Penang, and vowed to build ten thousand affordable homes.

But despite the huge expenditures, Najib remained stubbornly unpopular in Penang. At the Psy concert, the prime minister went on stage as a warm-up, asking the concertgoers whether they were ready for the South Korean singer.

"Yes," they screamed back. Then he asked whether the crowd was ready for his coalition to take back power in the state.

"No," they roared.

Low's gambit had backfired.

Najib was panicking, and he was making a fool of himself. Anwar Ibrahim, the former deputy prime minister who had just been released from jail after serving several years in prison for sodomy, was on the rise. A gifted speaker, Anwar was leading a coalition of opposition parties, and polls showed he might win the election on May 5. Najib was desperate not to go down in the history books as the first UMNO leader to be cast from office, so he turned to Low for money.

For over three years, Najib and his wife, Rosmah, gave Low cover to run 1MDB, without asking questions. His wife enjoyed her jewelry and mansions, and his stepson had become a movie mogul. Now Najib needed his own gusher of cash to avoid catastrophe. Low knew he had to deliver money to Najib, but the problem was that much of it was tied up in other endeavors. On top of that, Anwar in February had published his election manifesto. One campaign pledge was particularly distressing to Low. The opposition leader wanted to know the purpose of 1MDB, which had little to show for $7 billion in debt. If elected, Anwar promised, he would close down the fund.

To ensure that didn't happen, Low set about raising even more money. Once more, he relied on Goldman Sachs.

The World Economic Forum, held each year in the Swiss ski village of Davos, is a microcosm of elite networks that span the globe, attracting world leaders, Wall Street titans, and chief executives of Fortune 500 companies. The events, in which panels of experts debate high-minded topics like radical Islam or the "democratic deficit" in front of audiences, is only the public face of Davos. In rooms open only to the chosen few with special white VIP passes—the highest in a color-graded hierarchy—the real dealmaking occurs.

In late January, Michael Evans, a Goldman vice chairman in New York overseeing "growth markets," had an important person to see on the sidelines of Davos: the prime minister of Malaysia. Evans's audience was with Prime Minister Najib, brokered by Tim Leissner—just the kind of meeting between a Wall Street banker and a world leader that was typical at the event in the Swiss Alps. In public appearances at Davos, Najib was in his element, deepening the impression of Malaysia as a beacon of democracy in the Islamic world, and himself as an urbane technocrat.

"We have to take care of the young people, we have to give them jobs," he told Fareed Zakaria of CNN during an interview on the sidelines of Davos.

But here, with Evans and Leissner, Najib had a strikingly different agenda. After pleasantries with the two bankers, Najib brought up the role Goldman had played selling bonds for 1MDB in 2012, and asked if the bank was willing to do so again, getting the money to the fund quickly and quietly, just like before. Goldman's top management, advised by Leissner, had been expecting more 1MDB business. But Najib's demand, less than three months since the fund last tapped the market for almost $1.75 billion, was almost too good to be true.

The prime minister said the fund wanted to raise a further $3 billion. Such a staggering sum would mean another major payday for Goldman.

To explain the need for speed, Najib said he had an opportunity to partner with Aabar, the Abu Dhabi fund, to build a new financial center in Kuala Lumpur, to be named the Tun Razak Exchange, after his father. The hope, he said, was to make Kuala Lumpur one of the foremost banking centers in Asia. The Abu Dhabi fund was to put in another $3 billion, the prime minister went on.

Of course, Goldman would be more than willing to help out, Evans replied. Normally, Wall Street banks send in bankers armed with proposals—documents laying out structuring, yields, potential investors—but here Goldman appeared to have won the mandate through a casual conversation. When David Ryan, the bank's Asia president, heard about this, he was suspicious. But again, Gary Cohn and Mark Schwartz, the new Asia chairman above Ryan, were supportive. The wheels of Project Catalyze were set in motion.

In March, Goldman was ready to buy the entire $3 billion bond from 1MDB, but there was a hiccup. The fund wanted to deposit the money in a Swiss bank account at BSI. Goldman's lawyer on the deal, a Singapore-based employee of Linklaters named Kevin Wong, pointed out in an email that it was unusual to use such a small private bank for a $3 billion deposit.

In the end, Goldman shrugged off Wong's concerns. It wasn't as though BSI was on any blacklist for money laundering. In a presentation for 1MDB and Aabar, Goldman set forth what it understood its client's key objectives to be in the deal making. They included "maintenance of confidentiality during execution" and "speed." In other words, this was to be a fast and secret deal—although no one at 1MDB ever bothered to explain why these conditions were necessary. Indeed, Goldman's prospectus for the bond even stressed to would-be investors that the 1MDB-Aabar joint venture company didn't even yet have a well-defined business plan.

By now, Goldman had established a track record for this kind of transaction, and on March 19, the Hong Kong PFI desk, as with the earlier two issuances, bought the $3 billion bond in its entirety. This time, Prime Minister Najib, who also headed the Finance Ministry, signed a letter of support for the bond, meaning Malaysia's government promised to repay the debt in the event of a default. For the firm's work, Goldman made just short of $300 million in profits. In total, over just twelve months, the bank had earned nearly $600 million from selling three bonds for the 1MDB fund—two hundred times the typical fee. This amount of profit was too implausible to go unnoticed.

As Goldman was finalizing the bond in March 2013, Jho Low sent a BlackBerry message to Joanna Yu, an employee at

AmBank in Kuala Lumpur, warning her that "681 American pies" would soon be arriving from overseas into an account known as "AMPRIVATE BANKING—MR." The account, beneficially owned by Najib Razak, was a secret whose existence was known only to Low and a few key executives in AmBank, a Malaysian bank. Low ordered Yu to inform her colleagues that "PM" did not want his name, address, or identity card number to appear on the transaction. Low knew his actions at this juncture, so close to elections, involved a heightened level of risk.

Access to the account "shld be restricted n tracked so if someone took pic n access the a/c we will know," Low wrote.

The worst outcome, he added, was Malaysia's opposition getting hold of this information and leaking it. To hide the impact of a transaction this large, Low and Yu discussed ways to break it up into tranches so as to lessen the impact on the ringgit, Malaysia's currency.

Only days later, Goldman deposited the proceeds from the $3 billion bond with BSI, and $1.2 billion immediately was purloined, moving through the Curaçao funds into a British Virgin Islands company. The shell firm, Tanore Finance Corporation, was controlled by Fat Eric. Then, in two separate transfers, $681 million moved from Tanore to the prime minister's secret account. The correspondent bank for both wires was Wells Fargo, which Low used, along with J.P. Morgan, for most of his large transactions involving U.S. dollars. Seemingly unperturbed by the lack of a beneficial owner's name on such a large transfer—a glaring red flag—Wells Fargo let it through, just a tiny drop in the pool of trillions of dollars that U.S. correspondent banks process every day.

Low had set up the AmBank account for Najib in 2011 with the help of Cheah Tek Kuang, the bank's chief executive. Low had gotten to know Cheah, who was in his sixties, after he returned from Wharton, almost a decade earlier. He had borrowed from AmBank to finance Wynton's early deals. When Low explained the need to set up a secret account for Najib, Cheah had been willing to oblige, drawn in by Low's promises of business opportunities, including a chance to advise on 1MDB's plans to IPO its power assets.

The following year, Low had arranged for $170 million from the Goldman-prepared power-plant bonds to fill Najib's account. To avoid questions, Cheah and Low had seen to it the account was marked as one used for internal bank transfers, meaning it would not be visible to compliance staff. The Australian and New Zealand Banking Group, known as ANZ, owned a minority stake in AmBank, giving it the right to appoint executives and board members. But ANZ's management had no idea about this secret account's existence. Joanna Yu, a middle-level AmBank executive, was tasked with taking instructions from Low about incoming wires and outgoing checks. Najib had used most of the initial infusion to pay off crony politicians, as well as on jewelry and a $56,000 expense at Signature Exotic Cars, a high-end car dealership in Kuala Lumpur. Now, with the elections approaching, the account was about to become a lot more active.

With such a large movement of cash, Low wanted a "friendly" bank on both sides of the transfer. To be safe, Tanore Finance opened an account with Swiss-based Falcon Bank, which was owned by Aabar and controlled by Al Husseiny, Low's associate. He also drew up fake loan agreements that purported to show the $681 million was a loan from Tanore to the "AMPRIVATE BANKING—MR" account, which the loan documents falsely made out to be owned by a company under the Finance Ministry, not the prime minister. But Low's risky maneuvers and slapdash creation of supporting documentation were getting difficult for even the most pliable banker to permit.

At Falcon's headquarters in Zurich, Eduardo Leemann, the bank's chief executive, couldn't believe the amateurishness of the loan documents. Although Low was trying to be careful, he was also rushing, and he found it hard to stay on top of all his varied schemes. On March 25, the day of the second wire transfer, Leemann patched Al Husseiny into a conference call to discuss the worrying transaction.

In his fifties, Leemann was a Swiss national and former head of Goldman Sachs's private-banking business. He had joined Falcon in the 1990s when it was still called AIG Private Bank. Leemann was no stranger to huge flows of dubious money, but what Low was trying to do risked landing him in trouble, and he was scared.

"Mohamed, the rest of the documentation, which our friend in Malaysia has delivered is absolutely ridiculous, between you and me... This is... gonna get everybody in trouble," Leemann said, his voice shaking with emotion. "This is done not professionally, unprepared, amateurish at best. The documentation they're sending me is a joke, between you and me, Mohamed, it's a joke! This is something, how can you send hundreds of millions of dollars with documentation, you know, nine million here, twenty million there, no signatures on the bill, it's kind of cut and paste... I mean it's ridiculous!... You're now talking to Jho, and tell him, look, you either, within the next, you know, six hours produce documentation, which my compliance people can live with, or we have a huge problem."

Falcon's chief executive next called Low himself to convey the message: "The documentation which we have received, Jho, it's a joke. It is not good," he said. Leemann was particularly worried that other banks, especially U.S. correspondent banks, would raise a red flag over the transfer, alerting authorities that something was not right. He said Falcon had hired an outside counsel to look at the transfer from a legal perspective. "If any other bank just makes a 'peep!' and this gets reported... we are gonna have a huge problem."

Low moved quickly, tapping Al Husseiny to find a solution. He was having to rely more and more on his high-placed friends in banks like BSI and Falcon to keep the money moving, threatening to make this scheme unmanageable. By now he was dealing with too many flows to keep it all straight in his head—money to the prime minister, to his business deals, for mansions, parties, and more.

Jasmine Loo, his friend and 1MDB chief counsel, noticed he was putting on more weight, a sure sign of stress with Low, and he himself noted to others he was having problems sleeping at night. But he plowed on, too deep to stop. And despite Leemann's concern, Falcon Bank processed the money after Al Husseiny, the bank's chairman, vouched for the legitimacy of the transfer.

Armed with dirty 1MDB cash, the prime minister had a powerful weapon to win the 2013 election. As the vote approached, Low managed the account, diverting hundreds of millions of dollars to the prime minister's allies across the country. He barraged Joanna Yu with BlackBerry messages, ordering her to move chunks of money from Najib's account to ruling-party politicians. Frustrated with having to arrange hundreds of checks, she started to refer to Low as "Fats" behind his back. Some of the money moved to politicians via the private account of Nazir Razak, another of the prime minister's brothers and head of CIMB bank. The deluge of cash was an enormous advantage for Najib over an opposition without access to that kind of financial backing.

On Election Day, May 5, Najib averted disaster, clinging to power with the most slender of margins. Low had delivered yet again, and the prime minister was grateful. But it was a Pyrrhic victory. Not only did the government's coalition fail to win back Penang, it also lost the popular national vote. Najib remained in power only because of electoral rules that reserve more parliamentary seats for Malay-dominated rural areas. Sophisticated urban voters, many of them Chinese-Malaysians, had turned out in droves for the opposition, sick of the money politics. Anwar Ibrahim claimed election fraud, but the system was skewed against him.

Low's patron was still in power. But there was a new problem on the horizon. With Najib still in office, Low was able to avoid a full dissection of 1MDB's business by a hostile new government. But the unbridled spending on the elections, and Goldman's outlandish profits, were starting to attract attention from journalists. The *Edge*, Malaysia's weekly English-language newspaper, had raised questions about 1MDB's investments in PetroSaudi, including the unexplained, abrupt resignation in December 2009 of the fund's chairman. But the *Edge*'s journalists had failed back then to uncover solid evidence of wrongdoing, and instead turned to other stories.

Now, the paper's owner, Tong Kooi Ong, the multimillionaire who had made enemies due to his closeness with opposition candidate Anwar Ibrahim, ordered a fresh reporting effort. Over the summer, the *Edge* published its most detailed investigation yet on 1MDB. In a two-thousand-word story, the paper laid out how 1MDB had raised over $10 billion but invested only in power plants. It gave a skeptical account of how the fund claimed its $1.8 billion investment in PetroSaudi had miraculously been turned into a deposit in a Cayman Islands fund worth $2.3 billion. The piece noted Low's role in setting up 1MDB's predecessor fund, but made no other mention of him.

International journalists also had started to hear about Goldman's huge profits, mainly from other investment bankers in Southeast Asia, many of whom were getting heat from their bosses in London and New York for losing out on the business of the century. Even Gary Cohn, Goldman's president, boasted about the fees during meetings with journalists in New York.

Around the elections, the *Wall Street Journal* published a story under the headline GOLDMAN SEES PAYOFF IN MALAYSIA BET, in which reporters Alex Frangos and Matt Wirz detailed how Goldman had made $200 million raising bonds for Sarawak's government and 1MDB. The amount was, in fact, three times higher, but the story broke into the open the highly unusual Goldman windfall. A Goldman spokesman defended its role, saying clients sought out the bank for its ability to "deliver complex financing solutions" not available on "public markets."

Then, in August, a business weekly called *Focus Malaysia* published a cover story titled "Just Who Is Jho Low?" It mentioned Low's influence with Abu Dhabi funds and raised questions about his deals, including the purchase of EMI, suggesting his money might have originated with 1MDB, although the piece offered no proof. Those who worked at the fund did all they could to put the media off track. "The role of Jho Low as far as 1MDB is concerned is zero," Shahrol Halmi, the chief executive, was quoted by *Focus Malaysia* as saying.

Reporters were nipping around the edges. Was Low alarmed? Far from it. The latest $3 billion hadn't gone only to Najib and politicians. Hundreds of millions of dollars flowed to Low, and he went out to celebrate his patron's election victory by amassing an art collection fit for a Hollywood billionaire.

Chapter 31

Art No One Can See

New York, May 2013

Low was tingling with nerves, his heart beating fast as he clutched his phone. "Thirty-seven point five," he breathed.

At the other end was Loïc Gouzer, a Swiss specialist in contemporary art at Christie's, the 250-year-old British auction house. Gouzer was standing at the edge of the auction hall at Christie's New York headquarters, a grand, high-ceilinged room at Rockefeller Plaza. Between him and the auctioneer, affluent collectors and onlookers, who had come for this sale of postwar and contemporary art, sat in tight rows of seats, watching the bidding unfold.

Gouzer signaled to the auctioneer a bid of $37.5 million. The auctioneer chuckled.

"Will it work this time?" he said.

Low had just upped his offer by a million dollars, more than previous increments of $500,000—what's known in the auction trade as a "jump bid," or an attempt to scare off your rival.

On the side wall of the auction room hung the work that was the target of the bidding war: *Dustheads* by Jean-Michel Basquiat. A 1982 masterpiece of two figures with wide eyes, evoking African tribal masks, constructed in colorful red and green with acrylics, oil sticks, spray enamel, and metallic paint on canvas, the nearly seven-foot-high piece was among Basquiat's most sought-after pieces. The former Brooklyn graffiti artist had died aged twenty-seven in 1988, limiting the supply of his work. Prices for Basquiats had been steadily climbing.

Another anonymous bidder on the phone went up by $500,000; Low's aggressive jump bid had failed to see the rival off. The amounts kept rising—$38 million, $39, $40, $41, $41.5, $42, $42.5—as the bidders matched each other. Taking a breath, Low launched another jump bid—$43.5 million—and Gouzer signed to the auctioneer. There was a pause. No response on the other phone line.

"It's worked. I think," the auctioneer said, bringing his gavel down with a thud. "Sold at forty-three million five hundred thousand."

With the buyer's premium—a commission charged by Christie's—the price tag came to $48.8 million, a record for a Basquiat painting.

The private room at Christie's, from where Low was bidding, erupted. Leonardo DiCaprio, Swizz Beatz, Joey McFarland, and others congratulated the Malaysian for clinching the bidding war.

Only ten days after the Malaysian elections, Low marked Najib's victory by purchasing one of the world's most expensive paintings. It was a moment of victory and supreme hubris. He had arranged after the vote to open an account at Christie's in the name of Tanore, the shell company which by this point had received $1.2 billion from the latest Goldman bond. And he was set on building a world-class art collection.

No one except Low knew how much he had taken over the past four years, and even he was stretched to stay on top of it: more than $1.5 billion from the PetroSaudi phase from 2009; $1.4 billion from the first two Goldman bonds in 2012; and now over $1.2 billion more. On top of this, over $1 billion in loans from the pension fund for Malaysia's civil servants to a 1MDB unit called SRC International had gone missing. More than $5 billion in funds, one of the largest-ever financial frauds, and it wasn't over yet. More than a billion had been frittered away, more than a billion went into property and businesses, and more than a billion was used to pay off the prime minister and other conspirators.

To resolve this crazed theft, Low wagered an IPO of 1MDB's power plants would bring in billions of dollars. Yet he never spent long cogitating the endgame. Bernie Madoff bet he could always find new investors in his pyramid scheme, which ran more than four decades. But Madoff's fraud, like many other examples before, collapsed when he could no longer lure new dupes, whose money he needed to pay "profits" to other investors.

Low believed government funds were limitless and he could just keep on spending. State leaders were able, unlike individuals, to forgive their own administration's debt; Low had promised Patrick Mahony, the director of investments for PetroSaudi, that Najib would eventually agree to write off hundreds of millions of dollars. When corrupt organizations take over a country's apparatus, whether in Russia, China, or Malaysia, its members feel emboldened. They are not common criminals but an elite, shielded by privilege from the normal reaches of justice.

Prime Minister Najib's father, himself a leader, but of another era, had envisioned Malaysia as a proud democracy. The success of Low's scheme highlighted just how far the nation had strayed from that dream. The country's best minds increasingly were leaving, preferring a life in New York or London over the struggles in Malaysia. It was the kind of brain drain that had stunted the growth of nations from India to Indonesia, whose most ambitious citizens gave up on their troubled homeland and sought a better life elsewhere.

Western financial institutions, from Goldman to auditors and private banks, had unwittingly helped Low get away with it, impoverishing Malaysia. As Low amassed his art collection, he paid no heed to the 60 percent of Malaysian households who lived on less than $1,600 a month. The 1MDB fund had amassed $10 billion in debt, which would weigh on future generations. Prime Minister Najib boasted the country would attain developed-world living standards by 2020. But the leaders of the country, as they enriched themselves, were failing to achieve this. With national income of $10,000 per person, a fifth of the United States's level, Malaysia was stuck in the middle-income trap, no longer poor but not yet rich. In an earlier era, Japan, South Korea, Singapore, and Taiwan had reached developed-world status. Now, rampant corruption was condemning Malaysia, as well as Brazil, Russia, and a number of other nations, to mediocrity. But the elite—and those serving them—continued to thrive.

Low didn't scoop up only the Basquiat that evening. He also bought two works by Alexander Calder for over $8 million. It was a record-breaking night for Christie's, with $495 million in sales, the largest haul in auction history. That year, global art market sales topped 47 billion euros, a jump of 150 percent from a decade earlier, according to the European Fine Art Foundation. The growing cost of fine art, like that of real estate on the Upper East Side of Manhattan or in London's Knightsbridge, was partly due to the innate worth of the painting or the residence, coupled with limited supply. But it was also a reflection of the amount of dirty money in the market, and that night at Christie's was a glaring example of the problem, even if the auction house was not aware of it.

Low craved art to boost his cultural prestige—so he could tell Swizz Beatz, also an avid collector, about his latest Basquiat. But he did not display the works or appreciate them. Art had an advantage over other assets: It was hard to trace and could be

turned into cash in an instant. Low needed somewhere secret—
and safe—to house his new collection.

In Geneva, seven low-slung, white-colored warehouses sit just
south of the city center. This is not the old town, where private
banks like Pictet and Julius Baer have offices overlooking the lake,
but an industrial estate a short drive away. The warehouses look
just like any nondescript building, with storage vans parked outside, and to a passerby they could be a depot for a major logistics
company, except the complex is secured more tightly than any normal warehouse, with iris scanners on the doors. This is the Geneva
Freeport, a warehouse for the überelite to stash their possessions—
gold bars, bottles of rare wine, and, most recently, art.

Freeports have a long history in global commerce as a place
for traders to temporarily deposit commodities or other goods
without incurring local taxes. Authorities were willing to forgo
the revenues if it led to more economic activity and investment.
The Geneva Freeport, majority-owned by the state of Geneva,
started out in the nineteenth century as a tax-free waypoint for
grain, timber, and other commodities. Over time, wealthy individuals began to use the Freeport to move gold or other possessions into or out of Switzerland, and, eventually, deposited goods
there for longer periods of time. Without legal limits on storage
periods, the rich could use the Freeport to keep their possessions indefinitely out of the hands of tax authorities back home.

By 2013, Switzerland's Finance Ministry estimated the value
of goods inside came to more than 100 billion Swiss francs, including 1.2 million pieces of art and 3 million bottles of fine wine. If
opened to the public, the warehouses would have been the finest museum anywhere, with more works than the Louvre or the
Prado. Not only were there tax benefits, but this was a discreet
place, and authorities asked few questions about the provenance
of the items inside. It was a money launderer's paradise. Perhaps

Low learned about the Geneva Freeport from Al Qubaisi, who had cars there, including a Bugatti Veyron and a Pagani Huayra.

In the early phase of his scheme, Low concentrated on mansions and hotels, as well as gambling and parties. In the United States, property agents didn't have to declare the names of buyers who used cash, and Low had been able to hide behind a wall of shell companies. But there was still the physical property, which was immovable in times of crisis, and Low was beset by a nagging worry someone would find out he owned the Time Warner penthouse or the Bird Streets mansion in West Hollywood. Recently, U.S. real estate news sites had reported on Riza Aziz's purchase of the Park Laurel but mistakenly named the sellers as Rothschild bankers involved in the transaction, and Low had kept his name out of the media. He also had bought stakes in companies like EMI and Viceroy Hotels; he'd even acquired a British lingerie brand called Myla—apparently Rosmah's favorite—with proceeds from the 2013 bond. Again, these were assets that could not be easily liquidated.

Even Swiss private banks weren't the redoubt of secrecy they once had been. In 2013, the U.S. Justice Department launched a program that permitted Swiss banks to avoid criminal prosecution if they agreed to come clean about abetting U.S. citizens to evade tax. Low could sense it was getting harder to use banks; even BSI, which soon would start cooperating with the Justice Department over its U.S. clients, had started to query his transfers, and it would be difficult to rely anymore on Falcon's Leemann. As the focus on 1MDB got more intense, Low was looking for the perfect movable and untraceable asset.

The art market fit the bill. The Financial Action Task Force viewed the art world, much like the jewelry trade, as one of the last great unregulated financial markets in the world. Its dealers, from small-time auctioneers in New York, Hong Kong, or Geneva to global behemoths like Sotheby's and Christie's, were under no legal obligation to disclose the identity of their customers, and even they sometimes didn't know the beneficial owner behind anonymous shell companies that bought Monets or Rothkos. While Swiss bank secrecy had been eroded, the Geneva Freeport did not have to list its clients. A Swiss art warehouse owner called Yves Bouvier, who was involved in the Geneva Freeport, in 2010 opened a similar fortress for the rich in Singapore, near Changi airport. The *New York Times* dubbed these entrepôts the "Cayman Islands of the art world."

Occasionally there was a chink in the armor of secrecy, like in 2013, when Swiss customs officers on a routine inspection of the Geneva Freeport impounded nine artifacts looted from Libya, Syria, and Yemen, ranging from Roman-era bas-reliefs to Greek statues. But for Low, the art world, and these depots shrouded in secrecy, offered a sanctuary.

Low and McFarland often attended auctions in New York, renting skyboxes, secluded rooms overlooking the main auction floor from where they could watch unobserved and make telephone bids in anonymity. Low's group had a reputation as parvenus at snobbish Christie's, which was founded in London in the 1700s, and whose employees looked down on the nouveau riche even as the auction house took their money. McFarland sometimes bid for Tanore, and he acquired a Mark Ryden for $714,000 and an Ed Ruscha for $367,000. Christie's executives saw Low and Tanore as interchangeable and believed the young Malaysian was building a corporate collection. But Low attempted to dissociate himself from these acquisitions—at least on paper—by using Fat Eric and McFarland. For one auction, Low used the Eric Tan Gmail account to reserve a skybox at Christie's for twelve guests.

"It better look like Caesar Palace [*sic*] in there," one employee wrote to a colleague about the skybox. "The box is almost more important for the client than the art."

That night, Low bought a van Gogh—*La Maison de Vincent à Arles*—for $5.5 million. The company's earlier payments to Christie's, from its account at Falcon Bank, had gone through. But this time, Falcon's compliance kicked up a fuss over the huge amounts of art purchases that Tanore had been making, and Low—again using the Eric Tan email address—had to apologize to Christie's for a delay in paying for the van Gogh. In the end, he had to pull money from elsewhere.

In all, between May and September 2013, Low, via Tanore, bought $137 million in art. But Low had picked up more via other channels, such as the van Gogh, as well as works by Lichtenstein, Picasso, and Warhol, and by the end of the year he possessed art worth an estimated $330 million. He stashed it all in the Geneva Freeport and then set about covering up the evidence of how it had been financed. To do that, Low wrote a series of letters—supposedly from Eric Tan—offering him the artworks bought by Tanore as a gift.

In the letters, "Tan" said he was giving Low the art because of the "generosity, support and trust you have shared with me over the course of our friendship, especially during the difficult periods of my life." All of the letters ended, absurdly, with a rider stating that the gift "should not in any event be construed as an act of corruption." Low was exhibiting signs of sloppiness: It was risible that someone would hand over $100 million in art for no consideration. McFarland also got a painting from "Tan"— the cheaper Mark Ryden work—but no one could enjoy these testaments to human creativity; they were locked away in the humidity-controlled vaults of the Geneva Freeport.

Now, Low had hundreds of millions of dollars in a very safe place. But there was one asset even more transportable than art: jewelry. To keep Rosmah happy, and perhaps even attract a famous woman, in keeping with his newfound status, Low embarked on a jewelry-buying spree.

Chapter 32

Jewelers and Bankers

Aboard the M/S Topaz, *French Riviera, July 2013*

The mood among those aboard the *Topaz*, Sheikh Mansour's superyacht, berthed just off the French Riviera, was celebratory. The boat had taken four years to build, at a cost of over $500 million—the value of five F-35 fighter jets—and it was an apt backdrop for Najib to celebrate his recent election victory. Sitting in a horseshoe of chairs, laid out in one of the yacht's staterooms, the prime minister was talking business with Sheikh Mohammed, the crown prince of Abu Dhabi, who also was Sheikh Mansour's brother.

Low helped arrange the meeting in early July 2013. The group also included Michael Evans, the Goldman vice president who met Najib at Davos, and Tim Leissner. As he held forth, Najib was in an ebullient mood. The money Low had put at his disposal had kept him securely in power. And now Abu Dhabi was preparing to pour money into a financial center that would carry the Razak family name, with Goldman standing by to help. Turning to Evans and Leissner, the prime minister heaped praise on the bankers for their role so far and promised it was just the tip of the iceberg.

"Do you see any other bankers on this boat?" Najib joked.

After the meeting, Najib and Rosmah hosted a private

dinner in Saint-Tropez for around eighty people, with most of the attendees from Malaysia and the Middle East. As always, Jamie Foxx, by now a good friend of Low's, was on hand to play the piano and sing.

One Goldman banker not there was David Ryan, the Asia president who had raised a series of questions about the 1MDB bond business, and had retired the same month aged only forty-three, abruptly ending a stellar career at the bank. He had been right to question the 1MDB business, but his warnings had gone unheeded.

The *Topaz*, the very boat on which the bankers stood, had been partly financed by the first set of bonds Goldman had sold, and now Low had spent 3.5 million euros to rent it for a week, drawing on 1MDB's latest bonds. He had paid off his debt to Najib through his role in the elections, and the prime minister was content as Low continued to deliver a stream of Arab royalty to his doorstep. But he also had to think of Rosmah. He'd turned her son into a Hollywood producer and procured for her a dream mansion in London's Belgravia, but there was one possession Rosmah craved above all others: diamonds.

That summer, while the *Topaz* was idling off the coast of France, Lorraine Schwartz, the famous U.S. jeweler, flew into Monaco, and Low whisked her to the yacht. He had bought jewelry from Schwartz over the years, getting to know her well—he told friends he was going to see "Lorraine"—but this order was of a different magnitude.

Low had talked up Schwartz to Rosmah, impressing the first lady by the depth of his connections. Schwartz's career had blossomed in the 2000s after Halle Berry wore one of her pieces on the red carpet, and her loyal customers ran the gamut of Hollywood stars. In June 2013, Low had texted the jeweler with a very specific request: He said he needed an eighteen-carat "pink heart diamond vivid or slightly short of vivid. On diamond necklace urgent." By early July, Schwartz had found the perfect specimen. Low thought of sending Al Husseiny to pick it up for a viewing, but in the end Schwartz traveled out to France, without knowing the identity of the customer.

As Schwartz boarded the yacht, Low ushered her into a room, introducing the jeweler to the assembled group. It included Al Husseiny, Rosmah Mansor, and one of her Malaysian friends, and soon they were passing the shimmering diamond around between them, gasping over its beauty. In the diamond trade "vivid" is the top of a hierarchy of color intensity, and the diamond appeared to conceal a light shining from within. The group discussed different designs for the necklace to hold the diamond, which at twenty-two carats was even more exquisite than Low had requested. The group concurred: Making the chain out of interlinked smaller diamonds would be a perfect fit for Rosmah.

Two months later, in late September, Low's Bombardier jet circled above New Jersey's Teterboro Airport, a favorite landing spot for billionaires looking to get quickly to Manhattan. The plane touched down, and Low disembarked with Riza Aziz, Fat Eric, and Joey McFarland. They had been gambling and partying in Las Vegas, but Low had to get to New York for a meeting with Rosmah, whose husband was in town for the United Nations General Assembly. Najib loved rubbing shoulders with world leaders, and he rarely missed the chance to attend a summit, or give a speech about his "Global Movement of Moderates." On this trip, the prime minister had pushed for a meeting with Lloyd Blankfein, Goldman's chief executive. The bank was happy to oblige one of its top clients.

Rosmah was more concerned with jewels. A few weeks earlier, Low had fired off an email to Lorraine Schwartz, using the Eric Tan Gmail account, requesting she show the necklace to the first lady while she was in New York. He asked Schwartz to invoice Blackrock Commodities (Global), another shell company nominally owned by Tan, and made to look like Blackrock, the U.S. investment company. (Low also told people the company represented "Black"—for Rosmah's heart—and "rock"—because she loved diamonds.) It was important, Low informed Schwartz, that all this was kept under wraps.

"Please as mentioned on many occasions, do not state Mr. Low's name on email as he is just the introducer and not the buyer! V sensitive!" Low wrote to Schwartz's assistant, using the Eric Tan Gmail.

After the elections, Najib wired back $620 million to Tanore, and some of that money ended up in an account held by Blackrock at DBS Bank of Singapore. Using the Tan email address, Low told DBS compliance that Blackrock was a wholesale buyer of jewelry, to justify tens of millions of dollars in inflows. Queries from DBS's compliance department delayed the payment to Schwartz, but eventually Low, as usual, was able to urge bankers along, and the wire went through. The price was $27.3 million, making it one of the most expensive pieces of jewelry in the world.

The necklace wasn't ready yet, but Rosmah was keen to see the designs. The couple had taken to staying in the Mandarin Oriental, on Columbus Circle, just off Central Park. Low's Time Warner penthouse was basically part of the hotel—it was located above the guest rooms—allowing him to move easily to their suite without rousing media attention. On September 28, Low joined Rosmah and Schwartz in the room, where the jeweler showed her client various sketches of how it would look. They met with Rosmah's approval. This was the largest of a series of diamonds that Low bought for Rosmah, but it was not the last.

While Rosmah concerned herself with jewelry, the prime minister was looking for more investments, and he turned again to Goldman. In a meeting room in the Mandarin Oriental he gave a pitch about Malaysia to a high-powered client meeting put together by Blankfein. Malaysia was so important for Goldman that Blankfein had roped in some of the biggest names in U.S. finance to attend. Still on a postelection high, Najib extolled Malaysia's economy. The attendees included John Paulson, the hedge-fund owner who pocketed $4 billion trading credit-default swaps during the crisis; and David Bonderman, founder of TPG Capital, the private equity firm. Najib's daughter, Nooryana, had joined TPG in London after Georgetown, and was now working for them in Hong Kong.

Leissner had been working hard to keep a lockdown on the Malaysia business, following Najib and Rosmah around the world. Goldman's profits had awakened other Wall Street and European banks who now were attempting to get in on the action. As his prestige within Goldman grew and he became wealthier, Leissner's lifestyle also changed. After dating a range of ordinary women, the German banker now was with a star.

Back in March 2013, flush with triumph from Goldman's latest bond, Leissner had boarded a Cathay Pacific flight from Hong Kong to Kuala Lumpur to attend the city's Formula 1 race. The modern Sepang circuit, opened in the late 1990s near Putrajaya, was a symbol of Malaysia's emergence as a modern country and had won the right to host a Grand Prix. Like Singapore's race, the event was an excuse for the monied classes from around Southeast Asia to get together, make deals, and party.

On the plane, Leissner was seated in business class next to a glamorous woman a few years his junior, and he was struck by her appearance. The woman was six feet tall, with long black hair, pronounced cheekbones, and full lips. She seemed familiar. Soon after takeoff, the woman, Kimora Lee Simmons, a television personality and former U.S. fashion model, began to pile her bag and clothes into the spare middle seat that separated her from Leissner. Both passengers were frequent fliers, and Cathay Pacific had promised each of them use of the extra space. When Leissner complained to her, a heated disagreement ensued.

Simmons was well known in the United States for her reality-television show, *Kimora: Life in the Fab Lane*, which charted her efforts to build a fashion business while looking after her two daughters with former husband Russell Simmons, the founder of Def Jam Recordings. If the altercation started fiery, it turned smoldering, as Leissner and Simmons began to hit it off. They both were extreme extroverts who liked to talk. By the end of the four-hour flight, the Goldman banker proposed to her—the kind of grand gesture he liked to make to women.

They didn't marry immediately. But Leissner started to bring Simmons with him on business trips, and she too got close to Najib and Rosmah. In Asia, face time is crucial to business success, and Leissner was shadowing Najib after the elections, from the South of France to the United States. Before New York, he had accompanied Najib and Rosmah on a visit to San Francisco for an event to open the office of Khazanah, Malaysia's main sovereign wealth fund. It was nothing special—just a regular corporate public relations exercise—but was spiced up by the presence of Simmons.

Discretion was not her strong suit. With hundreds of thousands of followers on social media, Simmons lived in the public eye. In Malaysia, she posted on Instagram a picture from the Khazanah launch, showing her in a red off-the-shoulder dress, accompanied by Rosmah in a green-colored Malay-style top.

"In #SanFrancisco with my friend Datin Sri Rosmah," she posted to her followers, using a Malay honorific.

It clearly wasn't the first time they had hung out together. She posted another photo of herself with Leissner and Najib. The men were both in open-collared white shirts and jackets, and Leissner, his head now shaved and his face thinner, looked piercingly into the camera, while Najib smiled. It was a rare snapshot of the Goldman banker with the prime minister.

Leissner married Simmons at the end of 2013, around nine months after they met. Many at Goldman, whose executives like to stay out of the spotlight, even eschewing social media, were aghast as the German banker and Simmons's romance began to land them in *People* magazine. The bank was hooked on the profits from Malaysia, but it did not need the attention.

Some bankers at Goldman, led by Leissner, were dependent on Low. The Malaysian's desire to keep doing deals—building his empire—had them excited about the potential for even more business. Low's company, Jynwel, had taken a minority stake in EMI Music Publishing, but now he wanted to lead a major acquisition, to become a genuinely famous investor. Better still, a sizzling business deal could generate profits to put his scheme on a solid footing.

Chapter 33

Bona Fide Business

New York, July 2013

The view from the restaurant where Jho Low and Steven Witkoff, a New York property developer, were holding a celebratory dinner gave out over Central Park South. The diners could see the famous Plaza Hotel, and nearby, the tired-looking Helmsley Park Lane Hotel, a forty-seven-story building from the early 1970s. The estate of Harry Helmsley, the legendary New York real estate baron, had been auctioning off properties since his death in 1997, followed by that of his wife a decade later, and the Park Lane was the crown jewel.

With sweeping vistas over Central Park, the hotel was a prime candidate for redevelopment. After a heated bidding war for the property, Witkoff and Low emerged victorious, with an offer in July 2013 to pay $654 million. The Malaysian had clinched the deal by agreeing to finance a $100 million down payment—more than double the usual amount for a transaction like this. As the pair tucked into dinner, they discussed plans to tear down the building, replacing it with a "billionaire tower," the kind that were sprouting up across New York, a city awash in foreign money.

After the financial crisis, New York developers like Witkoff increasingly were taking minority stakes in projects, relying on deep-pocketed foreign partners to stump up the majority of financing costs. After Jynwel's role in the acquisition of EMI Music Publishing, Low was scouting for a deal in which his company could take the lead and further embellish the story of family money. The Malaysian heard about Witkoff's interest in the Park Lane from Marty Edelman, one of the United States's top real estate lawyers, and he asked for an introduction.

With a shock of curly white hair, Edelman had studied at Princeton and Columbia, before spending more than thirty years practicing law in New York, lately with Paul Hastings, a white-shoe U.S. law firm. He was fast-talking and likable, known for working all hours and developing personal relationships with clients. Over the years, he had built up contacts in the Middle East via multiple business deals. Edelman became an adviser to Mubadala, and Abu Dhabi's Crown Prince Mohammed often sought his advice on cross-border real estate deals; he even weighed in sometimes on affairs of state. Executives at Mubadala had introduced Low to Edelman, and the lawyer set up a meeting with Witkoff.

Yet again, Low had leveraged his powerful connections, and Witkoff saw him as the real deal. That he seemed to have bottomless financing didn't hurt. Low agreed to fund 85 percent of the deal, with Witkoff's investor group taking a 15 percent stake. In response to an emailed request for details about his funding from a Witkoff executive, Low responded: "Low Family Capital built from our Grandparents, down to the third generation now." Another Witkoff executive told Wells Fargo, which was lending money for the project, that Low's capital "derives from a family trust."

In the months ahead, the Witkoff group discussed how to develop the Park Lane. Due to New York's zoning laws, part of the original hotel needed to be incorporated into the new structure. The investors hired Herzog & de Meuron, the Swiss architects, who envisaged an almost one-thousand-foot tower with an undulating facade and a raised podium. The architect's sketches showed the sleek building, set for completion in 2020, towering over its neighbors on Central Park South. Low was excited. He suggested putting outdoor swimming pools on the exterior decks of the five penthouses, which the partners hoped would sell for more than $100 million apiece.

The deal for the Park Lane closed in November 2013, and Low paid his initial $200 million investment with money taken from the latest Goldman bond and sent on a dizzying journey through shell companies, bank accounts of family members, and U.S. law firm trust accounts. Low was on his way to developing a high-profile property that could make his name. At the same time, he was playing another angle.

Until now he'd seen corporate deals as a way to add credibility to his family-wealth story, but perhaps he'd been looking at it from the wrong angle; instead of an endpoint for stolen cash, maybe he could use corporate acquisitions as a way of moving money elsewhere. Once he bought a major asset, and then sold it, the money would be gold-plated—the respectable earnings from a deal. The Park Lane offered him a way of moving hundreds of millions of dollars in one fell swoop.

In December, Low agreed to sell a minority interest in the project to Mubadala for $135 million. Most of the proceeds from this sale ended up in the private accounts of Low, his brother, Szen, and his father, Larry, at BSI in Singapore. Here were the proceeds from the sale of a stake in one of New York's most ambitious real estate developments, hopefully rubbing out all traces of links to the $3 billion Goldman bond.

Low still needed to reward Ambassador Otaiba for the latest deal involving Abu Dhabi. This was the least the ambassador expected for making all these connections for Low. In a meeting in December with Awartani, Otaiba's business partner, Low promised to send the pair money by the end of the year. Then, he set about laundering the proceeds of his stake sale to Mubadala through yet another corporate acquisition, and Goldman, of course, would be involved.

Low had been deepening his connections at Goldman, and had gotten to know Hazem Shawki, the bank's Dubai-based head of investment banking, who heard pitches from the Malaysian. One of them involved a plan for Low to take over Coastal Energy, a Houston firm controlled by legendary Texas oilman Oscar Wyatt Jr.

Low, informally advised by Goldman, approached Coastal in 2012 about a takeover, but the firm didn't believe he could come up with cash and told him to find a bigger partner. Now armed with cash from the Park Lane sale, Low returned with none other than IPIC, the Abu Dhabi fund controlled by Khadem Al Qubaisi, who had helped funnel money out from the first 1MDB bonds sold by Goldman. IPIC's Spanish energy unit—Compañía Española de Petróleos, SAU, or Cepsa—agreed to partner with a Low-controlled shell company to make a $2.2 billion offer for Coastal.

Before an agreement with the U.S. energy company could be reached, Goldman's compliance department told its bankers to stop working with Low or his entity on the deal, again citing concerns over his wealth. It was the same reason Goldman's private bank had given to reject Low for an account a few years earlier. As a result, Goldman switched to advising Cepsa, the IPIC unit, even though its bankers were aware that Low was still involved. Eventually, Wyatt Jr. agreed to sell, and Low invested $50 million in the deal, with Cepsa funding the remainder of the purchase price. One week later, Cepsa transferred $350 million into Low's shell company, ostensibly to buy out Low's share in the partnership. He had made 600 percent on his money in a matter of days.

Shawki, the Goldman banker, who was now working with IPIC, told executives at the Abu Dhabi fund that the payout to Low was to reward him for scouting out the Coastal deal. Unknown to Shawki, in reality it was nothing less than corruption, the spoils shared between Low and Al Qubaisi. In public, Goldman denied knowledge of any agreement between Cepsa and Low's shell company.

The Malaysian used some of the proceeds to buy an office in London's Mayfair district, which became the headquarters of Myla, his lingerie brand. If anyone inquired, Low could say the money came from a sale of his stake in Coastal Energy, which he acquired after offloading a share in New York's Park Lane hotel.

His plans to build a corporate empire were on track. No one, from major New York real estate developers to bankers and lawyers, knew the truth about him. Low and Al Qubaisi continued to act as if the money in the firms they oversaw was their private property. But as Low closed the Park Lane deal, an unexpected development risked bringing his scheme to an abrupt end.

Chapter 34

140 Gigabytes

Bangkok, Thailand, October 2013

Since leaving PetroSaudi in 2011, Xavier Justo had tried to put the server out of his mind. He toured Southeast Asia with his girlfriend, Laura, a Swiss-French woman whom he later married on a secluded beach, and the pair were now developing a luxurious villa on the Thai resort island of Koh Samui, a short flight from Bangkok. The spacious main house and guest villas were nestled into a terraced hillside, with a lap pool and tennis court down below. Palm trees surrounded the property. It was Justo's dream island, a place to start a new life. But plans for a financial consulting business had failed to bear fruit.

As the villa's construction costs mounted, Justo remembered the money PetroSaudi promised but never paid. He played his card.

For over two years, Justo had nursed his grievances. The former PetroSaudi employee was bitter over how his former friend, Tarek Obaid, had thrown him out of the company without the payout he desired. What's more, Justo had heard from friends that Obaid was bad-mouthing him around their hometown of Geneva.

In the fall of 2013, Justo had contacted Patrick Mahony, PetroSaudi's director of investments, by email, informing him that he had damaging information. In fact, he had a copy of PetroSaudi's computer server. A 140-gigabyte treasure trove of almost five hundred thousand emails and documents from PetroSaudi, the server's contents painted a picture of how Low, Mahony, and Obaid had worked to take money from 1MDB, including emails in which the PetroSaudi principals talked about how to cover the hole. For two years, Justo had sat on the server, fearing the consequences of making its contents public. Now, he was losing his patience and set up a meeting with Mahony, in Bangkok to negotiate.

As he sat in Bangkok's Shangri-La Hotel, waiting for Mahony to turn up, Justo knew he was about to make a very dangerous move. The hotel, set on the banks of the churning Chao Phraya River, had a resort-like feel, with palm trees and a laguna-style swimming pool, offering respite from the bustle of the chaotic Thai capital. When Mahony finally appeared, Justo's heart jumped.

Justo began by recounting how he felt duped by PetroSaudi, which had agreed to pay him millions of Swiss francs in severance but then had scaled back the amount dramatically. Now he wanted 2.5 million Swiss francs—money he believed was due to him. Mahony was cool to Justo's demands. There was no evidence to suggest wrongdoing, he said. PetroSaudi would absolutely not pay him any cash. They parted without an agreement.

Justo barraged Mahony with emails, trying to get him to agree to the payment.

"The official side paints a nice picture but the reality is commissions, commissions, commissions," he wrote in one email.

For four years now, Mahony had avoided any blowback on the deal, perhaps believing the involvement of Prime Minister Najib and a Saudi prince protected him. He must have been rattled by developments but still felt untouchable. In one email, he issued a dark threat to his former friend and colleague.

"What troubles me so much is the way I see this situation ending—with the destruction of you."

Rather than cow Justo, the dark threat emboldened him to look for a suitable buyer for his data trove. No candidate immediately sprang to mind. As he thought over what to do, a former British journalist with ties to Malaysia was just getting interested in Jho Low. Soon, their paths would cross.

In December 2013, Clare Rewcastle-Brown sat at the dining room table in her fourth-floor central London apartment, tapping away on a MacBook Pro. She was preparing a piece for her blog, *Sarawak Report*. Born in the Malaysian state of Sarawak in 1959 to a young British police officer and nurse, Rewcastle-Brown spent her childhood years playing in the jungle and swimming in the warm sea, sometimes tagging along as her mother visited villages to work as a midwife. After returning to the United Kingdom for boarding school in the late 1960s, Rewcastle-Brown eventually got a job as a reporter with the BBC World Service, but she had never forgotten Sarawak. She'd started *Sarawak Report* in 2010 as an attempt to hold Taib Mahmud, Sarawak's chief minister, to account for the environmental destruction and corruption in his state.

Now fifty-four years old, with long brown hair and bangs, Rewcastle-Brown was married to the brother of former British Prime Minister Gordon Brown. Though connected to Britain's establishment, Rewcastle-Brown believed strongly that politicians must answer for their actions. When Taib claimed *Sarawak Report* was part of a plot to recolonize the state, she reveled in taunting the powerful figure on her blog, with little fear about making enemies in high places. But this latest story was not about Sarawak.

Weeks earlier, Rewcastle-Brown had started to hear rumors from sources in Malaysia about Red Granite, the film company run by Najib's stepson, Riza Aziz. Few among Malaysia's elite bought into Riza's claims of Middle Eastern funding, and Rewcastle-Brown picked up on gossip in Kuala Lumpur that Malaysian state-owned entities might have financed the film company. Intrigued, she traveled to Los Angeles to gather more information about Red Granite. During her reporting, she came across a lawsuit, filed in Los Angeles over the summer by the producers of *Dumb and Dumber*, the 1994 comedy starring Jim Carrey and Jeff Daniels.

Red Granite had bought the rights to a sequel—*Dumb and Dumber To*—but it had shut out the producers of the original film. In July 2013, Red Granite filed a lawsuit seeking to exclude the producers, Steve Stabler and Brad Krevoy, from involvement in the movie. Stabler and Krevoy countersued, claiming a contractual right to involvement in any sequel. Red Granite had only just settled with Alexandra Milchan, a producer who had sued after the firm booted her from *The Wolf of Wall Street*, and now it was involved in another legal tussle.

McFarland and Aziz's "misconduct and hubris will cause Red Granite to crash and burn," Stabler and Krevoy claimed in the lawsuit. The pair lacked experience to successfully produce motion pictures themselves, the suit continued, and although Red Granite apparently had "family money" from Aziz, the venture would not succeed with cash alone. Then the producers hit home, summarizing what many in Hollywood were whispering about these upstarts behind their backs.

The Red Granite executives' "experience producing motion pictures during their short tenure in the industry consists of cavorting at nightclubs with Paris Hilton and making dinner reservations at posh restaurants in New York and Los Angeles." (The following year, both sides withdrew their suits after an agreement that included executive producer credits on the film for Stabler and Krevoy.)

To Rewcastle-Brown, something wasn't right—it seemed greater than a squabble between a bunch of movie producers. She began to comb through interviews that Riza and Joey McFarland had given to the *Hollywood Reporter* and *Los Angeles Times*. As Red Granite had attracted notice—at the Cannes Film Festival in 2011 and now before the U.S. theatrical release of *The Wolf of Wall Street* on Christmas Day 2013—the pair had been coy about their finances. They talked vaguely about money from the Middle East and Asia but declined to give more specifics. In one interview, Riza said how he had "skin in the game."

This made no sense to Rewcastle-Brown. How could a former junior banker, with Najib as a stepfather, have enough capital to launch a film company? It was a mystery she wanted to solve.

Chapter 35

Leo's Wall Street Indictment

New York, December 2013

On December 17, a windy, subzero winter's night, with a flurry of snow, the guests milled around outside the Ziegfeld Theater on Fifty-Fourth Street in Midtown Manhattan for the premiere of *The Wolf of Wall Street*. On the red carpet, McFarland and Aziz posed with DiCaprio, Margot Robbie, and Jonah Hill. McFarland was in his element, boasting about his gray Brioni suit on his Instagram account. Wearing a dark blue suit and maroon tie, Low couldn't help but attend, despite his earlier efforts to keep out of the limelight. He had to be there to celebrate this extraordinary achievement.

In just a few short years, Low had gone from being a low-tier Malaysian financier to effectively bankrolling one of the splashiest Hollywood films of the year—and one about a fraudster. Just as Belfort for a time had enjoyed the fruits of his scheme, Low couldn't miss out on this evening. He wanted to share his success with those closest to him, and the business partners he yearned to impress. Low's guest list included family members, his girlfriend Jesselynn Chuan Teik Ying (seated next to his mother), Jasmine Loo of 1MDB, Swizz Beatz, Khadem Al Qubaisi of IPIC, Steve Witkoff, and Martin Edelman.

Low posed with the Red Granite founders on the red carpet,

but he didn't take part in the photos with the main cast. He was snapped with DiCaprio, though, milling around before the performance. The pair had remained close. A month earlier Low had attended the star's thirty-ninth birthday party in TAO Downtown in New York's Chelsea district. That night, McFarland had made Page Six of the *New York Post* for ordering bottle after bottle of champagne. Low's parties, and DiCaprio's attendance at them, were by now embedded in Hollywood lore, even getting a mention in a song on the soundtrack for the film *22 Jump Street*. The party anthem, "Check My Steezo," featured the lyrics:

> Jho Low! I see you Jho Low! / Got Leo at my party taking shots never solo / Grade-A chorizo followed by sea-bass Miso Miso, / Me so loco. . . .

The Red Granite principals and Low had assiduously cultivated DiCaprio, whom they hoped would star in *Papillon*, or if not that, then another one of their upcoming movies. A few weeks after the *Wolf of Wall Street* premiere, Low, posing as Eric Tan, sent DiCaprio a $3.3 million painting by Pablo Picasso as a late birthday present. The oil painting—*Nature Morte au Crâne de Taureau*—was accompanied with a handwritten note. "Dear Leonardo DiCaprio, Happy belated Birthday! This gift is for you," it read. Then, Low told a Swiss gallery that was storing a $9.2 million Basquiat—a collage entitled *Red Man One*—to transfer ownership to DiCaprio. The order, made in a letter also signed by DiCaprio, indemnified the actor from "any liability whatsoever resulting directly or indirectly from these artwork." The actor also got a photograph by Diane Arbus—cost $750,000—from Low.

In private, DiCaprio was happy to accept these gifts. On the red carpet, he was in a more philosophical mood. Some critics of the film—including voting members of the Academy who heckled Scorsese at an official screening before the Oscars— complained it glamorized Jordan Belfort's fraud and was more likely to spawn financial malfeasance than serve as a cautionary tale. DiCaprio had carefully prepared his retort.

"This is an indictment of all of Wall Street. But it's an indict- ment about something that's in our culture, this incessant need to consume and this incessant need to obtain more and more wealth with complete disregard for anyone except yourself," he told one interviewer.

Two days after the premiere of *The Wolf of Wall Street*, Rewcastle-Brown let rip in a post titled "Wall Street Greed / Malaysian Money—EXPOSE!" It was typical Rewcastle-Brown, a mix of speculation and reporting, spiced up with acerbic asides and tabloidesque headlines. The piece boiled down to asking one enormous question: Who had paid for the film? Skilled at rounding up interviews and photos available on the web, point- ing out inconsistencies, Rewcastle-Brown noted how Riza and McFarland had suspiciously refused to detail Red Granite's financing. Her piece linked to a story on a U.S. real estate web- site about Riza's $33.5 million purchase of the Park Laurel apart- ment. Where was the money coming from?

Perhaps Jho Low—whom Rewcastle-Brown described as a close friend of Rosmah and Riza—could have put up the money himself, she speculated. The little-known Malaysian financier was on the red carpet for the premiere, and seemed to be close to DiCaprio, attending his recent birthday event at TAO Down- town. Rewcastle-Brown's piece, peppered with photos of Low— alongside Paris Hilton in Saint-Tropez, holding champagne in a nightclub, at the *Wolf of Wall Street* premiere—was the most intense scrutiny yet of his activities. She had a sizable following in Malaysia and was edging toward the truth. The post ended with an acute observation:

> Many may wonder if the link to the top political players in Malaysia and friendship with the PM's step-son might account for Jho Low's easy access to investment income or indeed if he is the front man for others.

This was too much for Red Granite, whose lawyers quickly fired off a letter demanding a retraction and an apology, which Rewcastle-Brown ignored. There was no Malaysian money in the film, the letter said. Talents of the caliber of Scorsese and DiCaprio, it went on, never would have gotten involved if the financing was tainted.

Chapter 36

The Oval Office

New York, December 2013

Leonardo DiCaprio ducked into the Four Seasons restaurant on Fifty-Second Street in Midtown Manhattan and made his way to a private room. Since the late 1950s, the restaurant had catered to the city's business elite to the point that, in the 1970s, *Esquire* magazine coined the term "power lunch" to refer to the meetings held between lawyers, bankers, and ad executives over steaks in the Grill Room, with its leather sofas and wood-paneled walls. Jordan Belfort, too, dined there, and DiCaprio and Margot Robbie, who played Belfort's second wife, filmed a scene for *The Wolf of Wall Street* in the Pool Room, dining under the indoor trees near the water feature.

The night before, after the film's premiere at the Ziegfeld, DiCaprio had moved on to the after-party at the Roseland Ballroom, a converted ice rink, also on Fifty-Second Street, with his "Wolf Pack" in tow, friends like Orlando Bloom and Tobey Maguire. DiCaprio's schedule was packed, and the next morning he was at the Four Seasons to meet members of the Academy, the six-thousand-member body of former actors, directors, and other movie professionals who vote on the year's Oscar winners.

He was running late to catch a plane and didn't really have

time for the lunch event, put on by Paramount Pictures, the film's distributor. Scorsese was already en route to the airport and wouldn't make the lunch. But DiCaprio's presence was crucial, and he made his way around the room, greeting Academy members. The glad-handing was important public relations. The Academy was dominated by old, white males, and several of them had shown hostility to the film, with its gleeful depiction of sex and drugs. After ten minutes, DiCaprio made his excuses and exited quietly, befuddling some in the room, leaving Margot Robbie to animate the event with jokes about the awkward sex scenes between her and DiCaprio.

After years in the business, DiCaprio had gotten used to the usual flurry of events that follow a major film release, but the next meeting on his schedule was more enticing. Outside the Four Seasons, a car was waiting to take the actor to the airport, where he would fly on to Washington, DC. There he would deliver a DVD of the film to President Barack Obama.

As usual, Washington was a few degrees warmer than New York, and there was no snow, but DiCaprio was wrapped in a dark coat and cap as he went through White House security. Accompanying him was a small group that included Scorsese, Riza Aziz, and Norashman Najib, the son of Malaysia's prime minister. Escorting them to see the president was Frank White Jr., one of Obama's foremost individual fund-raisers. With pronounced cheeks and an easy smile, White was an entrepreneur who made his fortune providing information technology support to the U.S. government, including the intelligence community.

In the 2008 elections, he raised more than $10 million as a "bundler"—a supporter who collects small individual contributions and delivers them to a campaign. By 2012, White was national vice chair of the president's reelection campaign. Born and raised in Chicago, where he'd studied at the University of Illinois, he also had family ties to the White House—his sister was married to Michelle Obama's cousin—and was a regular attendee of state dinners. He was also deeply entwined with Jho Low.

During the 2008 campaign, White got to know Prakazrel Samuel Michél, better known as Pras, a former member of the 1990s hip-hop band the Fugees, and Shomik Dutta, who had worked as an investment banker at Morgan Stanley. After the Fugees and a short-lived solo career—"Ghetto Supastar (That Is What You Are)"—Pras was looking to reinvent himself as a businessman. A longtime fixture on the Hollywood party scene, he'd heard from a nightclub promoter about these showy events a young Malaysian was throwing, and by 2012 was a regular at Low's parties. Like DiCaprio and Scorsese, Pras saw Low's billions as a business opportunity, and the pair became close. He started to tell his new friend about Frank White, a political operative he'd met on the campaign trail, and Low was entranced.

Low moved quickly, trying to figure out a way he could benefit from a connection to White. Could he leverage the new contact to acquire influence in the United States, as he had done with Otaiba in Abu Dhabi and Prince Turki in Saudi Arabia? On the face of it, Low's ambition seemed laughably lofty. But Malaysian connections were enticing to some in Washington at that moment. Since taking office, Obama had been keen to befriend Najib to deepen U.S. influence in Asia, part of the president's much-vaunted pivot to East Asia. Some in the White House and State Department, as well as retired diplomats, including old hands like John Malott, a former U.S. ambassador to Kuala Lumpur, had urged caution about Najib, pointing out the prime minister was showing increasingly antidemocratic tendencies.

In 2013, after losing the vote of ethnic Chinese and Indian Malaysians, the prime minister turned to solidify his Malay

base. Despite initially pledging to repeal it, Najib and his government had used a colonial-era sedition law to prosecute opposition leaders, students, and critical academics.

But the White House, especially Deputy National Security
Adviser Ben Rhodes, clung to its vision of Najib as a transforma-
tive prime minister, not least because of constant lobbying from
Jamaluddin Jarjis, a former Malaysian ambassador to Washington who now was special envoy to the United States. A senior
UMNO politician and one of Najib's closest friends, Jamaluddin
was an architect of efforts for closer U.S.-Malaysia ties, and he
was agitating for Obama's staff to organize an official presidential visit to Malaysia. (It was his daughter who interned at Goldman Sachs in Singapore and had an affair with Tim Leissner.)

To build his connection to the White House, Low got
involved with efforts to reelect Obama to a second four-year
term. Pras Michél would be his conduit. In 2012, Low sent $20
million from an offshore company he controlled to two companies owned by Pras. The money was ostensibly a "gift," but the
musician used one of these firms to make a $1.2 million dona-
tion to a super PAC called Black Men Vote, which supported
Obama's campaign. It was a risky move for Pras, as donating
money to a candidate on behalf of another person is a violation
of federal campaign-finance laws. A lawyer for Pras later said the
musician was the victim of a "false narrative."

Low also reached an agreement for Frank White to scout for
projects and act as a cheerleader for Malaysia with the Obama
administration. For that, White was paid handsomely; Low in
2012 arranged for $10 million in 1MDB money to move to White
via MB Consulting, a firm controlled by Aabar's Mohamed Al
Husseiny.

In return, White went to work. In October 2012, he set
up a meeting between Obama and the Red Granite crew. Joey
McFarland posted a picture on Instagram of himself shaking

hands with President Obama at White's home. When the president won reelection in November, Low wanted to celebrate with
a visit to the White House. Later that month, White arranged
for Low to attend the president's holiday party. Low later showed
off a photograph of himself with Obama and the first lady to
friends. But on another occasion, White House security personnel turned Low away at the door. It seemed the U.S. government
had growing reason to be wary of this young Malaysian with a
mysterious past.

Undeterred, Low doubled down on his investment in White,
an association he hoped could influence White House policy.
In May 2013, White set up DuSable Capital Management in
Washington with Pras and Dutta, the banker who also had
worked as a special assistant in the White House. Soon after,
the fund told the Securities and Exchange Commission that it
was planning to raise $500 million to invest in renewable energy
and infrastructure projects. The plan was for Aabar to put in
the majority of the capital, with White investing a small amount
himself. DuSable registered as a lobbyist for 1MDB, and by the
end of the year, White was arranging for another White House
tour—this time for DiCaprio's group.

DiCaprio and Scorsese did in fact hand over a DVD copy
of *The Wolf of Wall Street* to President Obama, but there was
little publicity for the visit. The administration didn't want to be
seen unduly influencing the upcoming Oscar race. *The Wolf of
Wall Street* was viewed as an outside challenger to *Dallas Buyers Club*, *12 Years a Slave*, and *Gravity*. The famous director and
actor were spotted later in the day having tea at the W Hotel,
just across Fifteenth Street from the White House, but neither
of them mentioned the meeting with Obama in the barrage of
interviews that followed the film's public release a few days later,
on Christmas Day.

Between the release and the Oscars in early March, Low

headed off on his traditional end-of-year ski trip with friends and family. This year's destination was Aspen, Colorado. Low's guests included Alicia Keys, Swizz Beatz, Joey McFarland, and his girlfriend, Antoniette Costa. The town was awash with celebrities, and Leonardo DiCaprio, Tobey Maguire, Nicole Scherzinger, and her boyfriend, Formula 1 World Champion Lewis Hamilton, attended some of Low's gatherings.

At one dinner, the actor Dakota Johnson, the daughter of Melanie Griffith and Don Johnson, was sitting next to Low, who thought she was a random stranger. Now used to fraternizing with bigger stars, Low had no time for Johnson.

"She ate food and didn't even say thank you afterward," Low complained to friends.

At one point, Low bumped into Paris Hilton, who also was in Aspen. He had remained friendly with Hilton, even though he saw her less now than back in 2010. The pair went to get pizza.

The chat that week, at the St. Regis Aspen Resort, centered on *The Wolf of Wall Street* and whether DiCaprio would finally win an Oscar. As he snowboarded, Low had good reason to be content.

The film would be extremely lucrative at the box office, earning more than $400 million globally, almost four times the cost of production. Despite his constant scheming, Low was exhibiting skill as an investor. Viceroy Hotel Group, in which he now owned a half share, had expanded, gaining a name as a five-star boutique chain. His 13 percent stake in EMI Music Publishing also was a winner, as the global music business recovered due to digital sales via streaming services. *The Wolf of Wall Street* was his most successful investment to date, and Red Granite had a promising pipeline of new films in development. If the company became one of the biggest producers in Hollywood, Low wagered, there would be oodles of cash to put back into 1MDB.

As the award season came around, *The Wolf of Wall Street* was expected to do well. In January, DiCaprio won a Golden Globe for his role as Jordan Belfort, using his acceptance speech to thank "Joey, Riz, and Jho" for taking a risk on the project. (Jho Low was also thanked in the film's closing credits.) But the big prize remained just out of DiCaprio's grasp yet again: At the Oscars, in early March, the Best Actor statuette was handed to Matthew McConaughey for *Dallas Buyers Club*. It was a terrible night for *The Wolf of Wall Street*, which, despite five nominations, failed to pick up any awards. For Low and Riza, sitting behind Bono and the Edge from U2 in the Dolby Theatre, the evening fell a little flat.

To top off their Oscar buzzkill, the movie wasn't even going to play back home in Malaysia. To comply with local morality laws, Malaysian authorities demanded more than ninety cuts, and Paramount Pictures, the film's distributor, together with Scorsese and Red Granite, had decided it wasn't worth the trouble.

But, no matter: An even bigger American import was soon set to land in Malaysia.

On April 27, 2014, Obama became the first U.S. president to visit Malaysia in five decades. The iconic image of the visit was a selfie that Najib took of himself and Obama. The president leaned in, beaming broadly, while Najib didn't quite know where to look as the camera snapped. "My selfie with President Obama," the prime minister tweeted moments later. The world had gone selfie mad months earlier when Ellen DeGeneres had taken one at the Oscars with Bradley Cooper, Meryl Streep, Brad Pitt, and other stars.

It was Najib's moment to shine on a world stage. The leaders had spent the morning at the National Mosque, where Najib's father was buried, and the prime minister used the visit to underline his special relationship with Obama. For years, U.S. presidents had avoided Malaysia, put off by former prime minister Mahathir's strident anti-Western rhetoric and the nation's authoritarian bent. Now, Obama was finally in Malaysia as part of a tour that also included close allies like Japan, South Korea, and the Philippines.

His deputy national security adviser, Ben Rhodes, who was also on the trip, called Malaysia a "pivotal state" in the region—a code for a bulwark against China. In recent months, Beijing had been taking a militarist approach toward enforcing its territorial claims to the entire South China Sea.

President Obama, keen to balance this aggression, promised in a joint statement with Najib to help train and equip Malaysia's navy. The statement also stressed the two leaders' support for a vibrant civil society. For some State Department officials who had counseled against the visit—given Najib's government was busy locking up opposition politicians—this last pledge was derisory.

As Obama toured Malaysia, Low bragged to contacts that he had played a role in the rapprochement with the United States. Just days before Obama arrived, 1MDB signed a multi-million-dollar deal with Frank White's company, DuSable Capital, to develop a solar-electricity plant in Malaysia. The 1MDB fund's management falsely described the deal to the board as a "government-to-government" endeavor, even though DuSable was a private entity.

Low was hoping Obama and Najib would highlight the joint-venture plan during the president's visit. But he was learning it wasn't as easy to stage-manage events with the United States as in the Middle East. For one, he didn't have an ambassador-level figure like Otaiba at his disposal, only Frank White—who although close to Obama, was a mere businessman and fundraiser. Only months later, the solar deal was scrapped, and

1MDB eventually paid $69 million to buy out DuSable's share in the joint venture. White had plucked a fortune from thin air. He'd later say the deal was "intended to provide renewable energy in Malaysia, create jobs in the United States and earn support for Malaysia in the United States," and at the time he had no knowledge 1MDB was the "victim of theft."

The president's visit turned out to be a major disappointment. If Obama's Malaysia trip hadn't worked out as planned, Low could take comfort in another development. In recent weeks, he had started to date one of the world's most striking women.

Chapter 37

Size Matters

The New Wonjo Restaurant, on Thirty-Second Street in Manhattan's Koreatown, sat under the shadow of the Empire State Building. It was a 24/7 establishment, with plastic menus in the windows and authentic Asian fare—exactly the sort of place Jho Low liked to head after a late night of partying. On this night, he was ensconced at a table with Joey McFarland and some other friends. It was cold outside—the "polar vortex" had sent temperatures plummeting at the turn of the New Year—and the group was eating Korean barbecue and soup after a night of karaoke, when Miranda Kerr, the Australian supermodel, walked in.

She had come from a formal event and was wearing a ball gown, at odds with the atmosphere in the down-to-earth eatery. With her soft brown curls, iridescent blue eyes, and trademark dimples, the thirty-year-old was instantly recognizable, and her elegant attire stood out in such a simple restaurant. She had come to see a friend who was part of Low's group and took a seat at the table. Before long, the model was engrossed in a conversation with Low about her skin-care line, KORA Organics.

As it became clear that Low was a major investor, a billionaire, even—with interests in EMI and the Park Lane, and ties to a Hollywood studio—Kerr peppered him with questions about how to develop KORA, the running of which she had recently taken over from her mother. As Low had accumulated power, and perhaps because of the built-up stress, some of his earlier charm and solicitousness had worn off, and he began to exhibit a rough edge of arrogance. At a recent gambling session in Vegas, he had told a British model called Roxy Horner that she needed to lose weight, pointing to her waist. She was offended, but Low had learned that, because he was paying, he didn't really need to care. Kerr, though, was a different prospect, and when she mentioned her desire to expand KORA, Low was careful to praise her financial acumen.

Kerr had grown up on the edge of the Australian Outback, in a stultifying farming town called Gunnedah, but she had left that world far behind. After winning an Australian modeling competition, aged only thirteen, she had eventually moved to the United States, where she became a Victoria's Secret model. In 2013, she earned $7 million, making her the second-best-paid female model in the world after Gisele Bündchen, and offers kept piling up—from H&M, Swarovski, Unilever—to promote products.

But a supermodel's earnings aren't enough to launch a major business, and Kerr was interested in what Low had to offer. She had tired of modeling and was looking to transform herself into an entrepreneur. The next morning, she had a package of KORA products couriered over to Low's apartment in the Time Warner building.

Back in October, Kerr had divorced actor Orlando Bloom, with whom she had a three-year-old son, and her tumultuous personal life was constant fodder for the tabloids. Her parents back in Gunnedah gave an interview to Australian television, bemoaning how their daughter had forgotten them and needed to come home to learn how to milk cows and ride horses. In the first months of 2014, Kerr would spend a chunk of time in New York, and almost every occasion she stepped out, a paparazzo would click her image. But despite the scrutiny, she managed to conceal a blossoming, and unexpected, romance with Low.

On February 2, the Malaysian invited her to watch Super Bowl XLVIII at the MetLife Stadium in New Jersey—it was her first—and she attended along with Riza Aziz and McFarland. Model Kate Upton and Katie Holmes, who were in another box, stopped by. Gossip columns noted Kerr was there to watch the Seattle Seahawks pull off the biggest upset in modern football history, defeating the Denver Broncos, but Low's presence went unnoticed.

In the ensuing days, Low set about wooing her in the only way he knew how. He texted Lorraine Schwartz, telling her he wanted a necklace with a heart-shaped diamond, costing between $1 and $2 million, noting that "[s]ize matters." The diamond necklace, inscribed with "MK," cost $1.3 million, and Low gave it to the model as a present for Valentine's Day, financing it with money washed through both the Park Lane and Coastal Energy deals.

Even to close friends, Low would say he was only "helping Miranda out," and to keep the relationship secret, the pair would go out accompanied by Kerr's agent, Kristal Fox. A few weeks later, however—at a party for Kerr's thirty-first birthday—it would have been difficult to overlook Low's romantic intentions. Low hired out a venue on Chelsea Piers in New York for a nineties-themed party and flew in Salt-N-Pepa, Mark Morrison, and Vanilla Ice to perform. As usual, Jamie Foxx was on hand to emcee, and DiCaprio, Bloom, and Swizz Beatz were among the hundred or so invitees.

For the weekend of festivities, Low had the *Topaz*, Sheikh Mansour's yacht, moored in the Hudson River, and bedecked with customized Miami-style glamor lighting and hundreds of balloons. After the partying, a helicopter flew Low, Kerr, and her Australian friends to Atlantic City for more gambling at the baccarat tables. It was like the old times, back during Low's Wharton days, although now he traveled by helicopter, not limousine, and he no longer cared whether Ivanka Trump would accept his invitation.

As he was wooing Kerr, Low also had to keep Rosmah Mansor sated, and in January 2014 he texted Lorraine Schwartz to see if she was in Los Angeles. The jeweler was in town and made haste to the Hotel Bel-Air, laden with luminescent diamond bangles and necklaces. Schwartz drove into the hotel, an exclusive Spanish mission–style retreat favored by Hollywood stars, set in twelve acres of gardens in the heart of Beverly Hills. Rosmah had checked into a plush suite with deep carpets and, after dinner with Schwartz and Low, she invited them up.

Schwartz unfurled her wares onto a table and Rosmah began to pick out items. She pointed at one eighteen-carat white gold diamond-studded bangle, and Schwartz set it aside. It cost $52,000, but Rosmah was only getting started. With the ease of a professional shopper, the first lady quickly picked out twenty-seven bracelets and necklaces. No one talks money in these elite circles, and it took a few months for the bill to arrive at Blackrock, Low's company. The total was $1.3 million—quite a moderate spending spree by Rosmah's standards. Low took care of the invoice, and he also picked up the $300,000 tab that Rosmah ran up at the Bel-Air hotel during her week's stay.

Between April 2013 and September 2014, Low used the Blackrock account to purchase $200 million in jewelry from across the globe: Las Vegas, New York, Hong Kong, Dubai. Even more portable than art, diamonds are extremely hard to track. The Financial Action Task Force, in a 2013 report, warned that money launderers and terrorists used the diamond industry as a conduit for illicit cash. In the United States, retailers like Lorraine Schwartz, or dealers in raw and cut stones, were under no legal obligation to conduct due diligence on clients. Even better, jewels could be transported without having to send money through financial institutions.

Not all the jewelry went to important figures like Rosmah. On one occasion, Low was in Las Vegas when he found out it was the birthday of a young Asian-Canadian model, a hanger-on in his group. On the way to dinner, Low spontaneously ducked into a Cartier store and came back out with a watch, passing it to her without any fanfare as a last-minute gift. The watch cost $80,000. But it was Rosmah on whom Low showered the biggest diamonds. Imelda Marcos had her shoe collection, at least 1,220 pairs left behind when she and her husband were driven out of the Philippines in 1986 by the "People Power Revolution." Rosmah would be known for her Birkin bags and jewelry, hundreds of millions of dollars of rings, necklaces, and pendants, arranged in specially made drawers at her residence in Kuala Lumpur.

From the outside, Low appeared to be accumulating prestige, and he no longer had to situate himself between formidable people—the ones who knew the secrets of how the world really works. He had become one of them in his own right. Dating a supermodel, he was pursuing deals and drawing the Malaysian prime minister and his wife ever closer. Those who hung around him, at the Super Bowl or over a dinner, still gossiped about his money. It was vaguely known he had links to Malaysia's prime minister, and it was taken as normal that such a relationship in a faraway Asian country could entail riches.

Anyone who was paying close attention, however, might have noticed an extra degree of restlessness amid Low's frenzied, globe-trotting schedule. As he whipped out his phone, excusing himself from a dinner or party, only he could see the obstacles that were piling up in his inbox, threatening to upend his scheme.

Chapter 38

Losing Control

Kuala Lumpur, Malaysia, March 2014

The 1MDB board of directors started their afternoon meeting with a recitation of the first seven verses from the Qur'an, known as the Al-Fatiha, for the crew and passengers of MH370, the Malaysia Airlines Boeing 777-200 jet that had gone missing in early March over the South China Sea. The plane, with 239 crew and passengers on board, was flying from Kuala Lumpur to Beijing, but just an hour after takeoff the pilot stopped making contact with air traffic control and, moments later, the plane disappeared from civil aviation radar screens.

In the weeks since, Beijing's official media had slammed Malaysia for leading a chaotic search effort, first focusing efforts on the South China Sea, north of Malaysia, before military radar showed the aircraft had gone missing over the Andaman Sea, to the west of the country. Failure to locate the plane debris, added to chaotic daily briefings, spotlighted the incompetence of Malaysia's government and was an embarrassment for Najib.

The board of directors intoned the Islamic verses but talk soon turned to another pressing matter at hand. Tan Theng Hooi, the managing partner in Malaysia for Deloitte Touche, had been invited to speak, and he brought some distressing news. Only weeks earlier, Deloitte had become 1MDB's third auditor and the fund's management was exerting huge pressure for a quick sign-off on the accounts for the year to March 31, 2013, which had been delayed by months.

Just as Deloitte was poring over the accounts, though, the firm's Southeast Asia regional headquarters in Singapore began to receive numerous emails and letters alleging financial reporting fraud at 1MDB. The complaints, Tan said, had touched on a number of issues, from 1MDB's claims to have $2.3 billion invested in an unknown fund in the Cayman Islands, to its overpayment for power plants, and a mismatch between its huge debt and minimal assets. An accountant with thirty years' experience, Tan appeared very keen to get rid of the problem.

"These allegations are not new and no evidence had been provided to Deloitte to substantiate these allegations. Deloitte was therefore unable to pursue the matter," he told the board.

One of the letters came from Tony Pua, a forty-one-year-old opposition politician, who quietly had been following the 1MDB issue for a few years. Unlike many politicians, Pua had a deep grasp of business; in a previous life he founded a technology company, before selling out to enter politics in 2008, winning a parliamentary seat the following year in a satellite town of Kuala Lumpur. Whip-smart, with a degree in philosophy, politics, and economics from Oxford University, Pua unsettled time-serving UMNO politicians, who were not used to his piercing questions and mastery of financial concepts. Unable to suffer fools, Pua, an ethnic Chinese Malaysian with spiky graying hair and a quick-fire delivery, was universally disliked in the ruling party.

He became intrigued by 1MDB in 2010, when KPMG had written an "emphasis of matter" about the fund's investment in PetroSaudi. Such arcane terms meant nothing to most folks, but Pua knew it signaled the accountants had concerns about 1MDB. He sat on the Public Accounts Committee of the Parliament, which was charged with overseeing state spending, and so agitated for the committee to investigate, but the chairman, an UMNO politician, had dragged his heels. By 2014, though, with articles in the *Edge* pointing out the fishy Cayman Islands fund investment, Pua had more firepower.

1MDB fired KPMG in January after the auditing firm had been unable to confirm the $2.3 billion the Malaysian fund claimed to have in the Cayman Islands was really worth that much—or whether it actually existed. Back in 2012, the 1MDB fund had sold its interest in a PetroSaudi subsidiary that owned the two oil drill ships to a company controlled by Hong Kong financier Lobo Lee. Instead of cash, 1MDB had received payment of $2.3 billion in the form of "units" in a newly formed Cayman Islands fund. It was a fictional transaction aimed at covering up the money that Low and others had taken from 1MDB in 2009.

Yeo Jiawei of BSI had misled KPMG that the Cayman Islands investment was backed by cash—not just shady "units." But the transaction just didn't seem right to the U.S. auditing firm. Refusing to sign off on the accounts, KPMG was dumped, just as 1MDB had fired Ernst & Young before it. Eager to build its business in Malaysia, Deloitte signed on.

KPMG's removal was a roadblock for Low, who needed an auditor to quickly rubber-stamp 1MDB's accounts. With $10 billion in debt and only $20 million in cash, the fund was in dire straits, hemorrhaging tens of millions of dollars a month, but Low had a game plan. The 1MDB energy unit was planning to list its shares on Malaysia's stock exchange. Hopefully big global institutional investors would snap up the shares, given Asia's economic outlook was still brighter than the West's, and the IPO would net $5 billion or more.

It was an optimistic assessment, but one that was crucial to keeping the scheme going, providing Low with the money he desperately needed to hide the fund's losses. Major banks, including Goldman Sachs and Deutsche, were feeding the optimism, telling 1MDB there would be ample appetite from global investors, keen themselves to win the mandate to advise on the IPO. Even an amount lower than $5 billion would be enough to fill financial holes and stop the scrutiny of 1MDB, Low anticipated, but first Deloitte needed to okay the delayed accounts.

Like KPMG, Deloitte's Tan had issues with the accounting of the Cayman Islands investment. To get around the problem, Low turned again to Mohamed Al Husseiny, asking for Aabar to guarantee the offshore money. This meant that the Abu Dhabi fund would cover the amount no matter what. It should have been a red flag for Deloitte, given the letters it had received alleging financial fraud at 1MDB, not to mention the fact that 1MDB already had ended its relationship with two major auditors. But a piece of paper from Aabar appeared to be good enough for Tan to get comfortable with the investment.

Auditors are meant to be independent, but Tan offered for Deloitte to help 1MDB with its media relations. With barely any business, and encumbered by huge borrowings, the only way for 1MDB to avoid a financial loss was to again revalue its land portfolio and book the profits, as it had done in 2010. In this way, 1MDB was hoping to show a $260 million profit.

Tan was not only supportive of this accounting, he also offered to explain it publicly to help deflect any negative media stories. Deloitte had been so helpful, in fact, that Tan asked whether his firm would be selected to audit 1MDB's many subsidiaries, including the energy unit that was gearing up for an IPO. The board confirmed Tan's request immediately, and its chairman, Lodin Kamaruddin, Najib's close aide, said he wanted Deloitte's "professionalism and objectivity" put on record.

Still, the board was adamant that 1MDB's management repatriate the Cayman Islands money, to help slash the fund's debt and to show the *Edge* newspaper and other critics they were wrong. Only Low, and perhaps a few associates like Al Husseiny and Yeo, knew the truth: There was no money in the Cayman Islands.

As dawn approached one night in May, Low made an unusual request of staff in a private gaming room at the Palazzo on the Las Vegas Strip. Drunk and in his element, Low called out for a watermelon. Some of those crowding around the baccarat table, many of them models, didn't know this short, pudgy figure who was putting down $200,000 bets at a time. The whisper went around that he'd financed *The Wolf of Wall Street*, a film that everyone was talking about, but there was something unhinged about him. He was on a losing streak, and when the Palazzo staff turned up with a watermelon from the kitchens, Low seized it and rolled it down the table—supposedly for good luck—sending cards flying. Still, the losses mounted, and guzzling Johnnie Walker Blue Label whisky, he started bellowing to staff again.

"Red T-shirts," he told a staff member waiting on him. "Everyone needs red T-shirts."

The staff hurried to comply, bringing in red Palazzo tourist shirts for the room of about twenty people, including Joey McFarland and Riza Aziz.

"My friend couldn't even watch," said one young woman who was in attendance that night. "He saw on that table all the money he would ever make in his life, his college tuition, car, home, everything. Won and lost."

It was typical Low, who on another drunk occasion had dropped $50,000 worth of casino chips on the floor, only recovering them when a shocked friend noticed the loss.

As the night of gambling at the Palazzo wound up at sunrise,

Low handed the casino staff a tip of $1 million, one of the largest ever at the establishment.

Ho Kay Tat in April wrote a strident column in the *Edge* calling on 1MDB to name the fund manager looking after its $2.3 billion in the Cayman Islands and to bring the money home. Then, in May, a Singapore newspaper, citing inside sources, named Hong Kong–based Bridge Global as the fund manager. When Lobo Lee later erased details, including his name, from Bridge Global's website, the newspaper noted the suspicious behavior. Low was furious—he believed there was a leak at BSI—and he ordered the bank to hunt down the source. The suspicion fell first on Kevin Swampillai, Yeo's boss, and Low made efforts to get him off the 1MDB-related accounts. Swampillai denied any involvement and refused to budge.

Over the summer, Low lurched from party to party, spending his days railing against unnamed "leakers." The facade of carefree revelry was starting to crumble, as Low became paranoid about a Judas in his ranks.

Around this time, he persuaded Yeo Jiawei, the funds expert at BSI, to come work for him. Yeo accepted. From this point on, Low didn't even want to speak on the phone or use email for important transactions, and he planned to tap Yeo's financial expertise, as well as having him courier top secret documents around the world.

The following spring, Low would invite Yeo to watch Floyd Mayweather Jr. fight Manny Pacquiao at the MGM Grand Garden Arena in Vegas, and the young Singaporean became hooked on the jet-set lifestyle. His proximity to Low had swelled Yeo's self-regard, and he sneered at those at BSI who didn't travel everywhere by private jet. He already had made millions of dollars, secretly funneling off fees paid by 1MDB to BSI and Bridge

Global to manage the Cayman Islands money and other investments. He began to buy multiple homes in Singapore and one in Australia. Now Low enticed him into his inner circle with promises of even more bountiful riches.

Yeo would pocket tens of millions of dollars more, but it came at a price, as Low morphed into a tyrannical—and insecure—boss. The banker stayed in contact with former colleagues at BSI, telling them stories about how Low would take calls on his private jet and start screaming. He was especially perturbed by details coming out about the Cayman Islands investment. Scared by the way Low was acting, so at odds with the mild manners he knew, Yeo began to believe his new boss was losing control.

Addressing 1MDB's board in July, Tim Leissner was doing the best he could to keep Goldman in the game to win the IPO business. The fund was in grave danger. In just two months, it had lost $140 million under the weight of hundreds of millions of dollars in interest costs. The fund needed an IPO of its energy assets, and quickly, to restore it to health. For two years, Leissner had championed the IPO, but now he faced a problem.

As part of the deal in 2012 to acquire Ananda Krishnan's power plants, 1MDB had given the billionaire the right to subscribe to the IPO at a cheap price. Now, Leissner was explaining to 1MDB's board how it would cost the fund hundreds of millions of dollars to buy back these rights before the listing. Some board members were outraged. The original deal seemed way too favorable to Krishnan, who already had received above-market prices for his power assets.

Some board members knew about secret charity payments of hundreds of millions of dollars by Krishnan-controlled companies to 1MDB. That was how run-of-the-mill graft worked in Malaysia: The government overpaid for an asset, and the seller made backhand contributions to UMNO, while politicians lined their pockets. Still, the terms seemed very good for Krishnan and his company, Tanjong.

"Is Goldman acting for 1MDB or Tanjong?" Ashvin Valiram, a Malaysian textile entrepreneur and board member, asked Leissner.

"Of course, we're representing 1MDB," the banker replied, trying to keep the atmosphere light. "Without this deal with Tanjong, the fund won't be able to undertake the IPO."

Finally, ties between Goldman and 1MDB were starting to fray. Earlier in the year, 1MDB had enticed banks to lend even more by offering them a role leading the IPO. The fund had secured a $250 million loan from a consortium led by Deutsche Bank, whose new country head, Yusof Yaacob, had been at Goldman. Finally, another bank was getting a look in.

Goldman itself, worried by the negative articles and focus in the *Wall Street Journal* on its huge profits, began to distance itself from the fund, and was not keen to get entangled in fresh lending. Leissner was furious when 1MDB selected Deutsche and Maybank to run the IPO, a lucrative assignment for both banks, and he turned to Jho Low to ensure a role for Goldman. For two years, Leissner had been using his accounts to move over $200 million in stolen 1MDB money, keeping millions and passing even more on as bribes. Just a few weeks earlier, Leissner and Low had chatted online about needing to get "cakes"— or diamonds—to Rosmah. Soon after, the banker would send $4.1 million to pay for even more jewelry for the first lady and others. *How was it that 1MDB was cutting Goldman out?*, he wanted to know. In the end, 1MDB appointed the bank as an adviser for the IPO.

At this juncture, Leissner was unsupervised, traveling the world, and spending large chunks of time in the United States with his new wife, Kimora Lee Simmons. The banker, through a limited liability company, put down $19 million over the summer for a base on New York's Upper East Side, a 4,600-square-foot, five-bedroom apartment in the Marquand, a 1913 Beaux Arts building just a stone's throw from Central Park, but he spent as much time in Los Angeles, at Simmons's Beverly Hills mansion, and flying to Asia. The following year, a British Virgin Islands company that Leissner controlled acquired the *Sai Ram*, a $20 million, 170-foot yacht with six cabins.

For years, Leissner had resented that Goldman never promoted him to a regional role, a consequence of his reputation as a cowboy who wouldn't hesitate to bypass internal permissions to get deals done. But in June, Goldman appointed him chairman of Southeast Asia; he was making too much money for the firm, and there were fears he might walk to another bank, taking his Southeast Asian relationships with him. Later in the year, Lloyd Blankfein, eager for Goldman to continue building its presence in emerging markets, held Leissner and Andrea Vella up as models to follow.

"Look at what Tim and Andrea did in Malaysia," Blankfein told a meeting in New York on how to build business in growth markets, rather than the increasingly heavily regulated U.S. "We have to do more of that."

Blankfein, Cohn, and other Goldman leaders, in the aftermath of the mortgage crisis, had pledged to put clients first and regularly preached good governance. Yet Goldman had made hundreds of millions of dollars and 1MDB was in disarray, at a high cost to Malaysia's people. The bank had turned a blind eye to irregularities, enabling the kind of industrial-scale corruption carried out in the past by Sani Abacha of Nigeria or Ferdinand Marcos of the Philippines. Those dictators had been crude—Abacha had sent trucks to loot cash from the central bank—but this was simply a more sophisticated way of taking money, one conducted under the noses of Goldman Sachs.

Leissner wasn't the only one interested in boats. Even as his scheme was starting to unravel, Low was making his biggest purchase yet. There was one asset he didn't yet possess: a mega-yacht. Since the previous year, Oceanco, a Dutch builder of custom yachts, had been constructing a three-hundred-foot vessel for Low, complete with a helicopter landing pad, gymnasium, cinema, sauna, and steam room. This wasn't going to match the *Topaz*, but it was still one of the most luxurious yachts in the world, and Low would be spared the ignominy of renting again from Sheikh Mansour and other tycoons.

As the shipbuilders were putting the finishing touches to the yacht at the Alblasserdam shipyard near Rotterdam over the spring, Low peppered Oceanco executives with demands to ensure every element was just so. In the same way he curated his parties, with performances, food, and drink organized down to the most minute detail, Low wanted this boat to be perfect.

"For owner's cabin, perhaps if you can get expert advice from Tempur specialists which is most top of the line and expensive with most functions for mattress," Low wrote in one email.

All those years ago in Penang, Low had borrowed a boat and pretended it was his family's. Now, this yacht would deepen the mystique of a little-known Asian billionaire—and keep hold of Miranda Kerr. Perhaps there was another reason: The yacht could be moved anywhere in an emergency.

Now, Low needed $250 million to pay Oceanco, and he had so many other financing requirements that he was starting to get reckless. Deutsche Bank's recent loan to 1MDB was meant to pave the way for the IPO of 1MDB's power assets. In 2012, the fund's management, without the board's knowledge, granted Aabar, the Abu Dhabi fund, options to buy cheap shares in the IPO. It was supposedly a reward for its parent IPIC's guarantee of 1MDB bonds—the payoff that Sheikh Mansour had been promised two years earlier.

To smooth the way for the listing, 1MDB's management claimed it needed to buy Aabar's options back at a cost of hundreds of millions of dollars, and Deutsche provided the money. Of course, Aabar's chief executive, Mohamed Al Husseiny, and chairman, Khadem Al Qubaisi, were conspirators; the options were just another ruse by Low to move money around. As soon as 1MDB got its hands on the Deutsche Bank loan, the fund's management sent the money to the look-alike Aabar, the same vehicle Low and Al Qubaisi had used to divert cash in 2012.

At this critical stage, Low could have deployed these funds to fill financial holes, especially the nonexistent cash in the Cayman Islands. Instead, he used the bulk of the money to pay for the superyacht, which was delivered in the summer. At this late stage, with politicians and journalists clamoring for the Cayman Islands money to be returned to Malaysia, it was irrational to be exacerbating the financial damage at the fund.

After years of getting away with the scheme, Low was blinded to the peril he faced. The first party on the yacht, complete with a dragon-shaped cake provided by Oceanco, was a birthday celebration that summer for May-Lin, Low's sister. He christened his new yacht *Equanimity*, meaning calmness and composure, especially in a difficult situation.

PART IV

BONFIRE OF SECRETS

Chapter 39

"No Cash. No Deal."

Bangkok, Thailand, June 2014

Clare Rewcastle-Brown, who ran the *Sarawak Report* blog, looked across the lobby of the Plaza Athénée hotel in central Bangkok for her contact. She was scanning for a Swiss man in his forties, and apart from those meager details, knew only the name and title: Xavier Justo, a former employee of PetroSaudi. When a bronzed and muscular figure approached, and introduced himself as Justo, she was taken aback. This encounter made even a muckraker like Rewcastle-Brown nervous. The meeting, in June 2014, had been arranged by an intermediary, and she was expecting a short, bald, bespectacled man. But then, it quickly became apparent that Justo, too, was deeply anxious, and that wasn't the demeanor of someone about to inflict harm.

"The people we're dealing with are ruthless and powerful," Justo said.

Justo was working on an alternative way to get the money he believed he deserved: find someone else willing to pay for the PetroSaudi documents he had taken.

His connection to Rewcastle-Brown had been a fortuitous one. After leaving PetroSaudi in 2011, Justo had traveled to Singapore for the city-state's Formula 1 night race. He was supposed to have met Tarek Obaid, the chief executive of PetroSaudi,

there for a negotation over the files, but his erstwhile friend had
not shown up. The trip, however, turned out fruitful in other
ways. By chance, he met people close to Mahathir, the former
Malaysian prime minister, and had given them his business card.

Nothing happened for more than two years. Then, in
the summer of 2014, those people had connected Justo to
Rewcastle-Brown, who was digging around, trying to find more
about 1MDB for her blog. She was eager to have a source with
information about PetroSaudi, who she hoped would help her
unravel what had transpired at the fund. Before meeting in person, Justo had supplied Rewcastle-Brown with a sampling of his
material, a single piece of paper with the heading, "Thousands
of documents related to the deal (emails, faxes and transcripts)"
and details of what the server contained. This was just the break
she needed to prove her suspicions about 1MDB and Jho Low. A
few weeks later, she traveled to Bangkok to meet Justo.

The server data was ready on a portable hard drive, detailing
the PetroSaudi phase of the scheme. But there was a condition:
Rewcastle-Brown had to pay $2 million if she wanted the infor-
mation. Justo defended the request by explaining this was simply money PetroSaudi owed him. She was a member of Britain's
establishment, with a brother-in-law who had been prime minister, but unlike Malaysia, that didn't grant her access to millions
of dollars.

Justo was adamant. "No cash. No deal."

Keen to get her hands on the documents, Rewcastle-Brown
set about finding someone who could pay. It would take her seven
months to secure a benefactor.

Low must have heard from the PetroSaudi executives about
Justo's demands for money. But he had no idea about this dangerous meeting between Justo and Rewcastle-Brown. What would
he have done if he did know? It was as if Low didn't take Justo

seriously. He could easily have arranged for a payoff of a measly few million dollars to the former PetroSaudi executive. But Low didn't seem interested in attending to the nuts and bolts of his scheme. He was too taken with his new love interest to focus on the mundane business of ensuring crucial information didn't leak out.

Wearing a green skirt and shirt, with purple floral patterns, Miranda Kerr stepped from the car in Munich and, as a small group of photographers snapped her picture, made her way into a branch of Escada. It was July 29, 2014, a hot Bavarian summer's day, and she was there to launch Joyful, a new perfume line for the luxury German fashion brand. The scent was meant to evoke simplicity, and Kerr's makeup was light, her brown hair falling naturally over her shoulders. As German models and television personalities drank champagne and chatted, there was a flurry of activity around Kerr, the kind that attended her wherever she traveled.

"Simple things, like, you know, a fresh bouquet of flowers makes me really happy, watching the sun rise or the sun set," she told one interviewer.

In the past few weeks Kerr's life had been anything but simple. Britain's *Daily Mail*, *HELLO!* magazine, and many other publications were speculating about a burgeoning romance between the model and James Packer, the Australian gambling billionaire. In June, Australian newspapers noted Kerr had been aboard Packer's superyacht, *Arctic P*, off the coast of Cyprus, and cited "inside sources" saying that, rather than a romance, she was looking to get the mogul to invest in KORA Organics. Her current investors, with a 25 percent stake, were the twin sons of Rene Rivkin, an Australian stockbroker who had been jailed for insider trading and later took his own life. But the model had grander ambitions for her company, which specialized in organic cosmetics, and she needed a big capital injection.

The speculation, however, was focused on the wrong billionaire. As Kerr finished up her work in Munich, Jho Low had arranged for a private jet to pick her up and whisk her to Naples in Italy. He had been planning this trip for over a month, even hiring a high-end concierge service to choreograph every element. Low ordered his new yacht *Equanimity*, piloted by British and American captains, to sail to the waters around Italy. With its Asian-inspired interior, constructed out of wood, bamboo, marble, and gold leaf, the boat helped Low stand out from the merely wealthy. It could accommodate twenty-six guests, but had even more berths for twenty-eight crew members, ensuring a sufficient staff-to-guest ratio. It would cost millions of dollars a year just to operate. This trip was to be much more intimate, although Kerr, as ever, was accompanied by her publicist, Kristal Fox.

Billionaires are today's royalty, and like a modern-day Louis XIV, Low thrived on being the center of orchestrated formality, each of his whims met immediately, whether by boat staff, private bankers, or art dealers. A few days earlier, Low had taken delivery from Lorraine Schwartz of a matching set of jewelry, comprising diamond earrings, a necklace, a bracelet, and a ring. A few weeks earlier, he'd sent Schwartz a picture of Kerr wearing Tiffany jewelry to give her an idea of the model's taste. Over the next ten days on the boat, as it sailed around Italy and to the Greek island of Corfu, Low gave the various pieces of jewelry to Kerr over elaborate set dinners.

Yet Low was straining to pay for all this opulence. Although some $5 billion had come out of 1MDB, the scheme had so many tendrils—so many payments to conspirators and business partners, and to keep up a billionaire's lifestyle—he was often hustling for cash. Recently, he had hired U.S. public relations firm Edelman to help counter the growing number of negative press stories about him, and he would later employ Schillings, the British reputation consultancy. Edelman's services were costing him as much as $100,000 some months.

As bills piled up, Low began to miss payments, including legal bills and salaries for the crew of *Equanimity*, forcing him to use his vast art collection as collateral for a loan from Sotheby's Financial.

To pay the $2 million invoice on Kerr's latest jewelry, Low again raided the fund. As he was such an important customer, Schwartz permitted him to pay a few months after the Corfu trip, but by September he needed to send the cash. Given how much he had taken from 1MDB, Low seemingly could have financed this relatively small amount from some pot of money somewhere in the world.

Instead, he was seized by the need to get as much out of 1MDB as he could, perhaps believing the upcoming IPO would keep the edifice from collapsing. He had already taken money from a Deutsche Bank loan to 1MDB in May—a late-stage flow of money that could have gone to shore up 1MDB's finances—and spent it on the *Equanimity*. Now, he set about trying to get a further $725 million in loans from Deutsche, ostensibly for the same reason: Before the IPO, 1MDB needed to pay off Aabar to cancel even more options that allowed it to take a stake in the listing.

Given the profits Goldman had made from 1MDB, Deutsche Bank was keen, but it couldn't muster this money alone. To rally other Middle Eastern banks to take part, Low wrote Ambassador Otaiba on September 10, 2014, using the Eric Tan Gmail account, requesting him to use his sway in Abu Dhabi to get other lenders on board. The ambassador duly obliged and wrote the managing director of First Gulf Bank, which, along with

Abu Dhabi Commercial Bank, and a Kuwaiti lender, joined a consortium led by Deutsche Bank. Goldman looked at taking part, but finally—after a number of years of obliviousness—the bank had questions about the fund's behavior and backed out. As collateral for the loan, 1MDB had posted its $2.3 billion Cayman Islands investment, but the fund's executives, when pushed by Goldman bankers, had been unable to show proof it existed, just a guarantee from the Abu Dhabi fund Aabar.

Mohamed Al Husseiny, Aabar's chief executive, helped the process along, urging Deutsche Bank employees to disburse the new loan quickly. Another Low associate, Terence Geh, a finance executive at 1MDB, also pushed Deutsche Bank to hurry up, citing Prime Minister Najib's desire to receive the money expeditiously.

Then, 1MDB requested Deutsche Bank send the first tranche of the $725 million loan directly to Aabar. It was an odd arrangement. Normally a bank, for compliance reasons, would send such large amounts of cash directly to the borrower. But Deutsche was satisfied by the apparent involvement of the Abu Dhabi fund. The perpetrators had tricked the bank: The recipient was another look-alike Aabar, set up by Al Husseiny with an account at UBS Bank in Singapore. Two days later, more than $100 million was diverted to a shell company controlled by Fat Eric.

It became clear from what occurred next why Low needed to keep pilfering the till: There were just so many people to repay for their services. The shell company sent $13 million to Densmore, a British Virgin Islands firm partially controlled by Otaiba, which had an account at BSI in Singapore, an apparent reward for using his ambassadorial position to help get the Middle Eastern banks on board. Khadem Al Qubaisi, who was Al Husseiny's boss, got $15 million.

And Low, of course, took his cut, sending some of the money

to Lorraine Schwartz. A few months later, he would buy Kerr yet more jewelry, a $3.8 million diamond pendant, making a grand total of over $8 million to acquire the supermodel's affections.

In September 2014, Mahathir Mohamad, the eighty-nine-year-old former prime minister of Malaysia, who remained a powerful figure in the ruling UMNO party, received a dossier of leaked information, including emails from 1MDB that showed Jho Low was involved in investment decisions. After years of speculation about his role at the fund, here was proof. Mahathir still wielded power at UMNO, and he began to engage in backroom dealing intended to force Prime Minister Najib to resign over this mess. The fund's huge debt risked toppling Malaysia into a crisis like Argentina, Mahathir wrote on his blog. This was not the *Edge*, a scrappy newspaper, but one of the nation's most powerful figures raising concerns about 1MDB.

Until now, journalists had only been able to speculate about Low and the source of his wealth. To counter the stories, Edelman, the public relations firm, put out a statement denying their client had received "patronage" from Malaysia's government. But now solid information was starting to leak out from the troubled sovereign wealth fund. Clare Rewcastle-Brown at *Sarawak Report*, who also got hold of the emails, published a piece titled "Jho Low's Spending and Malaysia's Development Money," in which she questioned why the fund had lied about Low's secret role.

"Malaysians are entitled to conclude that Low's record levels of spending in various billionaire hotspots," she wrote, "has largely been paid for by them."

At Deloitte's offices in Kuala Lumpur, the developments sparked panic. Its auditors were rushing to sign off on the accounts for the financial year to March 2014, which under Malaysian law were supposed to be submitted by the end of

September. The fund had never managed this in the past, but now a timely submission was crucial to getting the IPO under way by the year-end.

Concerned about its reputation, Deloitte was demanding a quick repatriation of the $2.3 billion in the Cayman Islands fund. The 1MDB board, apparently under the illusion there was money there, upped the entreaties on management to comply. Since first taking cash from 1MDB, Low had relied on accounting magic to make this problem disappear, but through three different auditing firms there it remained, like a pebble in his shoe. Before, he'd gone on taking more, and spending wildly, seemingly under the assumption he could cover it up with new trickery down the road. Now, as his desperation mounted, Low was coming to a stark realization: He would have to give up some real funds. The trouble was, he didn't have $2.3 billion at his disposal. He had to find another manuever—and it would be his most reckless yet.

Turning to Yeo Jiawei, the former BSI fund specialist, Low looked for a way out. *How could they turn a few hundred million dollars—the remainder of the Deutsche Bank money not used for jewelry and other purchases—into $2.3 billion?* This kind of alchemy was beyond even Low, but accounting tricks had worked for years to hide his thefts from 1MDB, so why not one last, monumental sleight of hand to fool Deloitte and the board? Yeo had an idea, and he looked to Amicorp, the Singapore-based financial company that administered funds in Curaçao, to put it into practice. To make it look like 1MDB was bringing the money home, Yeo devised a complex and circuitous flow of payments.

It was the craziest plan to date, so outlandish it appeared to have no chance of success. The idea was to transfer a portion of cash from the latest Deutsche Bank loan into the Cayman Islands fund. From there, 1MDB would then "redeem" this money, but immediately send it into a series of offshore vehicles set up by Amicorp, until the cash ended up back at the Cayman Islands fund. From here, 1MDB could again "redeem" the money. It was the *same* cash going in circles. The perpetrators sent a chunk of a few hundred million dollars through this cycle, and then repeated the process five more times, making it look as if 1MDB had redeemed $1.5 billion of its nonexistent Cayman Islands investment.

Satisfied by the money coming home, Deloitte in early November signed off on 1MDB's accounts. The auditor had missed the circuitous movement of cash. The fund had made over a $200 million loss, which was unlikely to entice investors to take part in the IPO, but it appeared to have quieted its critics. In a statement, 1MDB announced it had redeemed over half of the money in the Cayman Islands. Low looked to have performed a miracle, and perhaps the IPO would proceed, but there was still a problem.

Deutsche Bank had noticed something wasn't right, pushing Low further into a corner. Some bankers at Deutsche were suspicious about the Cayman Islands investment, the collateral for its loan. If the German bank asked for its money back, the investment fund would have been unable to come up with the cash.

The Malaysian needed some good publicity, and like many disreputable businessmen, he looked to philanthropy for a quick fix boost to his image. It was a sign of growing desperation.

Chapter 40

Generous Jho

New York, October 2014

As Alicia Keys and her husband, Swizz Beatz, introduced him, Low rose from his seat and made for the lectern at Cipriani Wall Street. Fervent applause rang out for the Malaysian, who was being honored at one of the highlights of New York's social calendar, the Angel Ball. A yearly event—organized by Denise Rich, a socialite and songwriter whose daughter, Gabrielle, had died of cancer—it attracted Hollywood stars, musicians, and business titans, and raised millions to fight the disease. A few months earlier, Rich had telephoned Low to inform him he would be honored as that year's "Angel Gabrielle" at a ball on October 19.

Dressed in black tie, Low took to the stage on the evening of the gala, and as the applause died out, he paused a moment to look out across the room. The banquet hall had once been home to the New York Stock Exchange, and its Greek pillars and high ceilings, centered around an imposing Wedgwood dome, exuded power and status. Low could see many people he knew well, and counted as friends.

There was Rich herself, whose former husband, Marc Rich, had fled to Switzerland after being indicted on federal charges of tax evasion, eventually being granted a pardon by President Bill Clinton. Nearby were Ambassador Otaiba and his wife, who also were being honored as "Angels of Inspiration" for their charity work. Sitting across from the pair was Jamie Foxx, who later that evening would perform, as would Alicia Keys and Ludacris. Lorraine Schwartz, too, was on hand, as were Paris Hilton and Richie Akiva, owner of 1Oak, a New York nightclub frequented by Low.

He began by telling the story of how, in February 2012, he'd undertaken his first-ever full-body medical checkup in Switzerland, only for a doctor to tell him he might have stage 2 lung cancer.

"I felt my world fall apart," Low said, sounding a bit stiff, as if trying to make sure he got the story right. "This was one of the changing moments of my life and I didn't know what to do."

He related how he called Al Husseiny—gesturing to his friend in the audience—who had connected him with a doctor at the University of Texas's MD Anderson Cancer Center, one of the world's top hospitals for treating the disease. After six months of tests, the doctors told him it was only an infection. The reprieve from cancer changed his outlook on life, Low said, and later that year he set up the Jynwel Foundation to make charity a bigger part of his life. The following year, in October 2013, Low pledged $50 million to MD Anderson to fund an effort to better diagnose cancer by feeding patient data into IBM's Watson supercomputer.

Here was Low, caught on camera, carrying on as he had for his entire life, the master storyteller mixing reality with half truths, all in the service of distracting anyone from looking deeper. What you claimed to be, you were, plain and simple. Perhaps Low had been worried about dying of cancer, but he used the speech to develop another fiction, one about his origins.

"I'd like to take this opportunity to tell New York a bit about my background," he said.

Some in the audience groaned inwardly as the speech went

on and on. But Low needed to make his moment count. He spun, once again, the old story of his grandfather, who had come to Malaysia in the 1960s and built a fortune—only now he told this story to an audience that included luminaries of New York business and entertainment. His grandfather, Low said, had started the Low tradition of philanthropy, giving to communities across Asia, including to "orphans." He recently had died, also of cancer, which Low said had inspired him to donate to MD Anderson.

"Everything he stood for inspires me every day," Low said.

The grandfather had died, Low undoubtedly loved him, but he was not as wealthy, or such a philanthropist, as his grandson made out. Neither was Low himself so charitable; the Jynwel Foundation had done little through 2012, while Low was busy raiding the 1MDB fund, even during his own cancer scare. It was true that the Jynwel Foundation had pledged more than $100 million to charities, although it had actually paid out only a fraction of that amount. Its activity began to pick up only in late 2013, just as negative media stories about Low were snowballing, and more so in 2014.

In order to change the narrative, Edelman counseled Low to publicize his charitable endeavors, including pledges of tens of millions of dollars to National Geographic's Pristine Seas endeavor and to the United Nations to save its news service from closure. Low was even planning to donate to his alma mater. At his request, an architect drew up plans for a new building at Wharton to be called the Jynwel Institute for Sustainable Business. Low was planning to make a $150 million commitment to build and operate the institute over thirty years, a munificent gesture, redolent of a Rockefeller or a Carnegie.

Low looked to have a handle on the situation, with Deloitte signing off on 1MDB's accounts, an IPO in the cards, and the rosy glow of a big philanthropic award. He arranged for Jynwel to make a snazzy corporate video. In the video, Thomas Kaplan, a U.S. businessman in whose New York financial firm Jynwel had invested $150 million, extolled Low for always standing by his promises. There were also cameos by Szen Low, Alicia Keys, and a top Mubadala executive.

"How do you quantify luxury and inspire synergies that create value for everyone whilst building trust and loyalty for a lifetime?" a narrator says breathlessly during the video, filmed in Abu Dhabi, New York, and the Caribbean. "For Jynwel, dynamic quality, exciting value creation, and loyal trust are the foundation. Nothing slips beneath."

Low even was in talks for what would have been his biggest corporate deal yet, a billion-euro bid alongside Mubadala to buy Reebok, the Boston-based sports-apparel company, from Adidas. Called Project Turbocharged at Jynwel, Low's firm, the acquisition would seal his name as a gold-plated investor. Swizz Beatz, who had a creative role at Reebok, was involved in the deal. The Malaysian traveled to Boston for negotiations, staying for weeks in a suite at the Four Seasons.

He also began talks with Tom Ford, the U.S. fashion designer who makes suits for James Bond, to take a 25 percent stake in his company. These were high-profile deals aimed at drowning out the increasingly loud noise about Low's past.

But he would not have time to finalize the negotiations. Back home in Malaysia, Prime Minister Najib's secret accounts were finally attracting some scrutiny, and Low was forced to hustle to stop a nosy Australian bank from getting in his way.

Chapter 41

Sacks of Money

Kuala Lumpur, Malaysia, December 2014

In early December, Joanna Yu, the AmBank employee who ran Prime Minister Najib's secret accounts, was in a panic.

"Very stressful these days. ANZ running the bank," she texted to Jho Low, referring to the Australian bank that held a stake in AmBank. "We need to close the accounts soonest please," she said.

Low texted back "okay" but seemed distracted, and as the month wore on, and the accounts remained open, Yu got increasingly worried. In a series of messages, she explained to Low how the situation was perilous.

Cheah Tek Kuang, the chief executive who had given cover to the enterprise, had stepped down to take on an advisory role. The new chief, Ashok Ramamurthy, was an appointee from ANZ, and he'd found out about Najib's secret business.

By now, the prime minister had a number of accounts at AmBank, and Ramamurthy was watching. Late in 2014, the new chief executive became fretful about a series of huge cash payments into Najib's accounts. In the last few months, the prime minister had been running short on funds, as he paid off politicians. Desperate to stop the accounts from becoming overdrawn, which would attract attention from compliance, Low arranged for an associate to make last-minute cash deposits, taking sacks of cash into an AmBank branch.

It was a huge miscalculation and alarmed Yu, who pleaded with Low to stop. Heedless of the advice, he kept sending the associate with sacks of cash—literally bundles of notes in bags—to AmBank branches. The deposits totaled only $1.4 million, but handing money over the counter like this had set off anti-money-laundering alerts at AmBank, and Ramamurthy was forced to act. The chief executive alerted the AmBank board and Bank Negara Malaysia, the central bank. Low was furious.

"This is confidential," he replied, ordering Yu to tell Cheah Tek Kuang to stop Ramamurthy from further disclosures.

It was too late, she replied, ANZ board members knew about the account now, and Cheah, who saw the writing on the wall, was retiring from the bank at the end of December.

At ANZ headquarters in Melbourne, Australia, overlooking the city's former docks, executives were disturbed by what they were finding out. It was a potential public relations disaster for ANZ, which was the largest single shareholder in the bank. Ramamurthy had been with the Australian bank for more than two decades, and Shayne Elliott, ANZ's finance director and one of Australia's most senior bankers, even sat on AmBank's board.

The bank had wanted to tap into Malaysia's growth—like many foreign retail banks that expanded in emerging markets during this period. But ANZ clearly had no idea about what had transpired at a bank it was supposed to control. It wasn't just a question of Najib's accounts: AmBank also had been lending to 1MDB, and the news stories about the fund were making ANZ executives nervous. To limit the potential damage, the board ordered AmBank to immediately drop out of any work on the IPO, which it was co-arranging with Deutsche and Maybank.

The revelations were also a dilemma for Bank Negara Malaysia. The central bank oversaw the country's financial

system, and it had failed to uncover one of the world's biggest
financial swindles. Cheah had informed Zeti Akhtar Aziz, the
sixty-seven-year-old governor of Bank Negara, about the prime
minister's account in 2011. He told her Najib was expecting
inflows of hundreds of millions of dollars in political donations
from Saudi Arabia—a story concocted by Low to explain the
torrent of cash.

That was the last Zeti heard of the matter. It was a deli-
cate situation, as it involved the prime minister, but Zeti now
ordered an internal review of his accounts. For more than a
decade, she had been at the helm of Bank Negara Malaysia and
was regarded as one of Asia's most skillful central bankers. This
issue threatened her reputation, and she wanted to get to the
bottom of it.

As the stress mounted, Yu was looking to change banks herself, scared about this scrutiny from ANZ and the central bank.
Protected in his bubble, served by sycophants, Low foremost
among them, Najib was among the few who didn't know the
noose was tightening, and he ordered that his accounts remain
open. The prime minister needed to keep his wife happy.

Just before Christmas, Najib, accompanied by Rosmah, and
their usual retinue of hangers-on and security, flew into Honolulu, the state capital of Hawaii, aboard a Malaysian government
jet. Days later, the pair breezed into a Chanel store in Honolulu's
upscale Ala Moana Center. The first lady perused the jewelry
and bags on display. Low had provided Rosmah with a $27.3
million jewel from Lorraine Schwartz. But for more mundane
purchases, those costing only a few hundred thousand dollars,
she relied on Najib's credit cards.

In the Chanel store, her items selected, Rosmah turned
to Najib to pay. The prime minister whipped out his platinum

credit card, with a $1 million limit, and handed it to the cashier. A moment later, a nervous Chanel employee informed Najib that the transaction was not going through. Annoyed, he tapped out a message to Low on his cell phone. The credit card drew from his AmBank accounts, which were funded by 1MDB money.

"My platinum cards are not going through Jho. Can u call AmBank Visa and Mastercard right away?" he wrote.

Low messaged Joanna Yu, who reassured him the prime minister's limit was still $1 million. After an awkward wait in the Chanel store, eventually the credit card machine burst into action, charging the Malaysian people another $130,625 for Rosmah's frivolity. It was just a drop in the ocean of her spending. Months earlier, on the Italian island of Sardinia, Najib had used his card to acquire 750,000 euros in jewelry for his wife.

Since 2008, Rosmah had spent at least $6 million using credit cards—her husband's, but also others in her own name—in a nonstop round of shopping stretching from Rodeo Drive in Beverly Hills, to Harrods in Knightsbridge, to Saks on Fifth Avenue. In private, she thought nothing of using government jets for her shopping trips. But after the Bersih antigraft protests in 2012 had targeted Rosmah's spending, she went on a public relations campaign to improve her image. Her wealth, she said, was due to a lifelong habit of saving.

"I have bought some jewelry and dresses with my own money. What is wrong with that?" she wrote in an autobiography.

But Malaysians weren't so easily fooled.

"She said she saved that money since she was small. That is impossible," said Anis Syafiqah Mohd Yusof, a twenty-four-year-old student from the University of Malaya, who organized a small protest against corruption, one of the many around this period.

In online blog posts, average Malaysians derided the first

family for their extravagant lifestyle. One site collected pictures of Rosmah with multiple Birkin bags. Those who protested did so at great personal risk—even of jail time—but the egregious corruption of this regime was becoming too much for many people to bear silently.

As Rosmah shopped, Najib had other business to transact in Hawaii. Two days later, on Christmas Eve, the prime minister met President Obama for a round of golf. Unaware of the trouble facing Low, Najib saw the chance to play the president as a triumph, another sign of his growing power and stature on a world stage. It was a rare honor: Obama golfed with British Prime Minister David Cameron and Vice President Joe Biden, but few foreign leaders had been given the chance.

To underscore his support of Najib, Obama had agreed to a round at the Kaneohe Klipper golf course, just a short drive from where the president was vacationing with his family. Despite the protests against Najib, Obama continued to view him as among the United States's best allies in Asia. But the round ended on an anticlimax.

On the eighteenth green, Obama made his first putt. As he struck, it was clear the ball was moving to the left of the hole. The president moved to tap the ball in, but picked it up before it missed again. Prime Minister Najib then stepped up, but he also missed a second putt. Obama consoled him with a pat on the shoulder, and the two leaders moved toward the clubhouse.

By December, Deutsche Bank was perturbed. The bank had dreamed of replicating Goldman's profits, but instead it was now dawning on executives that 1MDB had something to hide. Deutsche had lent hundreds of millions of dollars to the fund, which was obligated, as part of the loan agreements, to hand over financial information to the bank. But Terence Geh, the fund's finance executive, was refusing to cooperate. The bank particularly wanted details on the Cayman Islands investment, which was collateral for the loans.

The money was supposedly held by Brazen Sky, the 1MDB affiliate, at an account at BSI in Singapore, but Geh declined to hand any data over, citing government secrecy. If Deutsche found out there was no money there, it would recall its loans, plunging 1MDB into further financial distress and scuttling the IPO, which Deutsche was helping arrange. The 1MDB board also was anxious. In December, the fund's offices had received a visit from police after an UMNO politician close to Mahathir had made a complaint about possible fraud at the fund. They had gone away without taking documents but the raid spooked one board member, who worried aloud whether they could all be prosecuted for criminal breach of trust.

Deutsche Bank was not buying Geh's excuses, and, just before Christmas Day in 2014, Low took a drastic step, ordering senior executives at the fund to destroy all documents at 1MDB's headquarters in Kuala Lumpur. Low was a phantom presence at 1MDB, rarely in the offices but exerting his power through executives who would carry out his wishes without question. Most of the smart Ivy leaguers had left amid concerns about Low; those who remained were loyalists.

This demand, however, to erase the data of a multi-billion-dollar sovereign wealth fund reeked of desperation. Lower-level employees were told to bring their laptops and cell phones to the IT department, where staff wiped them clear of all data. Even information on the fund's mainframe computer was obliterated. As an excuse, executives told staff there had been a hacking of 1MDB—that was how *Sarawak Report* had obtained the emails—and this was the only way to ensure security.

The action was not rational. A company that's facing a hacking threat can simply take its servers offline. Not long after, the physical servers went missing, too. This was an attempt to erase history, and it was a sign Low was running out of options. For years, he had thrived, leveraging his proximity to Prime Minister Najib to run 1MDB in secret. Over the years, he exhibited an inhuman tolerance for risk. The flipside was that Low rarely looked to the future: He had no contingency plan, no idea of how to get out of this mess, and now he was panicked.

But his hapless maneuvering didn't work. There were copies of documents in multiple locations—Justo had access to some key ones—making it impossible for Low to smother all traces of the fund's existence. Deutsche Bank kept pushing for documents, and Geh eventually was forced to doctor 1MDB's accounts and Brazen Sky's bank statements at BSI to make it appear the cash was still there.

The 1MDB fund's chairman, Lodin Wok Kamaruddin, who was in close contact with Najib, informed the board, in a meeting on November 25, 2014, that there was no choice but to sell assets and wind down operations as soon as possible. Interest costs alone were more than $800 million per year and the fund was close to default. The IPO looked ever more like a pipe dream. Before the fund could be wound up, however, Xavier Justo pulled the trigger.

Chapter 42

The Exposé

Singapore, January 2015

Ho Kay Tat strode into the sunlit atrium of the Fullerton Hotel in Singapore, accompanied by his boss, chairman of the Edge Media Group, Tong Kooi Ong. The imposing gray-granite neo-classical building had served as the scrappy colony's Central Post Office in the 1900s but was now a well-known five-star hotel at the mouth of the Singapore River, towered over by the glass-and-steel skyscrapers of the financial district.

As the pair entered the Fullerton, Clare Rewcastle-Brown came over and informed them her contact was waiting in the lounge area. She had briefed them on a source with information on 1MDB, but they had been expecting a Malaysian, and they got a shock when Rewcastle-Brown led them to Justo, a tall, charming Swiss man sitting in a comfy chair. It was late morning, and over coffees, Justo showed a sampling of the emails from PetroSaudi, repeating his demand for payment of $2 million.

"We need to verify the authenticity of the emails first," Ho replied.

Although she refused to pay him herself, since meeting Justo, Rewcastle-Brown had been searching for someone to supply the money. The *Edge*'s publisher, Tong, was an obvious choice. Since founding the *Edge* two decades earlier, Tong had built up a staff of

350 people and a reputation as Malaysia's only true independent newspaper proprietor. He'd agreed to meet Justo, and brought along two independent IT experts to verify the information.

That afternoon, the group reconvened in one of the Fullerton's meeting rooms, where the IT experts pored over Justo's hard disk, taking a few hours to sift through the reams of emails and documents. The experts scoured for evidence of tampering, looking at the hidden metadata within files to ascertain whether anyone had made alterations after the date of creation.

Computer users leave a "digital fingerprint," and, though they could not be 100 percent sure, the IT experts concluded that, in their opinion, the files had not been tampered with. The group then discussed how to pay Justo. He didn't want cash, and he was worried a large transfer into his accounts might lead to complications with bank compliance executives. He left agreeing to find a way to receive the money at a later date, but handing over the hard disk.

"I trust you," Justo said to the group.

Rewcastle-Brown and Ho Kay Tat had their hands on the journalistic scoops of their careers.

Before they had time to sift through the hundreds of thousands of documents provided by Justo, the *New York Times* published a front-page story on Low on February 8, 2015. The *Times* piece, part of a series about dodgy foreign money in the Time Warner building, detailed his accumulation of U.S. properties and painted him as a bagman for the prime minister's family, buying apartments and mansions and passing them on to Riza Aziz. It noted how Low's story had changed, from being a "concierge" for rich friends to being a billionaire claiming that he was investing family money. The *Times* also pointed out how Red Granite's principals had once put forward Low as an investor, but of late had started mentioning Al Husseiny. And the newspaper noted Rosmah's penchant for expensive jewelry.

"Neither any money spent on travel, nor any jewelry purchases, nor the alleged contents of any safes are unusual for a person of the prime minister's position, responsibility and legacy family assets," Najib's office said in a statement to the *Times*.

The *Times* piece rippled through Malaysia, picked up by those news outlets that Najib couldn't control. The statement from the prime minister's office was the last straw for Najib's four brothers, who for years had complained inside the family about Rosmah's spending. The first lady was increasingly out of touch, a Marie Antoinette–like figure who recently had complained to a public gathering about the $400 it cost to dye her hair, a monthly wage for some Malaysians. The brothers decided to put out a rare statement to counter the inference that their father, Prime Minister Abdul Razak, had taken money while in office.

"We take issue with anyone who taints his memory, whatever the motive," the brothers wrote. It was a thinly veiled dig at Najib and Rosmah.

But it was too late to salvage the family name.

By late February, Rewcastle-Brown was ready to publish. After years of suspicions about 1MDB and Low, her story, posted on February 28, was headlined "Heist of the Century," and it drew back the curtain on the early days of the fund's operations. The piece showed with documentary proof how Low had siphoned money from 1MDB via Good Star, the first time anyone had detailed how Low took money from the fund in 2009. She embedded documents into her story to give it added heft: One email showed Shahrol Halmi, the chief executive, pushing Deutsche Bank to send money to Good Star; another document named Seet Li Lin as the investment officer for Good Star, the shady Seychelles company, linking it to Low; and there were agreements for Good Star to pay tens of millions of dollars to Tarek Obaid. Rewcastle-Brown had hit the mother lode, and days later the *Edge* would follow up with its own investigative scoop.

The news of Low's apparent theft caused a civil war within UMNO. A faction led by Mahathir called openly for Najib to resign. Some senior politicians even arranged to tap the prime minister's phone and heard him discussing with Jho Low a plan to put the blame for any corruption on 1MDB's Middle Eastern partners. Until the dust settled, Najib ordered Low to leave the country and keep a low profile. In public, the prime minister denied any wrongdoing at 1MDB but nevertheless ordered an official government investigation of the fund, led by the National Audit Department, a body tasked with checking state finances. The Public Accounts Committee of Parliament, headed by an UMNO politician, began to clamor for answers. The committee ordered Low to appear before it, but no one knew his location.

For years, Low must have been expecting this day to come. How could he believe it possible to take so much money, revealing parts of the scheme to a prime minister, a Saudi prince, Malaysian bankers, and the head of an Abu Dhabi sovereign wealth fund, while keeping the full contours of its audacity to himself?

In the days after the *Sarawak Report* scoop, Low acted as if he'd steeled himself for this situation all along. Many people, caught in the act of something much less felonious, would crumble and admit all. Najib was even talking to family members about stepping down. But Low was ready to fight. It was a survival instinct, for sure, but perhaps after years of fabrication, he found it hard to perceive the hard line that divided truth from falsehood. Maybe he really did believe he was benefiting Malaysia, building ties with foreign governments and raising the nation's profile.

As the news broke, the Malaysian was traveling the world on his jet, and he sent off a barrage of messages to his associates. He told Khaldoon Al Mubarak, the chief executive of Mubadala, that

Malaysia's government had found no evidence of wrongdoing. The reports were based on "fabricated" emails from PetroSaudi. "We expected these few months to be filled with noise, innuendo and misinformation from certain political quarters," Low wrote Al Mubarak. He blind-copied Ambassador Otaiba, showing his ally how he was trying to keep the situation under control.

"Please note the '*Sarawak Report*' exposé is sensationalized, filled with innuendo and baseless accusations," he messaged Joanna Yu at AmBank. Yu did not respond; she was too busy closing Najib's accounts. Finally, under pressure from AmBank's board and amid a constant shortage of funds, the prime minister had to acquiesce. For Yu, the scope of what she was involved in was revealing itself. Of course, she knew it was illegal to keep an account secret, even one controlled by the prime minister, and to hoodwink the central bank and the board. But the scale of Low's scheme was probably far from her imagination.

A few days after Low's last messages to Yu, Malaysian police raided AmBank. They moved through the bank's headquarters, a skyscraper close to the Petronas Towers in Kuala Lumpur, asking to be directed to Yu's desk, where they demanded she hand over her computer and phones. She complied immediately. There were no other senior executives left at the bank for the police to question. Her former boss, Cheah Tek Kuang, had gone into retirement months earlier. Ashok Ramamurthy had resigned as AmBank's chief executive in a hurry in early March, to return to a job with ANZ in Australia, and soon after he would leave the bank entirely.

In the wake of the *Sarawak Report* story, Malaysian law-enforcement agencies felt emboldened to take action, setting up a task force to investigate the 1MDB affair. The group included Bank Negara, the National Police, the Malaysian Anti-Corruption Commission, and the attorney general, the country's top public prosecutor.

The evidence taken by police about Najib's accounts, including Yu's phone messages with Low, painted an extraordinary
picture. In the ensuing weeks, officials at Bank Negara Malaysia,
under Governor Zeti Akhtar Aziz, combed through the documents
from the raid, revealing a stunning fact: The prime minister had
received more than $1 billion into his *personal accounts* between
2011 and 2014. The biggest payments, totaling $681 million, were
from an unknown company called Tanore, which had an account
at Falcon Bank in Singapore. Given the explosive nature of its discovery, the task force decided not to reveal the information to the
public for now.

The *Sarawak Report* story made no mention of Najib's
accounts. And, as yet, the central bank had no evidence the
prime minister had received money from the 1MDB fund, but
it began to cast its investigatory net in a wider arc. Bank Negara
reached out to Singapore's police for information on Jho Low's
accounts. The Suspicious Transaction Reporting Office wrote
back on March 13 that a company account at BSI in Singapore
owned by Low had received $500 million between 2011 and
2013 from Good Star. This was the company *Sarawak Report*
had mentioned, and it appeared to reveal another step in the
money flows, but it didn't connect 1MDB to the prime minister.

Still, the probe had momentum, and Singapore, normally
keen not to upset the equipoise of its lucrative private banking
world, began to dig in.

"If proceeds of crime have been transferred to Singapore, we
would like to consider whether an offense has been committed,"
Chua Jia Leng, head of the suspicious reporting office, wrote
Bank Negara.

Authorities in Malaysia and overseas were closing in. As
Low and Najib were trying to contain the fallout, another major
figure was in peril: Khadem Al Qubaisi of IPIC.

Chapter 43

Buttocks in a G-String

Tel Aviv, Israel, April 2015

Behind an office building in Tel Aviv, the flames of an impromptu bonfire melted the plastic of several USB sticks. Two men stood watching over the fire. One, Mohamed Al Husseiny, the chief executive of the Abu Dhabi fund Aabar, was there to ensure its contents were incinerated. Al Husseiny, who had helped Low take money from the 1MDB bonds arranged by Goldman, watched as singed bits of paper from a stack of burning documents floated into the sky. They included secret files and photos that risked bringing the career of his boss, Khadem Al Qubaisi, crashing down. The documents had been removed from Al Qubaisi's home and office in France by Racem Haoues, a French-Algerian man. Over years of corrupt deals, Al Qubaisi had made a raft of enemies, and Haoues was among them.

For years, Haoues acted as a glorified butler for Al Qubaisi, arranging cars, jets, and reservations while also occasionally passing messages between his boss and people making discreet payments. Haoues was handsomely remunerated, but he must have become increasingly envious as he saw Al Qubaisi and subordinates like Al Husseiny line their pockets with hundreds of millions of dollars in kickbacks. In a magnanimous moment,

Al Qubaisi said he would throw him a morsel—a stake in a big real estate play in Spain—but he later reneged on the deal. Soon after, in early 2015, Al Qubaisi fired him. But Haoues already had an insurance policy: Over time he had amassed a raft of compromising information on his former boss.

The documents included Al Qubaisi's bank statements, details of his multiple French properties, and payments on Sheikh Mansour's yacht, *Topaz*. Haoues leaked a selection of the documents to Clare Rewcastle-Brown, who published a story in late March 2015, just weeks after her exposé on Jho Low. The piece outlined how a Luxembourg company owned by Al Qubaisi had received $20 million from Good Star, Low's shell firm, in February 2013. It was accompanied by photos, also supplied by Haoues, of the IPIC managing director partying around the world. In one shot, he was dancing in a club while a topless model cavorted in an oversized cocktail glass. In another, he was making out with a woman on a sofa, behind some shisha pipes. Yet more photos showed him in clubs, wearing T-shirts with lewd images, including one that featured a close-up of female buttocks wearing a G-string. It was common for wealthy Gulf residents to shed modest Arab dress in the West, but these bawdy party photos were beyond the pale—especially after they were publicly disclosed.

Haoues had only given a drip of his total information to Rewcastle-Brown. According to a later complaint, filed and then withdrawn, Haoues, through an intermediary, set about trying to extract money from Al Qubaisi, warning that—if he did not pay—more material would come out. The material touching on Sheikh Mansour's business was extremely sensitive. Acting for his boss, Al Husseiny helped arrange a transfer of 30 million euros to Haoues in return for the destruction of the documents. After the payment was made, Al Husseiny traveled to Tel Aviv, where he and an intermediary for Haoues built their bonfire.

Al Qubaisi hoped further trouble had been averted. With the continued backing of Sheikh Mansour, he might have believed himself to be untouchable and more dominant than ever. Within the past year, Al Qubaisi had put his half a billion in 1MDB money to work, purchasing a penthouse in New York's Walker Tower for $51 million, and two mansions in Los Angeles for a combined $46 million. As chairman of Hakkasan Group, a nightclub empire owned by Sheikh Mansour, he had become one of Las Vegas's most powerful businessmen.

Around the time of Haoues's blackmail threat, Al Qubaisi launched the Omnia nightclub in Caesars Palace. Its name meaning "the sum of all things" in Latin, Omnia was the most expensive nightclub ever built, at over $100 million, and could host more than 3,500 revelers. Al Qubaisi's domain featured a 22,000-pound, light-emitting, kinetic chandelier, hovering like a UFO over the main dance floor, along with state-of-the-art liquid-crystal displays, "opera boxes" that looked down on the main club, and an outdoor terrace with views of the Strip. The opening night in March 2015 featured superstar DJ Calvin Harris (who was paid hundreds of thousands of dollars a night to perform), and Justin Bieber celebrated his twenty-first birthday at the club over the star-studded weekend of festivities.

But Al Qubaisi's optimism was misplaced. Crown Prince Sheikh Mohammed Bin Zayed Al Nahyan, the ruler of Abu Dhabi, had decided to take action. The dealings of his brother Sheikh Mansour, overseen by Al Qubaisi, had gone too far. The crown prince ordered a discreet investigation into Al Qubaisi. With his brother completely in the dark, investigators piled up evidence of financial wrongdoing, painting a picture of Al Qubaisi as a man who had grown too powerful, failing to respect the royals for whom he worked.

On April 22, 2015, a presidential decree ousted Al Qubaisi from IPIC, without explanation. A few months later, his subordinate, Al Husseiny, was kicked out of Aabar, the IPIC subsidiary. Al Qubaisi was in Spain at the time for business, and initially brushed off the change as a temporary issue and attended a football game between Real Madrid and Atlético Madrid in the evening. He didn't realize the seriousness of his predicament: Sheikh Mohammed was cleaning house. In the Gulf, the ruling families were protected; but Al Qubaisi was in danger.

For Low, Al Qubaisi's downfall removed one of his closest conspirators. It was unclear how deeply Abu Dhabi's rulers would probe—surely they didn't want to embarrass Sheikh Mansour—but Low recognized the ouster was dangerous for him, and he took immediate action.

Less than a week after the ax had fallen on Al Qubaisi, Low flew by private jet to Abu Dhabi on a damage-control exercise. With Al Qubaisi out of the picture, Low was laying the groundwork to put the blame on his former partner; if the full story about the money stolen via IPIC ever came out, Al Qubaisi, already a fallen man, could take the responsibility. Low had ensured his name wasn't attached to documents, but the signatures of Al Husseiny and Al Qubaisi were all over the place.

"There's rumors going round that I'm a buddy of Al Qubaisi, and money has gone missing. But it's an internal IPIC issue if some of the money 1MDB sent is not showing up in IPIC's accounts," Low told Shaher Awartani, Ambassador Otaiba's business partner, in one meeting.

In another meeting with the new head of IPIC—Suhail Al Mazroui, Abu Dhabi's energy minister—Low portrayed himself as a savior who could chart a course out of the wreckage left by Al Qubaisi. By now IPIC's new management had gone through the financial statements and were beginning to see that billions of dollars it should have received as collateral for guaranteeing

1MDB's bonds were missing. Alarmingly, the Abu Dhabi fund was on the hook for $3.5 billion in bonds that 1MDB had sold and didn't seem able to repay.

The Malaysian fund was on the brink of default. Deutsche Bank, finally aware of the problems with the Cayman Islands collateral, was demanding early repayment of its total $1 billion in loans. Low offered a solution: IPIC would stump up the $1 billion to avoid a default, and in return Malaysia's Finance Ministry, which Najib also headed, would agree to ensure IPIC was fully repaid in cash and assets. It was unclear how the fund would raise such money—the IPO was on hold amid all the bad news—but IPIC's new chief had little option but to accept. Al Qubaisi appeared to have been involved, and he was keen to keep a lid on the scandal. After speaking with Najib, Minister Al Mazroui agreed to the arrangement, and both sides soon after signed a formal deal.

Low had other problems bubbling that he needed to sort out in Abu Dhabi. Ambassador Otaiba was concerned about queries he had received from BSI. As Singapore authorities ramped up their probe, BSI had been forced to make a show of auditing all accounts related to 1MDB and Jho Low. The bank was in chaos. Hanspeter Brunner, the head of BSI in Asia, put Yak Yew Chee, Low's relationship manager, on unpaid leave in the spring.

In return for his bonus, the bank's head of compliance in Lugano attempted to wring a signed declaration out of Yak that he had received no "gratification" in dealing with 1MDB and Low. Unwilling to be singled out as a scapegoat, Yak took off to rural China to bide his time, and quickly fell into a depression brought on by stress. The bank's compliance department had begun to investigate all Low-related business, and that had led them to contact Otaiba and Awartani, whose shell company, Densmore, had an account at BSI.

"You should close your accounts. The bank is too much in

the limelight. I've moved out most of my major assets and will close the remaining accounts soon," Low advised Awartani in their meeting.

Then he set about enlisting his help. Low told Awartani he wanted to buy his own bank as a parking spot for his money—and that of friends and family—and had just the candidate: an Amicorp Bank affiliate in Barbados. Low had used Amicorp for many transactions, and its bank was on the auction block for $15 million. But Low needed a front, and he wanted to know if Equalis Capital, a Dubai-based financial firm controlled by Otaiba and Awartani, would be willing to acquire the bank. Already alarmed by the events of the past few months, Awartani was noncommittal.

Instead, Low shifted some of his accounts to Amicorp's bank. He also looked for other new places to stash his money. For help, he once again turned to Tim Leissner. The German Goldman banker was willing to help, writing a letter of reference in June 2015 to Banque Havilland, a small but illustrious Luxembourg private bank. At this stage, few banks would touch Low, but Leissner's letter, falsely stating that Goldman had conducted due diligence on Low's family wealth, opened doors.

Low was taking actions to shut down scrutiny of 1MDB and to hide his own assets. But this piecemeal approach wouldn't do. It was too reactive. He needed to make a more aggressive move—to fire a warning shot across the bows of anyone thinking of crossing him.

Chapter 44

Strongman Najib

Koh Samui, Thailand, June 2015

On a hazy, hot tropical afternoon in late June, Xavier Justo was relaxing at his villa on the island of Koh Samui. Suddenly, armed Thai police burst in and muscled him to the floor. Once officers had secured the suspect—tying his hands so tightly with plastic cuffs that his wrists bled—they ransacked his office, carting off computers and other documents. He was flown to Bangkok, where a convoy of police SUVs drove him across the city to a holding cell.

Two days later, still wearing his beach outfit—a gray Hugo Boss T-shirt, cream shorts, and flip-flops—Justo was paraded in front of the media in Bangkok. As the Royal Thai Police chief reviewed details of the case, five commandos in dark shades and brandishing machine guns stood ominously over Justo, whose hands were still cuffed. On a table nearby stood the computers taken from his residence. This was the kind of dramatic staging Thai authorities reserved for drug kingpins, not someone charged with attempted blackmail and extortion.

Awaiting trial, Justo was placed in a Bangkok jail with fifty other prisoners. The stench of urine and the lack of floor space, or even a mattress, made it impossible for him to sleep. He was relieved when a former British police detective, Paul Finnigan, who ran his own consultancy, turned up to visit. Finnigan was working with PetroSaudi, but he told Justo he was a police officer investigating the case.

Finnigan offered Justo a deal: Plead guilty to the charges and he would get out of jail before Christmas. Tarek Obaid would help him, Finnigan promised, but only if Justo was cooperative. A few days later, Mahony arrived at the jail cell, and made similar promises, according to a complaint Justo later filed. Stressed from the ordeal, and yet to have been given legal representation, Justo signed a twenty-two-page "confession," in which he apologized to PetroSaudi for stealing the documents and negotiating to sell them to the *Edge*.

This was phase one of a plan to discredit Justo, cast doubt on the authenticity of the emails, and blame Malaysia's political opposition for stirring up trouble for the prime minister. His resolve galvanized by Rosmah, who called the situation a "test from Allah," Najib was not going to resign so easily.

"We have been the victims of a regrettable crime that has unfortunately been politicized in Malaysia," PetroSaudi said in a statement.

The day after the arrest, the *New Straits Times*, an English-language newspaper owned by the ruling UMNO party, published a piece quoting an unnamed spokesman from Protection Group International, a London-based cybersecurity and corporate intelligence firm, as saying it had reviewed the leaked emails and found evidence of tampering.

The firm, owned by a former British Royal Marine, had been hired by PetroSaudi, but it had conducted only a review of a few documents available on the *Sarawak Report* website. Now, its private review for PetroSaudi was being plastered over UMNO's party mouthpiece. Only Najib, or other senior UMNO politicians, could dictate to the *New Straits Times* what to write. After its publication, Low quickly forwarded the story to Khaldoon Al

Mubarak of Mubadala, the Abu Dhabi sovereign wealth fund, to mislead his allies in the Gulf into believing that the PetroSaudi emails were somehow fake.

A month later, Justo was still languishing in jail, awaiting his trial, when a Singapore journalist turned up for an interview. The reporter had provided the questions ahead of time, and Finnigan supplied Justo with prearranged answers. Justo told the journalist how the *Edge* had failed to stick to its promises to pay him, and now he made a new claim: During the meeting in Singapore with Rewcastle-Brown and the principals at the *Edge* newspaper, the buyers had talked about how they planned to modify the documents he provided.

Justo repeated the claims in another meeting with Malaysian police officers, his answers scripted by Mahony and Finnigan. Justo had to help Malaysia's prime minister by blaming Rewcastle-Brown, and at all costs he was to avoid mentioning Jho Low, they told him. Since the publication of the *Edge*'s stories, Ho Kay Tat and four other staffers had been detained by Malaysia's police under the Sedition Act and then let go, in what appeared to be a clear act of intimidation. Najib's administration also recently had brought in a new law, on the surface aimed at curbing terrorism, but permitting suspects to be held indefinitely.

No evidence emerged supporting the claims of tampering; Justo was under huge pressure from Mahony and others to back their version of events. Ho responded with a note on the *Edge*'s front page, denying the newspaper had paid anyone or tampered with the documents. The publication, he wrote, had a "public duty to find and report the truth."

So far, Prime Minister Najib had stayed out of the fray, but that was about to change. The Malaysian government task force, led by Bank Negara and the Malaysian Anti-Corruption

Commission, had pored through thousands of financial transactions in the prime minister's accounts. The biggest incoming payments—$681 million from Tanore—were still a mystery, and the investigators were no closer to knowing who controlled the company or why it had paid money to Najib. Even governments could not easily see behind the veil of offshore secrecy, and Trident Trust, which had set up Tanore in the British Virgin Islands, only knew that Eric Tan was the ultimate beneficial owner, not Jho Low.

But investigators had been able to trace a much smaller amount of $14 million from 1MDB to one of the prime minister's accounts. The Malaysian Anti-Corruption Commission, whose job was to build major cases for the attorney general to prosecute, believed this smaller payment was sufficient grounds for criminal charges. But there was a hurdle: Some members of the task force, especially the National Police, were objecting to moving ahead to frame charges against a sitting prime minister. The only option was to leak the documents detailing Najib's financial transactions.

Just as the task force was looking for a candidate, we published a front-page story in the *Wall Street Journal*, the most detailed piece yet on how Najib had used 1MDB as a slush fund. The story caught the eye of an intermediary for the task force. A few days later, a Malaysian source met in London with Simon Clark, a *Journal* reporter, to confirm the veracity of the documents, which the intermediary handed over hours later. *Sarawak Report* also received them. The files, copies of wire transfer documents into Najib's accounts, as well as money-flow diagrams produced by the task force, were explosive.

Under the headline INVESTIGATORS BELIEVE MONEY FLOWED TO MALAYSIAN LEADER NAJIB'S ACCOUNTS AMID 1MDB PROBE, the *Journal* reported on July 2 how the task force had traced the money into Najib's accounts via 1MDB-linked entities.

After months of conjecture about the prime minister's involvement, and his fervent denials of wrongdoing, the story was a tipping point, splaying the issue across the pages of one of the world's most well-known newspapers. The *Journal* story was among the most-read online items of the year, garnering more than a quarter-million unique visitors online. Now the 1MDB story had a global audience. A few days later, we reported how Singapore was investigating payments made to Jho Low.

The *Edge* could have its publication license revoked, but now Najib was faced with the *Journal*, an organization that didn't rely on his goodwill to remain in operation. With few other options, the prime minister came out swinging, realizing this was a fight for political survival. Within a week, the *Journal* received a letter from Najib's lawyers asking for the newspaper to clarify its position on the story or possibly face a lawsuit. The *Journal's* lawyers responded that the paper was standing behind its piece. Najib also took to Facebook to paint the allegations as the work of Mahathir Mohamad, the former leader, who had intensified his calls for the prime minister to step down over 1MDB.

"Let me be very clear: I have never taken funds for personal gain as alleged by my political opponents," he said in a Facebook post. "It is now clear that false allegations such as these are part of a concerted campaign of political sabotage to topple a democratically elected Prime Minister."

The *Journal* story galvanized the Malaysian task force into action. Members of the group shared further password-protected documents on their investigation with the *Journal*. The password for many of the files: "SaveMalaysia."

On July 24, Attorney General Abdul Gani Patail informed Malaysia's police chief that he was drawing up criminal charges against the prime minister. He was preparing to take the document—known in Malaysia as a "charge sheet"—to a judge, the first step in seeking the prime minister's arrest. The document, laying out charges against Najib, noted how the payments were illegal under section 17 (a) of the Malaysian Anti-Corruption Commission Act of 2009, a provision proscribing the giving or receiving of bribes and that carried a maximum jail term of twenty years.

Najib's room to maneuver was narrowing fast. Even Deputy Prime Minister Muhyiddin Yassin began to make speeches quoting from the *Wall Street Journal* and demanding a transparent investigation on 1MDB. But the police chief, supposedly part of the task force, decided to switch sides at the last moment, and informed Najib of his impending arrest.

Overseas, the prime minister was considered charming and a democrat. Only months earlier, he had given a speech at Malvern, his old boarding school in England, in which he thanked his teachers for instilling in him "decency, discipline and perseverance." A politician needs at least two of these, he quipped to laughter. No one perceived Najib as either decisive or ruthless. But now, fearing he could end up in jail, a steelier edge to his character came into focus. At this crisis point, raw power was all that mattered.

On July 27, 2015, three days after Najib got wind of the charges against him, he breezed into the ballroom of Kuala Lumpur's Hilton Hotel for a dinner to celebrate Eid-al-Fitr, Islam's holiest festival. Thousands of people, the great and good of Malaysian society, had assembled for the event, and the conversation revolved around the country's mounting political crisis. Most of the guests expected that Najib would soon be political history. Dressed in a Malay-style purple silk shirt, the prime minister took his place at a table reserved for VIPs, shaking hands with many of the UMNO politicians who wanted him gone. Only the prime minister knew the fury he was about to unleash on those disloyal to him.

The morning after the dinner at the Hilton, Attorney General Abdul Gani Patail arrived at his office to find the way barred by staff and security from the prime minister's office. Abdul Gani no longer had a job and could not even enter the office to collect documents, they informed him. An hour later, Najib replaced the head of the Police Special Branch, who had been instrumental in the probe into the prime minister's accounts. Later in the day, a fire broke out in police headquarters, destroying scores of documents.

Najib fired Deputy Prime Minister Muhyiddin and four other cabinet members, and he suspended the Public Accounts Committee's probe into 1MDB. The prime minister sought to cow other critics, including the media. The Home Ministry suspended the *Edge*'s publication licenses for three months, claiming its reporting on 1MDB could lead to public disorder. In one brutal house clearing, Najib had solidified his control on power.

Days later, British Prime Minister David Cameron flew into Malaysia for an official visit. He'd just given a speech in Singapore about how Britain needed to stop corrupt cash from flowing into London's property market, where Malaysians were among the biggest buyers. In private, he pressed Najib on the corruption claims, and Malaysia's human rights record. Najib was furious at the lecture by Cameron. His love affair with Western democracies was over.

As Najib battled to stay in power, Jho Low was forced to cancel his participation in a National Geographic expedition, which would include Leonardo DiCaprio, who was filming *Before the Flood*, his documentary about global warming. The *Journal* published its stories about Najib's accounts and Singapore's investigation of Low just as he was about to set off.

As he dealt with the fallout, Low sent his parents in his stead. DiCaprio, a Victoria's Secret model who accompanied the actor, Low's parents, and a group of National Geographic scientists spent three days flying helicopters over the receding ice sheet in Greenland and filming polar bears. Afterward, DiCaprio announced his foundation was donating $15 million to environmental organizations, including National Geographic, which Low also had funded.

By August, with the prime minister's crackdown in full swing, Low felt reassured enough to fly by private jet and helicopter to join the *Equanimity* in the seas off Greenland. For over a week, he went completely dark, visiting the National Geographic scientific camp, and stunning people who were seeking regular updates on developments.

"He literally traveled to the end of the earth and went completely offline," said a Middle Eastern contact.

Perhaps Low was feeling confident the worst was over. Maybe he wanted to make a show of business as usual, clinging to his image as a philanthropist. On his return, he nonchalantly wrote another contact: "I apologize for my late response as I have been on a conservation expedition in the Arctic with limited coverage."

Or maybe the trip was like a gambling session, a short break from people calling and demanding answers. He exhibited few other signs of confidence, and he seemed increasingly agitated that Najib would burn him. Over the summer, he told a 1MDB board member: "If they sacrifice me, I'll go nuclear. I was acting on the instructions of the boss." The prime minister had warned Low to stay out of the country as the crisis deepened, and he began to lay low in Bangkok, the capital of Thailand, and Shanghai, China's financial capital, where he stayed in the residences of the Peninsula Hotel. Unbeknownst to all but his closest contacts, he had also obtained a new passport from the tiny island nation of St. Kitts and Nevis.

In August, Switzerland's attorney general announced he had

launched a criminal investigation of 1MDB and frozen multiple accounts containing tens of millions of dollars. With many of his accounts in Singapore and Switzerland now shut, Low was being shunted to the furthest reaches of the global financial system, forced to rely more on Thai baht or Chinese yuan transactions.

The bonds between Low and Najib remained in place. But they were frayed, with all sides now watching their own backs, distrustful of those with whom they had conspired for years. When one contact asked Low about all the money that appeared to be missing, he was quick to assign the guilt to Rosmah.

"She is an avid purchaser of jewelry in the millions. Where is the money from?" he asked.

Around one hundred thousand Malaysians, many of them young, urban professionals, swarmed around the center of Kuala Lumpur on August 29, 2015. Wearing yellow T-shirts bearing the slogan "Bersih"—the Malay word for "clean"—they marched through the streets, protesting the growing evidence of mass corruption at the heart of their government. The Home Ministry had banned yellow T-shirts after earlier Bersih protests, declaring them a national security threat, but the demonstrators took no heed.

One demonstrator carried an effigy of Najib in a cage; others held up pictures asking how much an average family could purchase of different everyday products—KFC chicken, rice, hot chocolate—with $681 million, the biggest transfers into Najib's accounts; a popular caricature of Rosmah, with cartoonishly big hair, replaced her eyeballs with dollar signs.

There were Bersih protests in other cities, and by Malaysians living abroad, too. In Kuala Lumpur, many of the protesters stayed out all weekend, sleeping on the streets. Former Prime Minister Mahathir Mohamad, wearing a safari suit, attended the rally, repeating his call for Najib to step down. Some of the protesters, regular school teachers or office workers, were simply tired of the kleptocracy that Malaysia had become. Others were worried the state was taking an authoritarian turn, closing newspapers and detaining anyone who threatened the ruling party's hold on power. And there were fears the massive debt that 1MDB had incurred would weigh on Malaysia for years to come, leeching funds away from spending on education and social welfare.

"When you act against the media it seems like you have something to hide," said Sheila Krishna, a Kuala Lumpur taxi driver.

Now a strongman, Najib would endure no opposition. A federal court recently had sent Anwar Ibrahim, the popular opposition leader, back to jail for five years for sodomy, prompting criticism from the United States and human-rights groups. A couple of weeks after the Bersih protests, progovernment "red-shirt" protesters took to the streets. Some participants admitted to receiving small sums of money to attend. Over the coming months, the red shirts—many of them aggressive-looking ethnic Malays wearing bandanas—disrupted antigovernment protests and assaulted activists.

"Malays too can show we can still rise up," Najib said in a fiery speech, praising the red-shirt protesters.

Glimmers of hope remained: A High Court judge ruled the suspension of the *Edge*'s publication license was unlawful, and its journalists once again began holding Najib to account. Some protesters came back into the streets over the ensuing months.

But Najib's newfound authoritarianism scared many.

A deadly turn would cow even the bravest Malaysians into silence.

PART V

THE CAPTAIN'S RESOLVE

Chapter 45

Prosecutor in an Oil Drum

Kuala Lumpur, Malaysia, September 2015

Just after dawn on September 4, a workaholic Indian Malaysian named Kevin Morais got into a Proton Perdana sedan for his daily commute to the Malaysian Anti-Corruption Commission's office in Putrajaya, about an hour's drive from his northern Kuala Lumpur apartment complex. He would never arrive.

Since Najib's crackdown several weeks earlier, Morais had become steadily more enraged. The fifty-five-year-old, with a mop of black hair and a haggard tiredness about him, had studied law in London in the 1980s before returning to Malaysia, where he rose to the position of deputy public prosecutor in the attorney general's office. In Malaysia, corruption cases were plentiful, and Morais often worked weekends, darkening the bags under his heavily lidded eyes.

A few months earlier, Morais had—to those who knew him—begun to act strangely. The prosecutor was nervous about a case involving Prime Minister Najib and Rosmah, he informed a brother living in the United States. Fearful his phone line was tapped, Morais often talked to his brother in Malayalam, a language of southern India. He sounded frightened, and complained about the stress of his job. Morais didn't go into the details of his work, but he was temporarily assigned to the Malaysian

Anti-Corruption Commission. He was working on the money flows from 1MDB to Najib's accounts, and he had helped draw up the draft criminal charges against the prime minister.

After Najib removed Attorney General Abdul Gani Patail, Morais felt anxious about his own position. He had even begun worrying about his safety. Only days later, an anonymous leaker emailed a copy of the draft charges the attorney general's office had been preparing to Clare Rewcastle-Brown at *Sarawak Report*. When she published her story, making it clear why Najib had moved so aggressively to fire Abdul Gani, there was a witch hunt in the attorney general's office and the Malaysian Anti-Corruption Commission to find the source of the leak. Police arrested two officials from the commission and a prosecutor from the attorney general's office. Police filed an arrest warrant for Rewcastle-Brown, but she was safe in the UK.

The detention of the prosecutors caused panic at the attorney general's office, which was now controlled by a Najib loyalist. Scared into compliance, the Malaysian Anti-Corruption Commission put out a statement saying the money Najib received was a "donation" from the Middle East, a fabrication to protect the prime minister. Fretful of his central role, Morais took off to England for several days, where he had an apartment in a town near London. He talked to his brother of retiring from government service and even visited a solicitor to arrange his will.

The police soon released the detained lawyers. Morais returned to Malaysia and moved on to other work. As he drove to the office that early September day, the prosecutor tried to focus on his latest case, one involving a Malaysian Army pathologist charged with running a medical-procurement scam. A few minutes from his complex, the driver of a Mitsubishi Triton truck began to tail the public prosecutor. The truck followed Morais for a while, and then accelerated, ramming his car off the road. Its passengers jumped out, dragged Morais from the car, bundled him into their truck, and sped off.

Sometime over the next hour, the assailants murdered Morais, most likely by strangulation, before tying his corpse in a gunny sack, the kind used for storing agricultural products. They put the sack in an oil drum and filled it with liquid concrete, before dumping it in a swampy wasteland near a school. Then, the perpetrators torched Morais's car and removed its serial numbers before dumping it in an oil-palm plantation.

When Morais didn't arrive at work, anxious colleagues and family members alerted police. Just under two weeks later, using security camera footage to locate the Mitsubishi Triton, officers made several arrests and were led to the swamp, where they discovered Morais's body. It was a macabre sight, the corpse curled up in a fetal position, encased in concrete like a fossil, still wearing his tie. Police arrested seven people, including the Malaysian Army pathologist, who was charged with abetting the murder.

To Morais's family, the official story of his death just didn't add up. The brother was convinced Morais had leaked the draft criminal charges against Prime Minister Najib and someone had found out about it. He contacted Rewcastle-Brown, who told him the source, unknown to her, had sent the documents from a "jibby@anonymousspeech.com" email address. Jibby was the name of a close family friend of Morais. But Najib's critics also used "Jibby" as a derisory nickname for the prime minister. The sender remained a mystery.

The killing had an immediate chilling effect at the Malaysian Anti-Corruption Commission. Staffers were scared for their lives. But a few brave prosecutors, at enormous personal risk, continued to look for a way to ensure Najib was held to account. The prime minister may have seemed secure, but his power only reached so far, and, unknown to him and an ocean away, the case had reached the desks of several special agents in the U.S. Federal Bureau of Investigation.

Chapter 46

Special Agent Bill McMurry

New York, February 2015

For Special Agent William "Bill" McMurry, the story about Najib's wealth landed at an opportune time. A veteran FBI agent, McMurry had just been tapped to head a new international corruption squad in New York, and his team was hunting for a high-profile case. With sandy, straight hair and blue eyes, McMurry gave off the air of a middle-aged California surfer, although in reality he was a New Jersey native who had spent years fighting international crime based out of the FBI's offices in a downtown Manhattan federal building.

His biggest triumph to date was unraveling the case of Sister Ping, a Chinatown underworld figure who in 2006 was sent to jail for thirty-five years for her role in a human-trafficking enterprise. After the *New York Times* story on Jho Low's property acquisitions, McMurry's team was tasked with checking out the details. The *Wall Street Journal*'s coverage of Najib's accounts put the case at the front of the queue.

The FBI squads—there were also units in Washington and Los Angeles—were an intensification of an effort by the U.S. Justice Department and the FBI to combat kleptocracies, foreign governments from Russia to Nigeria and Venezuela, dominated by corrupt officials who steal from their treasuries for personal enrichment. It was not pure altruism. The United States for decades had been concerned that corruption would undermine free-market capitalism, making it harder for American firms to compete internationally. And then there were fears that kleptocracy—the word is from the Greek and means "rule by thieves"—would lead to a less stable world order, in which failed states like Afghanistan and Syria harbor terrorists.

"Corruption leads to lack of confidence in government. Lack of confidence in government leads to failed states. And failed states lead to terror and national security issues," was how Special Agent Jeffrey Sallet, chief of the FBI's Public Corruption Section, put it when announcing the international corruption squads.

Corrupt foreign leaders and officials had an Achilles' heel—they relied on the U.S. financial system to transfer cash and had a penchant for acquiring real estate in New York, Los Angeles, and Miami. The Justice Department set up the Kleptocracy Asset Recovery Initiative in 2010 to coordinate the work of FBI investigators and prosecutors to seize the U.S. and global assets of corrupt foreign officials. If those kleptocrats were no longer in power, Washington would transfer the proceeds back to the countries. In 2014, the Justice Department oversaw the seizure of more than $480 million in corruption proceeds hidden in bank accounts around the world by former Nigerian dictator Sani Abacha.

The 1MDB scheme, McMurry's team must have soon realized, was of a whole different magnitude. For one thing, Low just seemed so brash: His money-laundering techniques, although sophisticated, had been carried out through major banks, and there was a solid money trail. This was easier to deal with than Pakistani money launderers, who often would go into hiding for years and make their funds disappear through the informal *hawala* money-transfer network. Then there was the scale: The 1MDB affair was shaping up as the single largest financial scam of all time.

On the ground, Robert Heuchling, a thirty-four-year-old FBI special agent who worked for McMurry, was attempting to get his head around this mind-numbingly complex case. Slender with blue eyes and an athletic build, Heuchling studied journalism at Northwestern University before joining the U.S. Marines, and he had worked at the FBI for five years. McMurry made him lead on the case, by far the most weighty of his short career. Justin McNair, an agent who had forensic accounting experience, was another senior member of the group. Alongside a team of federal prosecutors, and with access to data from the U.S. financial system, as well as cooperation with law enforcement agencies in Switzerland and Singapore, the agents were making progress.

But there was a problem. Money-laundering cases are by nature multijurisdictional, making them time-consuming to investigate. On sprawling international cases, prosecutors rely on what are known as Mutual Legal Assistance Treaties, which allow for the sharing of information—documents, sworn statements, and the like—between law enforcement agencies. The United States had signed such a pact with Malaysia in 2006, and Switzerland had a similar agreement. Najib's administration, however, was declining to cooperate.

At first, Najib privately expressed confidence that Western nations would not pursue investigations into 1MDB, wagering Malaysia's status as a U.S. ally would buffer it from intrusions into what he considered a domestic matter. It soon became clear the foreign investigations were not going to melt away. At a meeting of public prosecutors in Zurich, Attorney General Mohamed Apandi Ali—the loyalist Najib had installed in the job—urged his Swiss counterpart, Michael Lauber, to abandon his investigation. Lauber refused.

The Najib administration also tried diplomatic channels to get the FBI to drop its probe, without luck. But the prime minister instructed his attorney general not to cooperate with overseas probes, and that left foreign investigators without access to crucial Malaysian banking documents.

Investigators in Abu Dhabi, where the scandal threatened to highlight the shabby business practices of Sheikh Mansour, were similarly keen not to air their dirty laundry in public. It was one thing to quietly remove Al Qubaisi from his position, but quite another to launch a full-blown probe that could embarrass a senior royal figure.

The broad contours of the scheme had appeared in the pages of *Sarawak Report* and the *Wall Street Journal*, but only the first heist, involving the $1.5 billion taken from 1MDB starting in 2009, was clearly drawn. The *Journal* began to focus on exactly how Prime Minister Najib had gotten paid in 2013, and the money trail led to Abu Dhabi.

Jho Low was perturbed by questions the prime minister had received from the *Journal*. Focusing on the money flows, we had figured out discrepancies between 1MDB's financial reports and those of IPIC. The Abu Dhabi fund had guaranteed $3.5 billion in 1MDB bonds sold by Goldman Sachs in 2012, and, in return, the Malaysian fund's financial statements showed it had transferred $1.4 billion in "collateral" to IPIC. The collateral was accounted for in 1MDB's accounts as a "non-current deposit," meaning it would be repaid by IPIC in the future, but was not at that moment available in cash. This struck us as strange. Why issue bonds and then pay almost half of the proceeds in "collateral" to the guarantor of the bonds? But what we discovered next deepened the mystery: IPIC's financial reports made no mention of receiving the money.

Around this time, we developed a crucial deep-throat informant. Referred to internally at the *Journal* as "Malaysian Source," or MS, the person had intimate knowledge of the workings of every aspect of what had transpired, yet because of personal involvement was also motivated to mislead us. The person passed wire-transfer documents to the *Journal* that appeared to show the $1.4 billion indeed flowed from 1MDB to Aabar, the IPIC subsidiary. MS was hoping we would accept this at face value and move on.

But the documents in fact showed the money had been sent to Aabar Investments Ltd.—the look-alike British Virgin Islands–based shell company controlled by Al Qubaisi and Al Husseiny. We searched offshore company databases and took the information to government sources in Abu Dhabi, who confirmed that IPIC and Aabar did not formally control this company. Although Abu Dhabi authorities didn't want to embarrass Sheikh Mansour, it was evident to IPIC's new management that Al Qubaisi could not bear the blame alone. The Persian Gulf suspected Jho Low and began investigating the matter.

Malaysian Source's efforts to mislead us had backfired, handing the *Journal* a scoop about the existence of this look-alike shell company—one of Jho Low's trademark methods for siphoning cash. We then wrote to Najib asking why IPIC had not received money that 1MDB claimed to have sent, citing Abu Dhabi investigators. The PetroSaudi fraud already had been laid bare, and now Low feared the uncovering of another major part of his scheme, the removal of cash from the 2012 power-plant bonds. He moved fast to keep a lid on the truth. Turning to Ambassador Otaiba and Al Mubarak of Mubadala, Low worked to stop the *Journal*'s story in its tracks.

He was particularly worried by our discovery that Abu Dhabi "investigators" had found no trace of the money. He was losing control of events, worried by our ability to communicate with Abu Dhabi officials. In an email, Low, using a pseudonym, sent across to Otaiba and Al Mubarak the questions we had asked Prime Minister Najib, attached to which he made his own request.

"Malaysian side is extremely concerned and wants to ensure strategy to [be] consistent and coordinated," Low wrote.

Najib was keen, he went on, to make sure Abu Dhabi did not formally investigate the missing cash. Instead the emirate should stick to the agreed story. Al Qubaisi was to blame, and a deal was in place for Abu Dhabi to cover the $3.5 billion in bonds, with Malaysia later repaying the Persian Gulf state with cash or other assets.

"Note: There are enough reviews on 1MDB being done by various regulators. There is a concern that an additional review done by an Abu Dhabi investigative team will open another unnecessary attack avenue for detractors," Low wrote.

Neither the Prime Minister nor the 1MDB fund, now headed by Arul Kanda, a slick financier in his early forties, who previously had worked at an Abu Dhabi bank and knew Jho Low, responded to the *Journal*'s queries. But after the newspaper reported about the missing Abu Dhabi money, the Malaysian fund reacted aggressively. A former high school debate champion, Arul Kanda took on the *Journal*'s stories with sharp-worded tirades that claimed the newspaper was part of a wide political conspiracy against Najib.

"The inability to substantiate clearly shows the shallow nature of its assertions and casts serious doubt on whether or not the *Wall Street Journal* editors themselves believe in the weak story, cobbled together by its reporters," 1MDB said in one statement.

Foreigners working as spin doctors for the prime minister's office and 1MDB took a similar tone. Paul Stadlen, a young British man who worked for Najib in communications, played a vital role in a strategy aimed at discrediting our pieces.

"The WSJ continue to report anonymously-sourced lies as facts," read one statement. "They are a disgrace to journalism."

Arif Shah, who was working for 1MDB, on a sabbatical from British public relations firm Brunswick Group, took us to task for taking sides in Malaysian politics, without proffering any evidence.

"I question the veracity of your sources, their intentions, and the documents they provide. A question for you—Do you think that you are being used to help oust the Malaysian Prime Minister," he wrote in an email.

Added to the money taken via Good Star, the *Journal* at this time estimated that at least $3 billion had gone missing from 1MDB. In the prime minister's office, there was discussion over what to do about our coverage. Threats of a lawsuit were not having the desired effect—in fact the *Journal* appeared to be going deeper, obtaining reams of documents, from 1MDB's board minutes to the National Audit Department's draft report into the fund, as well as copies of BlackBerry chats between Jho Low and conspirators like Joanne Yu at AmBank.

Some of these documents came from Malaysian Source, who wanted to show the scheme enjoyed the backing of Najib, Rosmah, and Al Qubaisi; others were provided by frustrated Malaysian civil servants and politicians, as well as Abu Dhabi officials and other sources.

The *Journal*'s stories illustrated how Najib was a central decision-making figure at 1MDB, and painted in detail how Jho Low ran the show. To shut our reporting down, the prime minister needed to scare us.

At 3 a.m. in late November 2015, Tom Wright's phone woke him as he slept in the Shangri-La Hotel in Kuala Lumpur. It was his colleague and fellow author, Bradley Hope, calling from the *Wall Street Journal*'s offices in Midtown Manhattan. Just minutes earlier, Hope had gotten a call from Malaysian Source, who had some alarming news: Najib's office was about to send the police to arrest Wright at his hotel.

The *Journal* was investigating Low's role in the 2013 elections, and Wright had flown into Kuala Lumpur from Penang the night before. While in Low's home state, he'd left his *Journal* business card, with his cell phone number, at the homes and offices of the Malaysian's associates. One of them alerted Low, who in turn told Prime Minister Najib. Malaysian Source told Hope that the government had tracked Wright down to the Shangri-La, a resort-like hotel near the Petronas Towers.

The police would soon make an arrest at the Shangri-La, MS informed him, feigning worry. It was a threat, dressed up as a warning, and the *Journal* decided to pull the plug on the reporting trip. After being woken in the middle of the night, Wright left Malaysia early the next morning, avoiding Kuala Lumpur's international airport, and traveling overland by taxi to Singapore's border with Malaysia instead.

At the border crossing, Wright worried he might get stopped, but he walked easily over into Singapore. Had MS misled Hope on purpose, hoping to scuttle our investigations into the scheme? Or had Najib, learning Wright had checked out of the Shangri-La, decided he had done enough to derail our coverage?

But the *Journal* had what it needed, and in December it published a detailed story about the role of 1MDB money in the 2013 elections, especially in Penang. Even ruling-party politicians had been willing to talk for the piece. Low clearly was not popular in his home state.

With no credible probe in Malaysia, the government and 1MDB could say what they wanted about the *Journal*'s coverage. But Najib was unable to stop the tide of investigations from the United States to Singapore and Switzerland. As the probes spread, Low's associates panicked.

In October, as the *Journal* dug into Low's activities, Patrick Mahony, the investment director of PetroSaudi, spoke on the phone with Laura Justo. She was angry, and she wanted her husband released from jail in Thailand. A judge in the Southern Bangkok criminal court had sentenced Xavier Justo in August to three years in prison for blackmailing PetroSaudi, and he was languishing in a dank cell with twenty-five other people.

The trial and sentencing had lasted only five minutes, but Laura believed Mahony could pull strings to get him out. In her view, Justo had played his part, signing a "confession" and telling a Singapore journalist, without evidence, that the *Edge* and *Sarawak Report* had planned to doctor the PetroSaudi server documents. She was alone with their baby, and urged Mahony to act. But Mahony wanted more.

"The only way that you can show you're ready to be team players is to go to the media, and to show that you're ready to denounce everyone who's conspiring against him," Mahony said.

He wanted her to say Clare Rewcastle-Brown was working against PetroSaudi.

"But are there guarantees he will get out earlier?" Laura Justo replied.

"You can help or not help," Mahony snapped, his voice visibly tense. "I feel for you. But I'm also in the shit. We're all in deep shit. There's a prime minister of a country who is in the shit."

"Who put us in this shit? Don't forget that. I can't give you any guarantees."

"For you it's a matter of money. But for us, it's a question of our lives, our family, everything," Laura replied.

"It's not just a matter of money, Laura. It's a matter of my future, my life," Mahony broke in. "I won't ever be able to do deals anywhere because of all this, okay!"

"But that's just work, money, I'm sure you have enough of that, so what's the problem? You're talking of the life of someone who's locked up in a hole."

"But, Laura, all my assets have been confiscated. I have nothing at the moment. What do you think, that I'm living the sweet life? That I'm not paying for this? I'm borrowing money left and right to pay my bills, to pay for my kids' school, okay. That's what my life's like at the moment."

The next month, with Justo still in jail, Mahony told Laura that tensions were mounting because of the probes into 1MDB in Switzerland and the United States. Investigators were wading through piles of material—bank transfer documents, property records, shell company registrations, and mountains of emails—to piece together what had happened.

They had no access to Jho Low, or even any of his inner circle, many of whom had gone to ground in places like Taiwan and Indonesia, but they were interviewing people on the periphery of events and were building up a picture. Mahony told Laura that Swiss investigators had nothing, that it was all for show.

But she had lost faith in Mahony's promises to secure her husband's release. In January 2016, Laura contacted the Swiss ambassador in Bangkok. A few weeks later, she submitted a dossier to Swiss authorities and the FBI detailing what had transpired. The file included secret recordings she had made of her conversations with Patrick Mahony.

Despite his show of bravado, Mahony clearly was troubled. The *Journal* had reported that the FBI was formally investigating 1MDB and Najib Razak. Soon Mahony would receive a subpoena from U.S. authorities to testify. Fearing the worst, Prime Minister Najib and Riza Aziz hired Boies, Schiller & Flexner, cofounded by the well-known U.S. lawyer David Boies, to represent them. The firm assigned a tough young lawyer called Matthew Schwartz to the new clients.

Schwartz knew something about financial crime. In a former life, he'd been a key member of the crack team that successfully prosecuted Bernie Madoff.

As Mahony appeared to panic, and Najib braced for the worst, Low was doing all he could to keep up appearances. And that meant continuing to party with his famous friends.

Chapter 47

Partying on the Run

Aboard the Equanimity, *South Korea, November 2015*

As the screws tightened, the *Equanimity* was sailing in the Northwest Passage, the famed iceberg-strewn route through the Arctic Sea that connects the northern Atlantic and Pacific Oceans. For years, Arctic pack ice made navigation almost impossible, but environmental changes had opened up the channel, and the *Equanimity*, with a steel hull designed to withstand contact with ice, became one of a small group of elite private ships to complete the journey. As it emerged into the northern Pacific around Alaska, the pilot set a course for the coast of South Korea. It was early November, and Low had arranged for friends and celebrities to fly into Seoul, before being whisked to the boat for a party to celebrate his thirty-fourth birthday.

Despite everything going on, Low's desire to be the center of an event and bestow favors had not diminished; in fact, those around the Malaysian saw that he looked forward even more to these immaculately concocted parties. The theme of this event was "togetherness," and celebrity guests auctioned items to raise money for the United Nations, before everyone sang "We Are the World." Guests drank fine wines, champagne, the Korean spirit soju, and espresso-flavored Patrón tequila, while the food included Beluga caviar, lobster bisque, and truffle pasta.

One room of the yacht was made into a "Rose Garden," the walls plastered with red roses with leaves plucked off. The guests, including Jamie Foxx and Swizz Beatz, wore cocktail dresses and tuxedos. This wasn't just another secret party, with phones checked in at the door: Low also wanted to poke fun at the allegations against him, to make it seem like these falsehoods were water off a duck's back. At one point, there was even a slideshow of positive media articles about Low.

But another video he requested—a montage of world leaders including Barack Obama and Vladimir Putin wishing him happy birthday—even the top party planners could not have achieved.

The Obama administration's love of Najib was fast cooling. Later that month, President Obama traveled to Malaysia one final time, for a regional summit, a visit that had been scheduled long before the 1MDB scandal hit the headlines. After meeting behind closed doors with Najib, the president told journalists he had expressed to the prime minister the importance of transparency and rooting out corruption. With Anwar Ibrahim languishing in jail, and Najib's crackdown on civil liberties at home, the words rang hollow.

Low continued to act as if nothing was up. Just a few months earlier, the Malaysian told friends he had bid $170 million for Picasso's *Women of Algiers* at Christie's in New York, but lost out to a Qatari buyer who paid $179 million, at the time the most expensive painting ever to sell at auction. After eleven minutes of telephone bidding, Low dropped out. Along with the Nimes mansion in Los Angeles, this was another purchase that was beyond even him. It was hard to grasp how Low was even considering such purchases after the media stories about 1MDB.

In December, he traveled to Courchevel, a ski resort in the French Alps, for his usual end-of-year party with his closest friends. In a villa on the slopes of the Alps, Low appeared calm, as if none of the news was fazing him. After days of skiing and snowboarding, the group partied back at the villa. It was a routine his closest friends—Joey McFarland, Swizz Beatz, Alicia Keys, Jasmine Loo of 1MDB, Fat Eric, and Low's girlfriend, Jesselynn Chuan Teik Ying, had followed over several winter ski holidays around the world: Whistler, Aspen, Courchevel.

Like the other holidays, the itinerary was carefully planned out to include private-chef dinners, snowmobiling, massages, and drinks. But Low's business-as-usual mien was a facade, and aspects of the trip even took on a sinister undertone at times. Low confided in some of his gathered friends that he was even worried about assassination, although he never said by whom. As usual, Low continued to travel everywhere with his bodyguards. He instructed Catherine Tan, his personal assistant, to ensure no one on the Courchevel trip posted pictures to Instagram, Facebook, or other social media.

His closest associates in the scheme—Eric Tan, Jasmine Loo, Yeo Jiawei, the former BSI banker, and Seet Li Lin, who worked at Jynwel—were too enmeshed in Low's scheme to pull out now. But the decision of celebrities like Swizz Beatz and Alicia Keys to continue to fraternize with Low, despite stories in the *Journal* and Singapore's probe into the Malaysian, was more surprising.

The conversation during the skiing trip, and a subsequent few days in London, revolved around how to change the narrative on Low. Until the last, those who had benefited from his largesse seemingly refused to acknowledge the mounting evidence of wrongdoing. Perhaps Swizz Beatz and Alicia Keys did not read the media, or they just discounted the stories about Low, or maybe they simply didn't care if the money funding the trip was stolen.

Joey McFarland, who owed much of his Hollywood career to Low, was vociferous in the support of his friend. The coverage of Low was biased, a political hatchet job, he told the entourage.

One evening during the vacation, he advised Low to publicize more of his charity work on Twitter to counter the negative stories. With the money still flowing, McFarland didn't appear to have doubts. But he more quickly became angered, as the stress of the situation began to rub away at his normal happy-go-lucky persona.

Red Granite's latest movie, *Daddy's Home*, starring Mark Wahlberg and Will Ferrell, had just premiered and McFarland wasn't yet ready to let go of the Hollywood dream. For now, the news about Low and 1MDB had not yet penetrated Hollywood, and Red Granite was still a going concern. On Instagram, McFarland kept up the appearance of a successful producer, although there were signs of trouble.

Some stars seemed to be distancing themselves. DiCaprio, for instance, had passed on taking the lead in *Papillon*, the company's latest feature, which was in preproduction, with Charlie Hunnam playing the role instead. DiCaprio hadn't even attended Low's latest yacht party off the coast of South Korea, and was not present at the latest auction at Christie's. Talk about Scorsese making *The Irishman* starring Robert De Niro with Red Granite also had gone quiet.

It was a worrying sign; the slow peeling away of Low's coterie of famous friends had begun. But the Malaysian had other—bigger—worries to contend with. The FBI's probe was scaring his business partners. To save his empire, Low turned to China.

Chapter 48

China Connection

Shanghai, China, April 2016

From his residence in the Peninsula Hotel complex in Shanghai, Low's life of exile from Malaysia was not too shabby. Situated near the Bund, the city's old colonial heart, the hotel and residences boasted two Michelin-starred restaurants. From his rooms, Low enjoyed unbroken views across Shanghai's Huangpu River to the modernistic skyline on the other side.

It was here in Shanghai, China's financial capital, that Low was fighting hard to keep hold of his businesses. With the FBI asking questions, Low's empire in the United States was in peril. Major banks no longer wanted to touch him, and Wells Fargo was refusing to push through its loan to finance the purchase of the Park Lane, Low's flagship development project with the Abu Dhabi fund Mubadala and the U.S. developer Steve Witkoff near New York's Central Park.

The project was all but scuttled, but Low had hatched a plan in Shanghai. Unwilling to give in, his latest maneuver involved enlisting the help of Shanghai-based Greenland Group, a Chinese state-owned developer. On April 26, Low fired off an email to Khaldoon Al Mubarak, the chief executive of Mubadala, outlining how he planned to sell his stake in the project to a minor Kuwaiti royal. The royal was simply another old friend of

Low—a nominee to keep the Malaysian's name off the books. The Kuwaiti would then sell a part of his stake to Greenland Group, which would help fund the project.

"In 2015, I have been faced with vicious, false and misinformed media attacks which resulted in challenges with respect to the [Park Lane] financing," he told Al Mubarak. But this deal, he added, solved the problem.

Low had again pulled strings with a state entity—this time in China—to solve a problem. His ability to enter the halls of power, getting to know the chairman of Greenland in Shanghai, held out a slim chance the project might not die—and he could get his money from the project out of the United States.

Fearing an imminent FBI action, Low was taking other actions to sell assets for cash. In April, he ordered Sotheby's to sell *Dustheads*, the Basquiat painting, which he had pledged as collateral for a loan. U.S. hedge fund manager Daniel Sundheim paid $35 million, almost $14 million less than it had cost Low three years earlier. The Malaysian began to sell other pieces of his art, also at fire-sale prices. When he'd bought art, it was exactly for this kind of emergency. The mansions and companies were harder to divest in a rush.

As the Malaysian was trying to save his Park Lane deal, the *Wall Street Journal* published the most detailed story yet about Low's involvement in Najib's secret accounts and his behind-the-scenes role at 1MDB. After the story published, Malaysian Source, our secret contact involved in the scheme, stopped all communication. MS realized it was not so easy to influence our coverage.

The *Journal* then tried to locate Low. Bradley Hope flew out to Shanghai, where a female receptionist at the Peninsula confirmed that Low was a longtime resident at the hotel. But when Hope showed up at the entrance to the hotel apartments, a burly security guard insisted no one by that name had ever resided there. When he returned to the receptionist, she looked at her computer again and noticed all records of Low's stay had disappeared. Hope then flew to Hong Kong, where the *Equa-nimity* had berthed for repairs. The captain said the owner wasn't on board. Low was nowhere to be seen.

Low's connections with Chinese state-owned companies proved helpful in another way. The 1MDB scandal had wrecked Najib's relations with Abu Dhabi and Saudi Arabia. The attorney general had tried to pass off the money Najib received in his secret accounts as a donation from Saudi Arabia. The Saudis had refused to publicly confirm this fiction, despite Malaysia's entreaties. The kingdom's foreign minister would only say he believed Najib did nothing wrong and that there had been some kind of donation to Malaysia, but he wouldn't commit fully to the false story being put forward.

What the prime minister needed now was a way to fill the 1MDB financial black hole. The fund had more than $13 billion in debt and needed to repay Abu Dhabi for bailing it out. But its assets were worth nothing like this amount. In a series of deals, Chinese state-owned companies agreed to acquire the bulk of 1MDB's assets: land in Kuala Lumpur and power plants. If completed, the deals would raise about $4 billion, still well short of wiping out 1MDB's debt, but a start to cleaning up the mess.

Low needed another—bigger—deal to make his problems evaporate. On June 28, 2016, he met in Beijing with Xiao Yaqing, the head of China's state-owned Assets Supervision and Administration Commission, a powerful body that oversees the country's public companies, and other Chinese officials.

By this stage, with Najib's backing, Low was acting like a Malaysian government minister, and he was there in China's capital to negotiate an audacious plan. In the meeting, Low and Xiao, accompanied by other Chinese and Malaysian officials, discussed a proposal for Chinese state-owned companies to build a $16 billion railway in Malaysia and a $2.5 billion gas pipeline.

But there was a catch. The projects' valuations, to be financed by Chinese state banks, had been inflated. One document drawn up by Low ahead of the meeting said the projects would provide "above market profitability" to the Chinese companies. Indeed, the rail budget was double an estimate made earlier by a Malaysian consultancy. Another document discussed how, in return, Chinese state companies would make payments that would "indirectly be used to repay 1MDB debt."

In the meeting, Xiao expressed how the public must believe "all initiatives are market driven for the mutual benefits of both countries," according to a Malaysian government summary of the meeting.

Here was the naked truth of China's "Belt and Road" initiative, an ambitious plan by President Xi Jinping to build infrastructure across Asia, the Middle East, and even Europe, forging alliances and growing China's prestige. In Malaysia's misery, and Low's troubles, Beijing saw an opportunity to develop a client-state relationship, and Najib even embarked on secret talks with China's leadership to allow Chinese navy ships to dock at two Malaysian ports.

At a meeting the next day, Sun Lijun, head of China's domestic-security force, confirmed that China's government was monitoring the *Wall Street Journal* in Hong Kong at Malaysia's request, including "full scale residence/office/device tapping, computer/phone/web data retrieval, and full operational surveillance," according to the Malaysian summary.

"Sun says that they will establish all links that WSJ HK has with Malaysia-related individuals and will hand over the wealth of data to Malaysia through 'back channels' once everything is ready," the summary reads. It was unclear whether China carried out its promises or was just stringing Low along.

Sun also promised to use China's "leverage on other nations" to get the United States and others to drop their 1MDB investigations.

The troubles at 1MDB offered a perfect opportunity for China to supplant the United States in Malaysia—just the latest sign of America's declining power in the region.

It was no surprise then that Najib turned away from President Obama, who had lost faith in Malaysia as a model Islamic democracy, and looked instead to China's authoritarian rulers.

Najib was quick to claim victory, saying the deals, and the end to Malaysian investigations, put the fund's problems behind the country. The National Audit Department had finished its probe into 1MDB, but the government classified it under the Official Secrets Act, attempting to bury its contents.

The Prime Minister continued to instill fear in his political opponents. In April, police arrested an opposition leader who had gotten hold of the National Audit Department's report, which showed billions of dollars of 1MDB money was unaccounted for. He was sentenced to eighteen months in jail for breaking the Official Secrets Act. When the *Journal* reported on the secret document, Najib threatened the newspaper with a lawsuit. A leader of the Bersih protests also was detained under a new law meant to fight terrorism.

There had been intimidation—a murder, even—of those involved in 1MDB investigations, and people were frightened. Yet some patriotic Malaysians held out hope that authorities overseas would not let their investigations drop. At the Malaysian Anti-Corruption Commission, which had recommended the prime minister's arrest, there was simmering anger over the mothballing of their investigation.

And so, a handful of investigators began to secretly feed information to the FBI. McMurry's team of agents had spent months disentangling the money flows. By July 2016, the Department of Justice was ready to take action. It did so in a way that caught Low, Najib, and other conspirators off guard.

Chapter 49

Glass Half Full

Washington, DC, July 2016

U.S. Attorney General Loretta Lynch stepped up to the microphone in a press room at the Department of Justice's offices on Pennsylvania Avenue in Washington, DC. Moments later, she announced the largest-ever asset seizure under the Kleptocracy Initiative. With the help of the Malaysian Anti-Corruption Commission, and other Malaysian officials who met FBI investigators in secret, the Bureau had pieced together the details of one of the biggests frauds in history.

Flanked by senior Justice Department and FBI officials, Lynch laid out how the U.S. government was seeking to seize more than $1 billion in assets bought with proceeds stolen from 1MDB—the largest corruption case on record—from mansions in New York, Los Angeles, and London, to a stake in EMI, a private jet, and the future proceeds from *The Wolf of Wall Street*, to name just a few. For maximum publicity, the Justice Department filed its lawsuit—*United States v. The Wolf of Wall Street*—at the District Court for the Central District of California, where Hollywood is located.

"The Department of Justice will not allow the American financial system to be used as a conduit for corruption," Lynch said. "Corrupt officials around the world should make no mistake that we will be relentless in our efforts to deny them the proceeds of their crimes."

This was the largest kleptocracy seizure in U.S. history, and Heuchling's team, together with Justice Department prosecutors, had painstakingly laid out every twist and turn of the scheme in clear prose.

The lawsuit named Jho Low—the first time he had been publicly referred to by a law-enforcement agency—as well as Riza Aziz, Khadem Al Qubaisi, and Mohamed Al Husseiny. (Later addendums to the lawsuit would name Tarek Obaid and "PetroSaudi Officer," a reference to Patrick Mahony.) Tim Leissner was referred to as "Goldman Managing Director," and his interactions with Jho Low during the meeting with Sheikh Mansour in Abu Dhabi were sketched out, although it would take more than two years for the banker's full role to come out in the public domain. But most shockingly, Prime Minister Najib Razak was thinly disguised as "Malaysian Official 1," the lawsuit describing him as a relative of Riza Aziz and holding a position of authority at 1MDB. (Later, the department would add Rosmah as the wife of "Malaysian Official 1.")

The allusion to Najib shocked the prime minister's entourage, which never thought the United States would take such a bold step. This was a civil lawsuit, looking to seize assets, but from here on Jho Low would avoid the United States, fearing criminal proceedings were also under way. Even Najib would keep out of the United States for a while, sending a deputy to the U.N. General Assembly in New York later that year.

The prime minister never expected the hammer of U.S. justice to land so close to his door. After years of privilege, of golfing with President Obama, of endless speeches to the United Nations, he felt untouchable. It was hard for Najib to even conceive of an independent justice system that would embarrass a sitting prime minister. It formed a stark contrast to his ability to shut down investigations at home.

In the days after Lynch's press conference, Najib told family members he was not aware of the scale of Low's theft. It was hard to believe—he knew for sure about the homes in Los Angeles, New York, and London that Low had bought and transferred to Riza Aziz. But it's possible the prime minister did not realize the full extent of Low's actions. The Justice Department said that at least $3.5 billion had gone missing, an estimate it would raise by a billion dollars within a year. A week later, in a feeble news conference, Najib pointed out that 1MDB did not directly own any of the assets named by the Justice Department. It was technically true, but beside the point.

The *Journal* had reported the Justice Department's suits just before Lynch's press conference. When Low read the story, he thought it was a big mistake, because U.S. authorities had not served his lawyers with any legal documents. The action scuttled Low's efforts to liquidate his stake in the Park Lane, or to sell any other U.S. assets. His mansions, art, even his Bombardier jet, were now frozen. Only the *Equanimity*, in the open ocean and out of reach of U.S. authorities, was still his to enjoy. But Low already had hundreds of millions—if not billions—secreted away in secret accounts around the world. And he remained free.

Watching from the sidelines, Bill McMurry, whose New York–based international corruption squad had led the investigation, perhaps felt this was a glass-half-full moment. Global Financial Integrity, a Washington-based anticorruption group, estimated that $1 trillion was drained from developing economies in 2012 alone, especially poorly regulated places like Brazil, China, India, and Russia. But McMurry had a more optimistic take.

By mid-2016, the FBI was ratcheting up its cooperation with foreign anticorruption agencies, including Brazilian investigators looking into the Petrobras scandal, in which the state-owned oil company made illegal payments of more than $5 billion to company executives and politicians. Brazil's attorney general already had secured convictions of scores of Petrobras officials, politicians, and businesspeople. And despite Najib's best efforts, the Justice Department was moving to punish those involved in 1MDB.

"There is undoubtedly a global push toward anticorruption that has never really existed, even just a decade or two earlier," McMurry told a seminar.

In a later news release, the FBI even praised the "tremendous courage" of the Malaysian Anti-Corruption Commission in pursuing its own investigation. It was as close as the FBI could get to thanking the commission's staff for secretly helping the Bureau with its own probe.

There was a glass-half-empty way of looking at events. Hadn't the system of checks and balances at banks failed to catch Jho Low's malfeasance for seven years because of the greed of financiers? Wasn't he still at liberty to enjoy a life of ease in five-star residences in China and Thailand, where he lived in the St. Regis apartments in Bangkok, or on his superyacht berthed in Phuket? In Malaysia, Najib's position appeared unshakable. What sanction had anyone from Al Qubaisi to Leissner and the BSI bankers faced?

What remained to be seen was whether the U.S. government—or Singapore, Switzerland, and Abu Dhabi—would launch criminal prosecutions against those involved. The U.S. kleptocracy action was a civil case—an attempt to claw back assets. But only jail time, not simply a slap on the wrist and a confiscation of assets, would serve as a real deterrent to this kind of transnational fraud.

Chapter 50

White-Collar Crime

New York, Fall 2015

In the fall of 2015, Goldman compliance executives sifted through Tim Leissner's official Goldman email account. After the 1MDB scandal hit the pages of the *Wall Street Journal* in July 2015, Goldman launched an internal investigation into its dealings in Malaysia. The German banker told Goldman executives conducting the probe that he barely knew Low. But they didn't take Leissner's word for it and carried out a review of his communications. Normally, Wall Street bankers are savvy about keeping sensitive business offline, either meeting in person or using private emails and phone messages.

But Leissner had been sloppy.

Earlier in 2015, the banker had prepared his unauthorized reference letter for Jho Low—to help him open an account with Banque Havilland in Luxembourg—from a personal computer. The letter never should have formed part of Goldman's internal inquiry. But someone on Kimora Lee Simmons's staff mistakenly sent the document to Leissner's Goldman email, and compliance executives uncovered it.

At Goldman's Manhattan headquarters, there was a heated

debate about how to deal with the 1MDB issue, which was turning into a public relations debacle. Some executives, not knowing the full extent of Leissner's wrongdoing, cautioned against
scapegoating him. Pablo Salame, cohead of Goldman's securities
division, rejected an internal suggestion that the firm's involvement in the mess could be blamed solely on him.

"Goldman Sachs did these deals," Salame told colleagues in
one discussion.

In public, Goldman Sachs stood by its actions, pointing out
it had taken risks in helping 1MDB raise money and was fairly
paid for its services. The bank said it had no idea of Low's role
at the fund and could not have been expected to know what
1MDB would do with the money.

Despite high-level Goldman support of the 1MDB business,
Leissner couldn't survive the evidence of his secret support of
Low to open the Luxembourg account. In January 2016, Goldman put Leissner on personal leave, and the next day he quit,
formally leaving the bank the following month.

In the following weeks, Leissner often was spotted at Club
XIII, a futuristic-looking nightclub in Hong Kong's financial district, where he told friends he felt betrayed by Goldman. Sporting
a graying beard and looking haggard, the banker complained it
was unfair he was being singled out, arguing that senior Goldman
executives in New York had signed off on these deals. Despite
the bank's denials, many executives at Goldman were aware of
Low's role in 1MDB but had not raised concerns, he claimed.

Andrea Vella, who structured the 1MDB bond deals and
allegedly kept Low's involvement from compliance, had been
promoted to cohead of investment banking in Asia. Gary Cohn,
Goldman's president and a big supporter of the 1MDB business,
became director of President Donald Trump's National Economic
Council in January 2017, a job he stayed in for a little over a year.

Leissner didn't go public with his grievances. He was still

engaged in negotiations with Goldman over deferred pay worth millions of dollars and he still must have hoped his role in the fraud might never come out. The banker had not expected to be fired, and it appeared he needed the money to finance his lifestyle with his new wife, Kimora Lee Simmons; around that time he even asked a friend for a cash loan of a few million dollars. Plus, there was the code among Goldman bankers to never talk about deals, even once you have left the firm.

He tried to build other businesses. With Simmons, Leissner had set up Cuscaden Capital, a British Virgin Islands–based venture capital fund. Cuscaden invested in Celsius, a U.S.-based energy-drink company, and he became cochairman. Leissner divided his time between Hong Kong and Los Angeles, where Simmons purchased a $25 million mansion in the gated Beverly Park neighborhood, a twenty-thousand-square-foot estate with an olive-tree-lined driveway leading to a seven-bedroom mansion. Neighbors included Rod Stewart and Denzel Washington. Simmons posted Instagram pictures with her husband on the ski slopes in early 2018. But the specter of legal proceedings continued to hang over Leissner.

FBI agents had begun to look at payments of hundreds of thousands of dollars by Jasmine Loo, 1MDB's former legal counsel and a close Low aide, into one of Leissner's personal accounts. The purpose of the transfers was unclear. The banker appeared to maintain other links to people close to Low. The *Wall Street Journal*, in November 2017, reported that Leissner and a Thai associate of Low's had attempted in late 2016 to buy a small bank in the Indian Ocean nation of Mauritius—but regulators there had blocked the acquisition.

Low's role in the Mauritius deal, if indeed he had one, was unclear. It also was unknown if Leissner kept in contact with the Malaysian. Once a ubiquitous presence at Hollywood parties and an international jet-setter, Low had seemingly fallen off the map as authorities tightened the screws. He was sighted in Bangkok and

Shanghai, but his associates couldn't get hold of him as easily as in the past. No one seemed to be sure where he was at any given moment.

In early 2017, Singapore banned Leissner from its financial industry for ten years in connection with the letter he wrote to the Luxembourg bank on behalf of Jho Low. Later in the year, the Financial Industry Regulatory Authority, a U.S. body, barred him from the American securities industry, after he didn't respond to requests for documents and other information stemming from his departure from Goldman. (Later, in early 2019, the Federal Reserve would ban Leissner and Roger Ng from working in the banking industry. Leissner would also be fined $1.42 million.)

Then in August 2017 the Justice Department made a bombshell announcement: It was pursuing a criminal investigation into the 1MDB scheme.

The Justice Department's earlier legal actions were civil proceedings, an effort to seize assets, not to put people behind bars. U.S. authorities had filed a number of additional civil lawsuits, targeting a growing list of assets, including the *Equanimity*, the proceeds from Red Granite's *Dumb and Dumber To* and *Daddy's Home*, the $8 million in jewelry Low had given to Miranda Kerr, and the $13 million in art presented to Leonardo DiCaprio.

The civil action, however, was just a way to tee up the main event: a criminal investigation. Before the judge in California could rule, the Justice Department, in August 2017, asked for an "indefinite suspension" of its asset-seizure suits to permit the FBI to focus on building a criminal case. It was a sign the U.S. government was seeking to prosecute individuals involved in the fraud, and did not want to show its hand in civil proceedings.

By the summer of 2018, the Justice Department, working through global banking information, had enough to seek Leissner's arrest. He was picked up on June 10 and immediately entered plea negotiations with the government. Two months later, the banker admitted to conspiracy to launder money and violate foreign antibribery laws for helping siphon money from 1MDB. He forfeited $43.7 million.

Leissner continued to cooperate with the Justice Department. The question now was whether others at Goldman would be sanctioned. In November 2018, the Justice Department unsealed Leissner's guilty plea, making it public for the first time. Authorities indicted Roger Ng, who was subsequently arrested in Malaysia and soon after extradited to the United States to face trial. He pleaded not guilty.

Andrea Vella was named as a co-conspirator, although he was not charged. The next day, Goldman put him on leave. He denies wrongdoing.

In almost a decade since the financial crisis, only one Wall Street banker—a Credit Suisse executive—had gone to jail, despite an economic collapse that had thrown millions out of work and lowered living standards. More than one thousand bankers were convicted for their roles in the savings and loan crisis in America in the 1980s and 1990s. In 2006, a court found Ken Lay, the former CEO of Enron, guilty of fraud. Since the crisis, though, the Justice Department had shied away from singling out individuals for white-collar crimes, preferring instead to reach deals with banks to defer prosecutions in return for hefty fines.

Goldman agreed in 2016 to pay up to $5 billion in a civil settlement with U.S. federal prosecutors to resolve claims stemming from the selling of faulty mortgage securities to investors during the crisis. Wall Street banks, including Bank of America and J.P. Morgan, in total paid more than $40 billion in settlements. Critics pointed out that Wall Street saw these fines as a cost of doing business that did little to alter behavior.

Now, the Justice Department was trying to determine whether

Goldman had reason to believe the money it raised for 1MDB was being misused, which could lead to a steep penalty under the Bank Secrecy Act, perhaps in the quantum of the $2 billion that J.P. Morgan paid for failing to stop Madoff's Ponzi scheme. The specter of a criminal indictment also continued to hang over the bank. The Federal Reserve, the Securities and Exchange Commission, and New York State's Department of Financial Services also were examining some of the bank's actions.

In fall 2018, Lloyd Blankfein stepped down as CEO under a cloud after over a decade running the bank, first through the mortgage crisis and now the 1MDB imbroglio. There was no sign he had done anything criminally wrong, but his legacy had been tainted. Within months of his departure, Goldman announced some of his compensation could be held back as a result of the 1MDB scandal.

After the release of the Panama Papers in 2016, detailing how the ultrawealthy use shell companies to conceal ownership of assets, there was a heightened global debate about anonymity in the purchase of multi-million-dollar assets. The United States was taking other measures to stop money laundering through its real estate sector. The Treasury Department launched a pilot program in 2016 forcing all-cash buyers of luxury properties in Manhattan and Miami to disclose their identities to the U.S. government. The rules targeted properties bought by shell companies and worth more than $1 million in Miami and $3 million in Manhattan. Title insurance companies, which are involved in most real estate deals, were ordered to carry out the checks.

More than a quarter of all home purchases made over a six-month period were flagged as suspicious, leading the Treasury Department to roll the program out in Los Angeles and other city areas, with a view to bringing in new, permanent regulations. Major loopholes remained—lawyers, for instance, could continue to cite client privilege to avoid giving up the names of beneficial owners involved in real estate transactions—but the United States was moving to deal with the problem.

Christie's, the auction house that sold Low many paintings, began demanding that agents looking to buy or sell works reveal the names of their clients. These rules were voluntary, but Christie's was taking action. There were still no regulations to effectively stop the flow of corrupt cash into nightclubs, casinos, and Hollywood movies, but the U.S. government hoped the shame of the 1MDB fiasco would make nightclub promoters, directors, and actors think twice before receiving money.

Leonardo DiCaprio and Miranda Kerr in 2017 voluntarily gave up the gifts they had received from Low to the U.S. government, and the actor even returned Marlon Brando's Oscar statuette, which was not named in the lawsuits. By then, he had a Best Actor Oscar of his own, for *The Revenant* in 2016.

Kerr had split with Low after the first stories about him began to emerge in early 2015. In May 2017 she married Evan Spiegel, the billionaire founder of Snapchat, cutting all ties with Low.

As for Strategic Group founders Noah Tepperberg and Jason Strauss, their interactions with Jho Low had played a role in building their business. In February 2017, Madison Square Garden Company paid $181 million for a controlling stake in a new company, TAO Group, which included their nightclubs.

Red Granite, in March 2018, agreed to pay $60 million to settle the Justice Department's efforts to seize rights to the film company's future profits. Joey McFarland maintained a public presence, attending the premiere of Red Granite's *Papillon* in September 2017 at the Toronto International Film Festival. On Instagram, he posted pictures with Charlie Hunnam, the film's star, from the red carpet.

McFarland also appeared to keep in touch with some of his old associates. In March 2017, he posted an Instagram picture from the Batu Caves, just north of Kuala Lumpur, the capital of Malaysia. That was where Riza Aziz, the cofounder of Red

Granite, had been cooling his heels since the Justice Department's asset-seizure lawsuit in mid-2016. Scared to travel back to the United States, fearing possible arrest, Riza was trying to do business deals in Asia with one of Najib's sons.

The exact whereabouts of Low remained unclear.

On March 27, 2016, Yeo Jiawei, the fund expert on whom Low had relied to hide money flows, arrived for a meeting at the Swiss Club in Singapore. Yeo was frantic as he made his way through the doors of the private club, a two-story, whitewashed former British colonial mansion with bright red shutters, and made his way to a café on a verandah out back.

There to meet him was Kevin Swampillai, his former boss at BSI, with whom he had conspired to take money from 1MDB. As they sat at the café, looking over the Swiss Club's lush garden, Yeo told Swampillai that he'd recently been arrested by Singapore police and let out on bail.

Fearing jail time, Yeo sketched out a plan of action. The pair should tell Singapore authorities that the 1MDB money they'd received into their personal bank accounts was actually investments from another financier. Swampillai was noncommittal.

The same month, Yeo used the encrypted Telegram instant-messaging service to contact José Renato Carvalho Pinto at Amicorp, whose Curaçao funds had disguised the flows of 1MDB money. In his Telegram message, Yeo told Pinto to destroy his laptop and avoid coming to Singapore in case authorities tried to interview him.

Yeo had made a huge misstep. Unknown to him, Singapore police were monitoring his actions, and now authorities had evidence that Yeo was obstructing the course of justice. He was soon back in jail.

As in the United States, Singapore seized assets: $177 million in property and contents of bank accounts, about half belonging to Jho Low and his family. Authorities in the city-state revoked BSI's banking license, the first time it had shut down a bank for more than three decades. The Monetary Authority of Singapore levied fines of over $20 million in total against eight banks, the majority to be paid by BSI and Falcon, with smaller penalties to Coutts, Standard Chartered, and others, for failing to stop money laundering. The financial penalties were paltry, but Ravi Menon, managing director of the Monetary Authority of Singapore, defended the city-state's response to the calamity.

"When you fine a bank billions of dollars, it hurts basically shareholders and other stakeholders. It doesn't hurt the board and senior management, and it doesn't hurt the individuals much. And that is what, in my view, is one of the failings of the current regime globally, that people continue to do wrong things because they've not been held personally liable and responsible," Menon said.

But Singapore's criminal sanctions could hardly be called draconian. After cooperating with authorities, Yak Yew Chee, Jho Low's personal banker, was sentenced to eighteen weeks in jail after pleading guilty to forgery and failing to report suspicious transactions. He handed over a few million dollars in 1MDB-related bonuses to Singapore's government but was allowed to keep millions more. Haughty and defiant through his trial, Yeo was handed a thirty-month sentence for witness tampering and a further four-and-a-half-year term for money laundering and other charges.

Three other people, comprising a subordinate of Yak's at BSI, the head of Falcon's Singapore office, and a Singaporean broker, got short sentences of a matter of weeks. Prosecutors said Jho Low was a person of interest, but authorities had no idea where to find him. Singapore's central bank referred Hanspeter Brunner, who had retired as head of BSI in March 2016, and Kevin Swampillai, along with a number of other BSI executives, to state prosecutors for further investigation, but more than two years later, authorities did not appear to have taken any action against either man.

Switzerland's attorney general's office also launched a criminal probe into the 1MDB affair. Investigators focused on the role of Jho Low and Al Qubaisi, but the office also named BSI as a target, and Swiss financial regulators ordered the bank to hand over 95 million Swiss francs in illegal profits. After 143 years in operation, BSI ceased to exist in 2017, its assets folded into another Swiss bank under orders from authorities.

Falcon Bank, owned by the Abu Dhabi fund Aabar, also was under criminal investigation in Switzerland. Like Brunner, Eduardo Leemann, the chief executive of Falcon who had complained to Jho Low about hundreds of millions of dollars of risky payments in 2013, before letting them through anyway, also retired in 2016. Unlike BSI, Falcon was allowed to remain in operation, but ordered to return over $2.5 million in illegal profits.

Mark Branson, chief executive of the Swiss Financial Market Supervisory Authority, the financial-sector regulator, worried publicly that Swiss banks were becoming more exposed to money laundering as they targeted wealthy clients in emerging markets. "Money laundering is no victimless crime. It allows criminals to profit from breaking the law. It also facilitates corruption and the abuse of power and privilege," Branson said.

As in the United States and Singapore, the proof of Switzerland's seriousness in combating white-collar crime would be in criminal prosecutions of Swiss bankers, not rhetoric.

Chapter 51

King Khadem Falls

Abu Dhabi, August 2016

In the fall of 2016, Abu Dhabi's police swooped, detaining Khadem Al Qubaisi. It was an unprecedented move for the Gulf emirate, where the dirty laundry of the elite is rarely hung out for public view. For years, Al Qubaisi had acted without boundaries, a seemingly omnipotent figure who had the authority to move around billions of dollars. The key to his untouchability was a close relationship with Sheikh Mansour.

The Justice Department lawsuits had forced the ruling Al Nahyans to take stern action. Al Qubaisi's role in the 1MDB scandal had been exposed for the world to see, bringing shame on Abu Dhabi. Someone had to pay. Al Qubaisi's tenure atop the world's financial system had come to a close with his dismissal from IPIC in 2015. Now he was taken into custody, along with Al Husseiny, the former head of Aabar. Authorities did so without fanfare—there were no public statements—but the arrests nevertheless marked a rare moment of accountability in the emirate. Though the men's assets were frozen, neither was formally charged.

Both men were held in a detention facility meant for criminals on their way to prison. In an interview with the *Journal* in early 2019, Al Qubaisi complained that he was being scapegoated to protect Sheikh Mansour. He said he had been chained to a window for twenty-four hours in a bid to get him to admit guilt and hand over his assets. "I did this deal, but I did it on behalf of the government of Abu Dhabi," he said. "They are putting everything on my back." The fate of Al Husseiny, who was not even a citizen of Abu Dhabi, was unclear.

From his bases in Bangkok and Shanghai, Low had been working to reach a deal with Abu Dhabi authorities to brush the scheme under the carpet. With Al Qubaisi's arrest, such hopes were fast ebbing away.

Instead, both sides became embroiled in a public scrape over who was liable to pay interest on 1MDB's bonds, which IPIC had guaranteed. The Malaysian fund defaulted, but Abu Dhabi was on the hook for payments, or would face cross-defaults by investors on its own debt.

The bigger issue of who should pay for the money Low and Al Qubaisi took remained unresolved. Abu Dhabi's negotiators argued this was not their problem, but they couldn't walk away because IPIC had guaranteed $3.5 billion in 1MDB bonds. There was also the issue of the $1 billion emergency loan that IPIC had made to 1MDB.

Abu Dhabi authorities had taken action against Al Qubaisi, but now the rulers wanted this embarrassment to melt away. IPIC took a $3.5 billion provision, basically an admission to investors that it never expected 1MDB to pay its debts, and then was merged into Mubadala, bringing an ignominious close to the $70 billion fund's thirty-two-year history. For years, Goldman, Morgan Stanley, and other banks had made huge profits dealing with IPIC, and now suddenly it did not exist.

The empire of Khaldoon Al Mubarak, the chief executive of Mubadala, which had done so many deals with Low, appeared to have grown even larger as IPIC now came under his control.

Abu Dhabi authorities and 1MDB continued to negotiate

how to sort out the debt problem, but it was unclear how the Malaysian fund would come up with the money it owed. The hopes that China would bail out Malaysia seemed to have been misplaced. In early 2017, one deal for a Chinese state–owned company to acquire a parcel of 1MDB's land fell apart, after President Xi Jinping's government declined to sign off on the arrangement. It seemed that Beijing didn't want to get involved in this imbroglio, even if it helped bind Malaysia closer to China.

Low's efforts to cover up the PetroSaudi phase of the fraud also were failing. In November 2017, Prince Turki, cofounder of the oil firm, was detained in a consolidation of power in Saudi Arabia. His father, the former king, had passed away, and Saudi's new rulers detained scores of princes and cabinet members, ostensibly for corruption. Prince Turki's fall was another blow to Low's prospects.

PetroSaudi's role in the 1MDB affair was a focus of investigations in Swizerland. While Prince Turki was detained, Xavier Justo was let out early, in December 2016, from jail in Thailand, and he returned to his family in Geneva. Angry over his treatment, he filed a criminal complaint in Switzerland against Tarek Obaid, Patrick Mahony, and Paul Finnigan, the former British police officer. (In January 2019, the *Edge* finally paid Justo the $2 million it had promised for the PetroSaudi emails.) Obaid and Mahony still ran the PetroSaudi business, although it had few real operations. Obaid continued to party and was snapped on a superyacht off the coast of Turkey in August 2016. Mahony was at home in London with his family. In May 2018, Switzerland's attorney general announced it had begun criminal investigations into two officers of PetroSaudi.

In June 2017, Bradley Hope received an intriguing message in his *Wall Street Journal* email. The message, from a mysterious group calling itself Global Leaks, offered him access to emails hacked from the computer of Yousef Al Otaiba, Low's associate and the UAE's ambassador to Washington.

"We have something extremely smoking gun and exclusive," the email promised.

The email was sent from global-leaks@inbox.ru, a suffix denoting Russia, but the location of the group was a mystery. Their motivation was crystal clear. Global Leaks approached a number of international news outlets at the time. In messages, they pointed out Ambassador Otaiba's role in Middle East politics, including his efforts in June 2017 to isolate the tiny Persian Gulf nation of Qatar.

Hope was interested in a different aspect to Ambassador Otaiba's life, one about which other news outlets had no clue: his connection to Jho Low. He asked the group to search their files and come back with anything related to Low or 1MDB. The haul was remarkable.

The emails gave a comprehensive picture of Otaiba's relationship with Jho Low and how the ambassador had benefited financially from 1MDB. They also showed how Otaiba, after the stories in the *Journal* and *Sarawak Report*, had cut off Low, who was desperately trying to get in touch with him.

The Abu Dhabi government attempted to discredit the emails, pointing out the hackers were backed by Otaiba's political enemies in the Middle East, but it did not go as far as to claim the documents were doctored. Otaiba remained in his position, appearing on Charlie Rose's talk show in the United States to discourse on Middle East politics not long after the *Journal* published a story in July 2017 on his ties to Low.

Ambassador Otaiba was a survivor.

Prime Minister Najib started to act as if 1MDB had never existed. He disbanded the fund's board and placed it directly under the Finance Ministry, which he also headed. After the Justice Department suit, Deloitte Touche said it had resigned as auditor, and cautioned that 1MDB's 2013 and 2014 financial statements—accounts that Deloitte had earlier approved—could no longer be relied upon. The cost of the corruption was set to impact generations of Malaysians.

Moody's estimated the government would be on the hook to repay about $7.5 billion of the fund's debt, a sum equivalent to 2.5 percent of Malaysia's economy. Foreign investors, worried over the 1MDB scandal, sold Malaysian assets, pushing the local ringgit currency down 30 percent against the U.S. dollar in just a few months.

About half of the fund's debt was in dollars, and a weaker ringgit made it even more costly to repay in local-currency terms. The fund was supposed to have created new jobs for Malaysians, but instead would be a burden on state finances for years to come. Most of the borrowings weren't due for repayment for a few years, but 1MDB's debt was a ticking time bomb, waiting to go off in the future.

Any hopes Malaysia would one day become a true liberal democracy were shattered. Many Malaysians, from top bankers to lawyers and officer workers, were tired of the direction of their country. The country's brain drain, a phenomenon which had pushed many of the country's brightest minds to live and work in the United States, the United Kingdom, Singapore, or Australia, was unlikely to reverse anytime soon.

Sticking by her husband's side, Rosmah became more staunchly anti-Western after the Justice Department suits described how she had received jewelry from Low worth almost $30 million. The attempts to use charity to burnish the images of those involved with 1MDB also did not stop. In September 2016, Rosmah was to have received a "Lead by Example" award at a gala dinner hosted by the United Nations Educational, Scientific and Cultural Organization and a U.S. charity at New York's Metropolitan Museum, in honor of her work for children's education in Malaysia. The organizers canceled the award at the last minute after queries from the *Wall Street Journal*.

Malaysia slipped more into China's orbit. To coincide with a visit to Beijing late in 2016, Najib wrote an editorial in the *People's Daily*, the Communist Party mouthpiece, saying former colonial powers should not lecture nations they once exploited. A few weeks later, at an Asia-Pacific summit that Najib also attended, President Obama, in his last few days in office, made an allusion to Malaysia, one that wasn't lost on its people.

"There are limits to our reach into other countries if they're determined to oppress their people," Obama said, "or siphon off development funds into Swiss bank accounts because they're corrupt."

The United States's influence was indeed constrained. As the Justice Department prepared its criminal case, it focused on Jho Low, the main target of its investigation. But ensconced in Bangkok and Shanghai, the *Equanimity* safely parked in waters nearby, he appeared out of the reach of American justice.

Epilogue

Phuket, Thailand, February 2017

From the jetty that jutted into the sparkling waters off Phuket, the southern Thai resort island, the hulk of the *Equanimity* was visible, even though the captain had anchored a few nautical miles from the palm-fringed shoreline to avoid scrutiny. Fishermen said the crew had recently come ashore for supplies. We had received a tip that Jho Low—despite the threat of arrest by the FBI and the jailing of his associates in Singapore—was planning a major party aboard the yacht.

As we continued to try to locate the Malaysian, it became clear that he had no appetite for a quiet life. Since early 2015, Low's world had narrowed considerably. Fearing arrest if he set foot in any Western country, he was living on the boat and in serviced apartments at the St. Regis in Bangkok and Pacific Place in Hong Kong.

Thailand, ruled by a military junta, was a safe harbor for Low. China, meanwhile, saw him as a strategic asset—a pawn who gave Beijing influence over Najib. He still had access to copious amounts of cash. It was a comfortable existence, if isolated.

Now married to Jesselynn Chuan Teik Ying and with a

two-month-old baby boy, Low kept his new family hidden. He forced Chuan to remain for days on the boat or at the apartments, leaving only for shopping trips or endless Chinese meals in malls.

Low struggled with his pared-down life. He hated being alone in a room, even for a few minutes, and relied on high-end consultants, including London-based Concierge, to provide a full-time staff of more than forty for the boat, many of them Westerners, including a pediatric doctor, nannies, and cooks. Locked out of the global banking system, he depended on Chuan and others to pay.

There were signs of stress; he slept even less than normal—just a few hours a night—and wore a sleep-apnea mask. On one family outing to Bangkok's aquarium, he raced through the exhibits in minutes, eager to get back to never-ending business calls.

He had not hosted a major event since the dinner on the *Equanimity* off the coast of South Korea in November 2015. But after a miserable period, Low was regaining confidence. He thought himself untouchable. A huge party, attended by big-name U.S. entertainers, would be the perfect way to show he was back in the game.

As 2016 came to a close, Low had struck a chord of optimism in a New Year message to close friends and family.

"2016 was the Perfect Storm; but the calmness and resolve of our Captain, led his loyal Sailors whom placed their lives with utmost trust in his leadership weathered the storm," Low wrote on WeChat, the Chinese messaging app. It was not clear whether Low was referring to himself, or perhaps Prime Minister Najib, but the intention was clear: He was ready for a fight.

Low's grandiose message was a rallying call to those closest to him, associates like Seet Li Lin, who was holed up in Hong

Kong, and Jasmine Loo and Casey Tang, former 1MDB executives who, like Low, also had been forced into exile from Malaysia. With international authorities closing in, Low had to keep them on his side.

And what better way to put himself back on the map than with a blowout celebration? With New York and Las Vegas off-limits, he'd have to make the party come to him. In typical fashion, he lined up some notable, if B-list, performers: Nelly, Ne-Yo, Nicole Scherzinger, and others.

We thought the event would be held on the *Equanimity*. Singapore had seized Low's Bombardier jet, and he was keen to ensure the *Equanimity* didn't suffer a similar fate. The yacht had sailed down to Australian waters. Every now and again, the captain appeared to switch off the transponder, making the boat virtually impossible to track. Then, in late 2016, the yacht appeared in Phuket, berthed at the luxury Ao Po Grand Marina on the northeastern coast.

We visited the marina in February 2017, but the *Equanimity* had left the facility only days earlier. It hadn't gone far, just down the coast, where it anchored offshore. We thought of ways to get out to the boat to view the party in person. But our tip had been wrong. The party would take place in Bangkok.

Located on the banks of Bangkok's Chao Phraya, the AVANI Riverside was a curious choice for Low to throw an event. The hotel was on the far side of the river, almost an hour's drive from the city center. But Low had a reason for choosing such a demure spot: He wanted the event to go unnoticed.

One of the party's planners, April McDaniel, an American who had done work for Tepperberg and Strauss, the U.S. nightclub owners, was clear about the need for secrecy given Low's very public troubles.

"With what's going on, they've got to be careful," McDaniel, who had started her own event-organizing company, told some guests.

It was clear the musical performers didn't really care about Low's track record, despite the U.S. lawsuits and extensive coverage in the *Journal* and other newspapers. For many of them, it was just another easy paycheck, courtesy of Low.

Nicole Scherzinger, the former lead singer of the Pussycat Dolls, who was due to perform after a dinner for more than fifty guests, had been picked up by a chauffeured car at the airport. On the drive into Bangkok, where Low still had some clout, he had organized for police to escort Scherzinger's vehicle through the city's infamously snarled traffic.

As the guests were seated for dinner, Low walked in accompanied by Swizz Beatz, the producer who had been by his side for years. Sitting around the room were his family, rich Thais, Chinese business associates, and a few celebrities.

After dinner, at around 9 p.m., Low grabbed a shot of Patrón tequila from the bar and surveyed his party. It was a pale imitation of his 2012 birthday in Vegas. There was no DiCaprio, no marquee names like Britney Spears. But he could still attract a crowd. And Swizz Beatz, of course, was on hand to help. The producer took a microphone and urged everyone to down their tequila shots, as the DJ turned up the music and guests filed out into an adjoining space-themed room for the after-party.

The party was ostensibly to celebrate the birthday of Low's elder brother, Szen, and a famous Chinese singer, Jane Zhang, was on hand to belt out "Happy Birthday." The whole Low clan gathered around as models brought out a birthday cake. Then, Nicole Scherzinger took to the stage to perform three songs. She was followed by two hour-long sets by singers Nelly and Ne-Yo.

Around midnight Cyber Japan, a group of female performers from Japan, emerged. As foam from a machine covered the dancers, they removed their clothes to reveal bikinis. Afterward, models who had been paid to attend jumped into the hotel's pool, inviting guests to join them.

Low smiled as he looked on, a glass of whisky in his hand.

Three months later, Nickie Lum Davis, a glamorous Asian American with high cheekbones, emailed Elliott Broidy, a California businessman who just a month earlier had been named a national deputy finance chairman of the Republican National Committee.

"Here's to the start of an exciting and prosperous adventure," she tapped, before pushing send. The pair were about to fly to Bangkok to see Jho Low.

Broad-shouldered, with a double chin and a ruddy complexion, Broidy had a checkered past. In 2009, he had admitted to giving gifts of $1 million to top officials at New York state's pension fund, which invested $250 million in Broidy's financial firm.

As part of a guilty plea, he forfeited $18 million to New York state. But he stayed out of jail, and by early 2017, his star was on the rise again. For years he had known Donald Trump, the New York real-estate developer who was running for president. And when Trump unexpectedly won in November 2016, Broidy looked for ways to monetize his proximity to power.

Broidy had gotten to know Davis, whose former husband was Jewish, through the pro-Israel political community in the United States. Davis's family background was equally eventful. Her parents, Nora and Gene Lum, had been the first to plead guilty in 1997 amid a Justice Department probe into illegal foreign financing of President Bill Clinton's reelection. Gene Lum later also pleaded guilty to filing a false tax return and was sentenced to two years in prison, while Nora was given five months in a halfway house and five months of home detention.

After graduating from Princeton, Davis worked as a political fund-raiser, but she also dabbled in entertainment, pitching a reality-television show called *Hip Hop Wives* around

Los Angeles. But those deals hadn't worked out, and in 2012 she entered voluntary bankruptcy proceedings.

In late 2016, though, a very lucrative opportunity landed at her door thanks to Pras Michél. The rapper said he had a friend called Jho Low who was in need of assistance. Under investigation by the Justice Department, Low was willing to pay tens of millions of dollars to anyone who could lobby President Trump to get the case dropped. She contacted Broidy, who seemed eager to help—and take advantage of his access to the White House. In a draft agreement from March 2017, between Jho Low and a law firm owned by Broidy's wife, a success fee was proposed. It was an astounding $75 million. (A later draft changed the payment to a flat fee, and it's unclear if the agreement was ever signed.)

In early May 2017, the pair, along with Pras, flew out to Bangkok to meet Jho Low and go over the details of a plan to extricate the Malaysian from this mess.

By now Broidy had gotten cold feet about dealing directly with such a clearly disreputable character as Low. He negotiated for a layer between them. Pras was willing to play that role, and his financial adviser set up several Delaware companies.

To aid in their efforts, Pras turned to an old friend who happened to work at the Justice Department, George Higginbotham, a forty-something bureaucrat who dealt with congressional affairs. He wasn't involved in the 1MDB case, but his background made him a good choice for coming up with ways to evade the all-seeing eye of U.S. law enforcement.

Pras and Higginbotham had even more to gain. Jho Low, to whom they referred as "Wu Tang" in e-mail communications, had agreed to pay $300 million to the Delaware company if President Trump ended the 1MDB investigations, according to court filings.

Shortly after the Bangkok meeting, Low used a Hong Kong shell company to wire $8.5 million to one of the Delaware companies controlled by Pras, the Justice Department alleged in court documents made public in late 2018. From there, the documents show, over $6 million flowed to the law firm owned by Broidy's wife, which, in turn, passed on $1.5 million to Davis's company. In December 2017, Larry Davis, Nickie's husband, donated $100,000 to Trump Victory, a fund-raising committee for the president's reelection in 2020, allegedly using the money sent by Low.

Broidy, too, went to work. Prime Minister Najib was set to travel to the United States in September to meet President Trump, and Broidy strategized to find someone in the Justice Department who could influence events. In the meantime, he wrote to John Kelly, Trump's chief of staff, pleading for the president to play golf with Najib during the visit.

It was just the kind of gesture of international friendship that the prime minister needed. (Broidy and his wife, via lawyers, denied ever discussing Low's case with Trump, White House staff, or officials at the Justice Department.)

On September 12, President Trump welcomed Prime Minister Najib to the White House. Malaysia's leader didn't have a long journey. He was staying with his entourage at the Trump International Hotel, only two blocks away. In the meeting, in the Cabinet Room, just off the Oval Office, it became obvious the prime minister was hoping money, again, would buy him a way out of the situation.

Under the austere gazes of George Washington and Benjamin Franklin, whose busts fill two alcoves at one end of the room, the prime minister and his large entourage took their seats as journalists filed in for a photo opportunity. Ranged on the other side of the room's large, elliptical mahogany table sat President Trump and senior U.S. Cabinet members. Turning to Najib, the president mentioned the importance of trade.

The prime minister saw his opening and began to talk about purchasing Boeing planes and General Electric jet engines from the United States. It was as if he wanted Trump to see what a trusted ally Malaysia could be, if only the Justice Department would stop meddling in the 1MDB affair.

To make his case, he appropriated the global language of finance.

"We come here with a very strong value proposition to put on the table," Najib said as the cameras flashed on the two leaders.

In the end, however, the visit was a dud. Najib hadn't even gotten to play a round with Trump, despite Broidy's intervention. And the U.S. justice system was proving much trickier to manipulate than Malaysia's. Just weeks later, Attorney General Jeff Sessions would give a public speech in which he referred to the 1MDB affair as "kleptocracy at its worst," a clear signal this investigation wasn't going away.

The FBI continued to build its criminal case, and, in February 2018, Low made a misstep, allowing the *Equanimity* to sail out of Thai waters down to the Indonesian resort island of Bali. Robert Heuchling, the FBI agent, and his team were watching, and they flew to Indonesia, persuading local authorities to seize the yacht. Low had lost control of his last major asset bought with 1MDB funds.

Low, it seemed, had failed in his efforts to bribe his way into Washington. He didn't give up, though, hiring several lawyers connected to Trump to fight his mounting legal challenges, including Chris Christie, former New Jersey governor; Marc Kasowitz, one of the president's lawyers; and Bobby Burchfield, who advised Trump on ethics matters.

While Low was strategizing about what to do in the United States, he could still bank on the support of Malaysia's most powerful individual, Najib Razak, who looked a shoo-in for reelection in May 2018. Yet again, Low had been overconfident.

At 2 a.m. on May 10, Najib and Rosmah, surrounded by family and a few close associates at their private residence, were in shock. As the final tallies from the country's general election were filtering in, the mood grew more somber. Despite the cash handouts and the gerrymandering, Najib's party had suffered a thrashing. In his arrogance, the prime minister had made no contingency plans for such an eventuality. Najib and Rosmah had underestimated the anger of the Malaysian people.

Some aides counseled Najib not to give up; perhaps he could use money to entice opposition lawmakers into his fold. There was fear, even within his own family, that Najib might call on the army. In the end, the prime minister's colossal defeat meant that—finally—he was out of options.

For the first time in the nation's history, Malaysia's opposition was in power.

Many felt a new era was dawning, but there was a risk of more division and rancor. Mahathir had campaigned on a pledge to reopen the investigations into 1MDB, Jho Low, and Najib—and, in his first remarks, he made a broad threat.

"Certain people were aiding and abetting a prime minister who the world condemns as a kleptocrat," he said. "Certain heads must fall."

In the days after the election, Najib and his wife attempted to flee to Indonesia on a private jet, but protesters mobbed the airport after immigration officials leaked details of the flight plan. Prime Minister Mahathir blocked the escape. In the ensuing days, Najib, Rosmah, and Riza Aziz were called in for questioning by the anticorruption commission.

Police raided Kuala Lumpur apartment units owned by

Najib's family and carted out $274 million worth of items, including 12,000 pieces of jewelry, 567 handbags, and 423 watches, as well as $28 million in cash.

At 2:30 p.m. on July 3, 2018, exactly three years after the *Wall Street Journal* reported on the $681 million that Najib had received, anticorruption officials arrested the former prime minister from his Kuala Lumpur mansion. The next day, Najib appeared in court to face charges, smiling wanly at a pack of reporters as a group of senior police officers marched him through the doors. It was a remarkable fall from grace for a man who, only eight weeks earlier, had operated outside of the rules set for ordinary Malaysians.

As a former prime minister, Najib was, however, spared the ignominy of handcuffs and the bright-orange prison garb usually forced onto corruption suspects. Instead, he stood motionless in a dark blue suit and maroon tie as he listened to the judge read out the charges: abuse of power—a reference to Najib's brutal cover-up in mid-2015—and three counts of criminal breach of trust. Each of the four charges carried prison terms of up to twenty years. He pleaded not guilty and was granted bail of $247,000.

By the end of the year, Rosmah Mansor, too, would be arrested, while authorities continued to investigate Riza Aziz. Najib's trial, which started in April 2019, was likely to roll on for months.

For Low, even as he maintained an outer serenity, the election defeat was a devastating blow. He had traveled to Thailand for election night and was preparing to pop champagne. Instead, he rushed to a suite in the Marriott hotel in Macau, where he summoned his extended family. They had spent the hours since the election in an increasingly hysterical atmosphere. Surely Low would be hunted?

The group, including Jesselynn Chuan—who by now had had another baby boy with Low—as well as associates like Fat Eric, and his mother, father, and brother, were panic-stricken. Low ordered special precautions, including the use of inconspicuous side doors to exit hotels and apartments.

He began to plot an escape plan. Singapore announced it had sought a Red Notice from Interpol for Low's arrest in 2016—an international arrest warrant that Thailand and China had not acted upon. Now, with Malaysia's new government issuing its own arrest warrant for Low and exerting pressure on Beijing to get him sent back to face justice, Low knew his predicament was dire. Two burly Chinese nationals, who organized Low's security, took center stage.

In Macau, the men who greased Low's movements in China sat tapping on computers while staff organized for Tumi suitcases, stuffed with cash and documents, to move in and out of the hotel suite. As Low's family members huddled in the rooms, they helped pack up paperwork while aides wiped down countertops with alcohol to avoid fingerprints. The women sat around dressed in Gucci, eating fast food from McDonald's while checking Instagram.

After Macau, the family moved to Hong Kong, then to another Marriott in the gritty Chinese city of Shenzhen, before uprooting back to Hong Kong. Low pushed Jesselynn Chuan to join the prestigious Royal Hong Kong Yacht Club, acting as his front, while he began negotiations to purchase a 120-foot yacht. It would be no *Equanimity*.

In the years since the scandal first broke, he had given up Las Vegas, London, and New York. Now, his only choice was to descend further into anonymity, presumably somewhere in China.

Beijing had a reason to offer protection to Low. In August 2018, Prime Minister Mahathir, on an official trip to China, announced that Malaysia was scrapping the infrastructure projects involving Chinese state firms. These were the corrupt deals that Low had brokered with senior Chinese leaders to help pay off 1MDB debt. It was a major embarrassment for the Communist Party that the details of this secret deal-making seeped out onto the front page of the *Wall Street Journal*.

Just days after Mahathir's trip to Beijing, Malaysian police filed criminal charges against Low for money laundering. China refused to hand him over immediately, while the two nations discussed ways to allow Beijing to save face by renegotiating the infrastructure deals. Three months later, the United States indicted him for money laundering and bribery, announcing Leissner's guilty plea at the same time. Days later, the Justice Department announced Higginbotham had pleaded guilty for his role in the U.S. lobbying efforts. And in May 2019, the Justice Department indicted Pras Michél for allegedly receiving money from Low and using it to help get President Obama reelected—a violation of campaign-finance rules that ban donations from foreigners. (Michél pleaded not guilty.)

Will Low ever face justice? For years, corrupt rulers have been looting their states; Prime Minister Najib Razak was just the latest in a line that stretches back decades—to the leaders overthrown in the Arab Spring of 2011, and, even further, to Sani Abacha of Nigeria, Suharto of Indonesia, and Ferdinand Marcos of the Philippines.

It's tempting to see this kind of corruption as a disease afflicting poor countries, where kleptocrats live in splendor at the expense of their long-suffering populations. But Jho Low's crime is a modern take on that old story. The money he took, by and large, was not stolen directly from Malaysia's treasury or through padded government contracts. Instead, it was cash that 1MDB borrowed on international financial markets with the help of Goldman Sachs.

In our global financial system, where trillions of dollars move daily and huge institutional funds are looking for the next great investment, sovereign wealth funds can raise inordinate sums at the drop of a hat—in 1MDB's case, even without a track record or a plausible business plan. Low's genius was he sensed that the world's largest banks, its auditors, and its lawyers would not throw up obstacles to his scheme if they smelled profits. It's easy to sneer at Malaysia as a cesspool of graft, but that misses the point. None of this could have happened without the connivance of scores of senior executives in London, Geneva, New York, Los Angeles, Singapore, Hong Kong, Abu Dhabi, and elsewhere. Low straddled both these worlds—Malaysia and the West—and he knew exactly how to game the system.

This truth wasn't lost on Malaysia's new government, whose attorney general, in December 2018, filed criminal charges against Goldman, accusing the bank of making false and misleading statements. It was a rare criminal move against one of the world's most powerful financial institutions, one which underlined the anger in Malaysia at the global financial system.

Yet Low knew that he could still count on others in the West to defend him if the price was right.

In the months leading up to the initial publication of this book in September 2018, Schillings, a U.K.-based law firm representing Low, sent scores of legal letters to online retailers and brick-and-mortar bookstores in several countries, threatening them with defamation lawsuits if they made the book available for sale. (On its website, Schillings describes itself as "the only business in the world to deploy—under one roof—intelligence experts, investigators, cyber specialists, risk consultants, lawyers and top people from the military, banking and government.")

Some bookstores were scared off, but most brushed off the unusual legal threat. A year after *Billion Dollar Whale* was first published, Schillings had not filed any legal actions, despite the book earning spots on bestseller lists in the United States and in Asia. How Low paid Schillings, given he was a fugitive, without access to the global banking system, is unclear.

In 2019, with Najib's trial underway and the legal cloud around Goldman Sachs growing, rumored Low sightings became the focus of dinner party conversations. People said they saw him in Shanghai, Taipei, and Hong Kong.

Someone so gregarious seemed unsuited to an underground life. Maybe he'd paid adequate bribes to survive a little longer in China. But one thing was for sure: as the dragnet closed, Low, finally, appeared to be running out of options.

Acknowledgments

Writing a book is a team endeavor, and we're fortunate to work with a group of talented journalists. At the *Wall Street Journal*, Patrick Barta, Paul Beckett, and Ken Brown were instrumental in the success of this project.

It was Ken's early obsession with this story that got us interested, and his sage counsel, as Asia finance editor, kept the project on track. From his position of Asia editor, Paul gave us cover to pursue in-depth reporting, a luxury we don't take for granted. His unparalleled news judgment and enthusiasm for the story gave us impetus. Patrick skillfully edited many of our pieces, ensuring the significance was not lost in a morass of detail, while making certain our facts were always locked down. All three were the earliest readers of our draft manuscript, and gave us invaluable (and honest!) feedback on structuring, character development, and even pointing out where we had fallen into cliché. Without them, we would not have completed this book.

Thanks to Gerard Baker, the *Wall Street Journal*'s former editor in chief, and our other bosses—Thorold Barker, Dennis Berman, Rebecca Blumenstein, Andrew Dowell, and Charles Forelle—for giving us the space and time to pursue this project. In an age of round-the-clock news, the *Journal*'s commitment to deep reporting marks it apart.

The *Wall Street Journal*'s talented team of lawyers and standards editors ensured we met the highest levels of accuracy for which the paper is known. They helped shape our coverage of an extremely complicated and contentious issue. They include Jason Conti, Jacob Goldstein, Craig Linder, Neal Lipschutz, Karen Pensiero, and Rob Rossi. The page-one editing team, led by Alex Martin, and later Matthew Rose, and including Mike Allen, Dan Kelly, and Mitchell Pacelle, skillfully shaped our pieces.

A number of fellow reporters played a significant role in the coverage of this story: Justin Baer and Mia Lamar led the reporting on Goldman Sachs; Jake Maxwell Watts was industrious following developments in Singapore; Kelly Crow detailed Low's art market purchases; while Simon Clark played an important early role in coverage. In Los Angeles, John Emshwiller and Ben Fritz followed the Hollywood angles, John Letzing covered investigations in Switzerland, and Nicolas Parasie monitored events in Abu Dhabi. Rachel Louise Ensign and Serena Ng looked at the arcane world of law funds.

Celine Fernandez's brave and tenacious reporting in Malaysia led to early breakthroughs on 1MDB's role as a slush fund. James Hookway and Yantoultra Ngui of the *Journal's* Southeast Asia bureau, headed by Patrick McDowell, covered the political reaction in Malaysia.

Paolo Bosonin and Tom Di Fonzo of the *Journal's* video department produced creative animations and a documentary on the 1MDB scandal, which greatly enhanced our coverage. The *Journal's* art department, led by Jessica Yu and MinJung Kim, crafted original ways of bringing the scandal to life through graphics.

Clare Rewcastle-Brown, whose *Sarawak Report* website broke the first stories on Jho Low, generously shared information and helped us understand the early stages of the fraud. Her website, replete with documents and screen grabs of social media sites before they got taken down, was a resource for us.

Alex Helan, who was making a documentary about Jho Low, also shared sources and carefully read our manuscript, proffering perceptive suggestions about how to improve the book.

To our editor, Paul Whitlatch at Hachette Books, a huge debt of gratitude. His deft early reading of the manuscript led us away from density and toward lightness. It's still a complex tale, but Paul's sense for a story helped make this a more readable work, and his skilled hand gave the prose more vigor. Thanks also to our agents, Steve Troha and Dado Derviskadic at Folio Literary Management, for seeing the potential in this project when it was just a short proposal.

Keith Richburg, director of the University of Hong Kong's Journalism and Media Studies Center, supplied a wonderful space to work on this book and free coffee, as well as carefully reading parts of the draft. Tiernan Downes, who read the draft at least twice, and Nadia Chiarina offered a palatial home in Jakarta for writing. Sue Wright and Mark Hope provided valuable feedback on style and substance.

A number of other people read the manuscript or offered important guidance; they include Sylvain Besson, Luca Fasani, Alex Frangos, Liz Hoffman, Mark Hollingsworth, Deborah Kan, John Lyons, Dejan Nikolic, Andrew Peaple, Raphael Pura, Brad Reagan, Justin Scheck, and Ben Wootliff. There are many others we wish we could thank, but for their safety or by preference they remain anonymous. We appreciate their trust.

Finally, our families—Tom's wife, Nina, and Bradley's wife, Farah—provided real-time feedback on draft chapters and endured our obsession over multiple years. Without their support, the book would not have been written.

Q&A with Tom Wright and Bradley Hope

The story you tell in *Billion Dollar Whale* has so many prongs: Malaysian politics, Middle Eastern oil money, Western financial institutions like Goldman Sachs, and even Hollywood celebrities. How did you first hear about the story? And when did you know you were onto something big?

Tom Wright: The first inklings of a story came in 2013, when our *Wall Street Journal* colleagues wrote about the huge profits Goldman was making in Malaysia. For the bank to make $600 million in Malaysia made no sense to us, and it was a red flag. The first hard evidence of fraud emerged in early 2015, when the *Edge*, a Malaysian newspaper, and the Sarawak Report, an investigative website, reported on Jho Low's alleged purloining of hundreds of millions of dollars from a state investment fund. We began to look into the story, and in mid-2015 a source provided us documents that showed Malaysia's then prime minister, Najib Razak, had received $681 million into his private accounts. This was explosive news, implicating a sitting world leader. But Malaysian politics was just the starting point: Over the next three years we showed how the money flowed into Hollywood, Las Vegas nightclubs, and even U.S. politics.

What is the state of the legal case now (April 2019)? Is there more than one country or legal authority bringing a case? How much more legal fallout do you predict is yet to come?

Bradley Hope: There are major criminal cases in the United States and Malaysia against the main players in the scandal and a whole litany of other smaller cases and regulatory actions in places like Singapore, Switzerland, and Luxembourg. The biggest question mark at this point is what will happen with Goldman Sachs, which is reportedly in talks with the Justice Department over a settlement. Not only is that the biggest institution wrapped up in the 1MDB affair, but it has the potential to be the largest financial settlement.

What happened to the Malaysian government in the wake of the scandal breaking, and how did the publication of *Billion Dollar Whale* play a role in it?

TW: In May 2018 the Malaysian people voted Najib out of power, and he was subsequently charged with money laundering and abuse of power. His trial began in April 2019 and is likely to run over many months. The publication of *Billion Dollar Whale* in September 2018 gave ordinary Malaysians access to the full scope of the fraud in an easily digestible narrative. The book became a bestseller both in the United States and in Asia, where it's been on the *New Straits Times* bestseller list for over six months. Everyone seemed to be reading it. Signings and public events for the book were mobbed. It was even cited by the finance minister in his annual budget speech and, of all people, Najib's lawyer read passages of it aloud during a hearing in the former prime minister's court proceedings, while trying to argue that the defense should have access to additional documents.

What does the 1MDB story have to say about the global financial system? Do you think major institutions will strengthen their compliance offices in the future?

BH: It shows that there aren't just loopholes, there are giant, yawning loop tunnels where criminals can move billions of dollars without being stopped. Bankers and even law enforcement thought that the global financial system had been tightened up to the point where crime was becoming more difficult. Instead, it's starting to look like we live in an era of kleptocracy, where thefts start in the billions and go up from there. Compliance teams will try to avoid repeats of tactics used in 1MDB, but that only means the next big fraudsters will use different techniques. The problems are too deep to be fixed with new protocols.

New reporting of yours in the *Wall Street Journal* that came out after the hardcover release linked 1MDB money and Jho Low to campaign contributions benefitting Donald Trump. In your opinion, was Low trying to influence the U.S. Justice Department?

TW: Low definitely attempted to get the Trump administration to drop its investigations. The *Wall Street Journal* reported that, at one point, $75 million was offered to Elliott Broidy, a businessman and Republican fund-raiser, and his wife if the Justice Department ended its probe into 1MDB. (Broidy and his wife deny any wrongdoing, and their lawyer said they never discussed the case with Trump, his staff, or anyone at DOJ.) And the FBI is now looking at whether a donation of $100,000 to Trump Victory in 2017 originated with Low. Of course, Low's efforts came to naught, and he was charged by the United States in the fall of 2018. The question now is whether Low, who is believed to be in China, will ever see his day in court in the United States.

As reported in the *Guardian*, Low, as part of his legal team, became a client of a law firm in England called Schillings that, on its website, states that it employs "intelligence experts, investigators, cyber specialists, risk consultants, lawyers and top people from the military, banking and government." Did Schillings try to prevent the book's publication? Do you ever feel personally targeted?

BH: It's important to remember that Jho Low, through his lawyers, refused our requests to so much as verify the spelling of his name or age. They provided no explanation of any kind for the events we portray in the book, despite our numerous requests. So it was really galling to see their strategy to stop the book unfold months later. Their team of lawyers worldwide sent letters to bookstores across many different countries around the world, threatening legal action if they were to sell the book and, in some, falsely suggesting that Low had not been charged with any crimes. Some of the letters were even hand-delivered. Bookstores aren't used to being targeted like this—it scared and confused them, and some retailers decided against carrying the book. Low and Schillings didn't carry out any of the threats. We never felt personally targeted, but it did really show us how the legal system can be used by people with millions of dollars to spend on baseless legal threats. We're proud that the book became a bestseller despite this elaborate and costly strategy on Low's part. Of course, one wonders where Low got the money to pay for all his lawyers.

The book shows how a number of high-profile celebrities, including Leonardo DiCaprio, Jamie Foxx, Swizz Beatz, and Miranda Kerr, entered Jho Low's orbit. How did someone like Low manage to worm his way into these Hollywood circles?

TW: The book exposes one of the entertainment world's worst-kept secrets: almost everyone is for sale. I think DiCaprio was attracted by the offer of almost limitless film financing. Although he's one of the biggest movie stars on the planet, he is still answerable to powerful studio executives. Low's money offered him independence from that. Others, like Jamie Foxx and Swizz Beatz, were paid handsomely to attend events, and they enjoyed the parties. Miranda Kerr, recently divorced from Orlando Bloom and looking to develop her cosmetics line, was intrigued by this Asian billionaire, and the pair soon were dating.

You write about avoiding the trap of placing the blame for scandals like 1MDB entirely on developing-world corruption, and the role of Western financial institutions. What can Western governments do to prevent the kind of behavior the book exposes?

BH: It sounds simple, but Western governments need to require everyone who might interact in a legal or accounting capacity with fraudsters, criminals, and money launderers to hold some legal risk for the actions of their clients. Lawyers, accountants, and offshore fund administrators should all have to prove they conducted due diligence before carrying out their work. Everyone has the right to privacy, but it's gone so far now that it takes law enforcement years to discover the true owner of an asset because of multiple layers of shell companies.